Social Media and Sports

Social Media and Sports

Galen Clavio, PhD

Indiana University

HUMAN KINETICS

Library of Congress Cataloging-in-Publication Data

Names: Clavio, Galen, author.
Title: Social media and sports / Galen Clavio, PhD, Indiana University.
Description: Champaign, IL : Human Kinetics, [2021] | Includes
  bibliographical references and index.
Identifiers: LCCN 2020005013 (print) | LCCN 2020005014 (ebook) | ISBN
  9781492592082 (paperback) | ISBN 9781492592099 (epub) | ISBN
  9781492592105 (pdf)
Subjects: LCSH: Social media in sports--History. | Communication in sports.
Classification: LCC GV568.3 .C53 2021 (print) | LCC GV568.3 (ebook) | DDC
  796.0285--dc23
LC record available at https://lccn.loc.gov/2020005013
LC ebook record available at https://lccn.loc.gov/2020005014

ISBN: 978-1-4925-9208-2 (print)

The web addresses cited in this text were current as of February 2020, unless otherwise noted.

Acquisitions Editor: Andrew L. Tyler; **Developmental and Managing Editor:** Amanda S. Ewing; **Copyeditor:** Michelle Horn; **Proofreader:** Hannah Werner; **Indexer:** Karla Walsh; **Permissions Manager:** Dalene Reeder; **Senior Graphic Designer:** Joe Buck; **Cover Designer:** Keri Evans; **Cover Design Specialist:** Susan Rothermel Allen; **Photograph (cover):** Mark Cunningham/MLB Photos via Getty Images; **Photo Asset Manager:** Laura Fitch; **Photo Production Manager:** Jason Allen; **Senior Art Manager:** Kelly Hendren; **Illustrations:** © Human Kinetics; **Printer:** Walsworth

Printed in the United States of America

10 9 8 7 6 5 4 3 2 1

The paper in this book was manufactured using responsible forestry methods.

Human Kinetics
1607 N. Market Street
Champaign, IL 61820
USA

United States and International
Website: **US.HumanKinetics.com**
Email: info@hkusa.com
Phone: 1-800-747-4457

Canada
Website: **Canada.HumanKinetics.com**
Email: info@hkcanada.com

E7852

Tell us what you think!
Human Kinetics would love to hear what we can do to improve the customer experience. Use this QR code to take our brief survey.

For Katie and my girls

Contents

Preface

Welcome to *Social Media and Sports*! You're probably reading this book for one of four reasons:

1. You love social media and want to learn how to apply it to sports.
2. You want to work in sports and need to learn about social media.
3. You're a journalist or content creator who wants to understand how social media works in sports.
4. You're in a class that requires this textbook.

Whatever your reason for reading, thank you and welcome. The purpose of this book is to look at social media usage in sports from different perspectives, many of which you may not have considered before. The book examines the history of social media as we know it, looks at the current state of the networks and audiences on social media, evaluates the roles that have emerged in sports media content, and looks ahead to what directions social media appears to be headed. Rather than simply trying to walk you step-by-step through how to use Facebook or Twitter and apply them to sports media, we're going to take a different approach.

This Book Is for You

I wrote this book for aspiring sports media professionals who wanted a deeper understanding of how social media works and how they can use it to further their careers. This certainly includes people who want to work specifically in professional social media positions with sports teams and leagues. However, it also includes people who want to work in journalism, public relations, broadcasting, advertising, and other media careers—the types of jobs where your primary job is *not* social media, but you still need to learn how to effectively use it if you want to maximize your career potential and more fully connect with audiences.

You should find this book to be useful regardless of your experience level in social media. Beginners, you're going to want to start using social media as soon as possible, because as the book points out, practical experience and repetition in using social communication are keys to becoming an expert. The book provides a series of touchpoints to consider as you embark on your professional social media journey.

Veteran social media users, you should find that this book takes a different approach to evaluating the social media space than the others that you have read before. Although the book talks a great deal about the backgrounds of certain social networks, the core approach of the book is to highlight the importance of understanding how networks reach audiences, how to choose networks that best suit the approach that your job requires, and how to think effectively about communication in a social space.

My Perspective

I started my career in an era where social media barely existed—and what little of it did exist certainly wasn't called social media. I went to college in the late 1990s, with a focus on becoming a sports play-by-play broadcaster. My classmates and I didn't realize it at the time, but we were getting our degrees and entering the media profession during the last gasp of the mass media era of communication.

While sports media students during that time would often get experience in more than one form of media, there was very little media crossover once you graduated. For instance, as a junior in college, I was the sports director at the radio station, a play-by-play broadcaster for football and basketball games, the school newspaper's beat writer for women's soccer, and a summer intern in the sports department at the local NBC affiliate. But even with all that experience, I knew I'd be leaving most of it behind as I entered the profession and focused on radio broadcasting, just as my print media colleagues would leave their radio experiences behind and focus on writing for newspapers.

My path after graduation was as a play-by-play broadcaster, and that led me to some interesting hybrid jobs in sports industry. I was employed by several teams in combination roles where I would do their broadcasts but also served as the team's media relations director, public relations director, webmaster, and salesperson—in some cases, all at the same time. These experiences gave me some real insights into how sport organizations operate, how job roles within organizations connect, and why communication skills are important no matter what role you have within a sport organization.

Since becoming a professional in 2001, I have witnessed an upending of the traditional separations between types of media content because written material, video content, audio content, and photographic imagery have been flung together into new forms and digital combinations. The roles of both sports and media professionals have expanded and merged, largely because media itself has expanded and merged. Facebook, Twitter, and Instagram have combined the previously separate functions of newspapers, radio, and television and created a media space where professionals are expected to produce professional writing, audio, and video—and know how to interact directly with an online audience. Similarly, sport organizations now use the same platforms as media organizations to communicate directly with the public. Teams and leagues use networks like Snapchat and Instagram to sell tickets, get fans excited, and attempt to frame their organizations by using written and visual messages.

While this merger of media forms has taken place, another significant revolution in media content has occurred within the world of sports. The rise of digital media has allowed content production to become democratized, and this new world has given people a new power of content creation. Athletes, leagues, and teams, all of whom were forced to rely on mass media to carry their messages to the public during the 20th century, can now create and distribute their own content, in many cases competing directly with journalistic entities for audience attention. Social media is often the battleground for this competition, with news outlets and sport organizations trying to attract the same readers and viewers for stories.

My Background

I have been a sports media professor at Indiana University for over a decade now, and I mainly work with undergraduate students who want to become sports media professionals. Our sports media program gets students involved in social media early, both in the classroom and via student media experiences. Students are expected to develop their social media skills, and social media platforms have become the primary conduit for content to reach the audience. Some students are aspiring writers or broadcasters, but most of them have become aspiring multimedia students operating in multiple forms of media and developing their skill sets in all areas simultaneously. That is the direction of the sports media world as we enter the 2020s.

I also have a great deal of experience instructing sport marketing and management students, particularly in the areas of social media usage, organizational interactions, public relations, and team and media interactions. I have taught and worked with undergraduate, graduate, and PhD students at two major universities whose primary focus is working in the sports industry, and I work closely with collegiate and professional organizations on various initiatives relating to the interactions between sports, media, and audiences.

In addition to my work with aspiring professionals, I have over a decade of experience as a communication researcher, focusing specifically on how social media is used by sports audiences, teams, and leagues. Since 2006, I have published over 50 scholarly articles on social media usage, from early studies on sports message boards and online communities to examinations of how and why audiences use social networks. Those research experiences have given me a unique perspective into why people use social media within the context of sports, and I provide that perspective throughout the book.

Why Do We Need This Book?

Social media has always been a rather tricky thing to write about in textbook form. Everything about social media seemed to change every few years, whether it was audience composition, the popularity of certain networks, or the integration of different kinds of technology. Textbooks about social media tended to either focus on the general phenomenon of online communication without going into much about how social media worked, or they would be too specific about particular social networks and then become obsolete when those networks inevitably changed. That's not a criticism of those books. Instead, it's a reflection of how new social networks are and how unique social media communication is versus other forms of media.

With all that said, as someone who uses social media personally and professionally within sports, I think there is a need for a book that looks at social media usage holistically, from the standpoint of someone whose focus is creating social media content in sports. This book fills a gap in the available literature by providing aspiring sports media professionals with a guidebook for how to think about social media networks, how to think about social media audiences, and how to integrate social media into their daily work.

How the Book Is Organized

This book is organized into 10 chapters, each concentrating on a different aspect of the intersection of sports and social media. The book spends time on every important conceptual and creative aspect of social media usage, including skill development, creativity, understanding audiences, structuring messages, and more. Here's a brief look at what each chapter includes:

- Chapter 1, "Social Media and the Sports World": A brief history of social media, how it has interacted with the sports world, and how sports-focused social media has changed into something different than it was when it first started

- Chapter 2, "Tools of the Trade": A primer on the resources available to those working in sports and social media, including software, hardware, and information sources to help you do your job better and more efficiently

- Chapter 3, "Creative Sparks": A look at the building blocks of effective online communication, including the importance of language and its usage, the need to consume the media you create, and the necessity of repetition

- Chapter 4, "Audiences and Networks": An examination of the people who consume social media content, how they differ from network to network, and how the way networks are built affects the types of audiences they can serve

- Chapter 5, "The Online Community": An evaluation of online audiences, how they act and interact on social media, why they make certain choices, and why discourse on social media can be worryingly hostile at times

- Chapter 6, "The Technology Curve": Examines how the evolution of communications technology has affected the utilization of social media while framing the current landscape of social networking into conceptual areas

- Chapter 7, "Framing Your Presence": Applies communication theory to social media to discuss the concepts of agenda setting and framing, why those concepts are important for sports media professionals to keep in mind, and how they can be applied to social networks

- Chapter 8, "Editorial Content": Explores the more traditional branch of sports social media usage, focusing on how journalists and independent content creators should use social media

- Chapter 9, "Industry Content": Outlines the tremendous growth in industry-based social content, with athletes, teams, and leagues employing their own content creators and distributing media that rivals content from traditional journalistic sources

- Chapter 10, "Holistic Social Media": An examination of some of the key human elements of social media work, including ethics, burnout, and mental health, and a discussion of the best ways to prepare for the future in a changing social media landscape

The order the book introduces material is intended to help you first understand the building blocks of effective social media usage in sports media and then gradually learn the broader aspects and implications of the genre. The first three chapters focus on the core components of social media creation. The next four chapters focus on understanding the social media environment and some of the key considerations that social media workers should keep in mind. The final three chapters take these building blocks and apply them to the fields of sports journalism and sports industry.

Each of the chapters end with a series of review questions. These questions help you to practically apply the lessons learned from the chapter by having you think about what has been discussed within the context of examples that are important to you.

In addition to the chapters in this book, we've also included a wealth of web materials that will be regularly updated. These materials delve into specific social networks and their ever-changing lists of features, allowing you to stay abreast of the latest developments in a constantly moving part of the sports communication field. Whenever you see this element, you'll know that support material exists on the web:

 Check out the web resource for more information on how to effectively reach sports audiences via the major social media channels.

Features

Here are some of the things you can expect from this book:

- *Examples from outside of sports.* Social media messaging is a copycat environment. Some amazing ideas originate in the sports media world, but most of the great ideas emanate from elsewhere. This book will liberally use examples from across the spectrum of social media, both to point out what makes these ideas good and to give you the chance to make the ideas better.

- *A bit of irreverence.* If you opened this book thinking it would be the same dry style of writing that most of your other textbooks use, it's time to adjust your expectations. As you will learn throughout this preface and the chapters that follow, effective social media needs to be engaging, entertaining, and contextually sensitive. No, you don't want to be cracking jokes after a player suffers a serious injury, but maintaining an outgoing style in your content creation and delivery approaches is a huge help in distinguishing your social media messaging from those who haven't yet learned that lesson.

- *Professional insights.* Throughout the book, you will notice several sidebars that feature interviews with experts on social media usage. These sidebars give depth and context to the text by providing you with perspectives on important aspects of social media usage that are applicable to the sports media field. Many of these sidebars feature analysis and commentary from scholars who have studied social media in sports since the early days of Twitter and Facebook. Other sidebars include insights from sports and social media professionals from both the sports industry and the field of sports journalism.

- *A straightforward approach.* The purpose of this book is not to cheerlead for the sports world or for social media. Both areas are imperfect reflections of the societies that surround them, and both have plenty of problematic elements. It is important for aspiring social media specialists to learn the positive and negative side of both worlds.

Think about it in these terms: As a social media specialist focusing on sports media content, you have two primary jobs. The first job is to understand the concepts and stories that emanate from sports and media well enough to relate them to an audience effectively. The second job is to understand the social media networks and tools well enough to craft and distribute those messages to the right audience. Pretending that there are no negative sides to the sports world or ignoring the pitfalls and danger zones within social media won't help you do either of those jobs to the best of your ability. The more you know, the better prepared you will be to do your job.

Instructor Resources

Instructors have access to an instructor guide that provides instructions on how to use the instructor guide and web resource; a sample syllabus; and chapter-specific files that provide a chapter overview, objectives, key points, a chapter outline, applied activities with sample answers, and answers to the end-of-chapter review questions.

Conclusion

My goal with this textbook is to provide you with the tools you need to effectively think about social media usage in sports and for you to use social media as a tool in your career in whatever aspect of the sports or media industries you are pursuing. The book gives you the insights you need to become an effective social media user and can demystify the social media environment for you.

Nobody should be scared at the prospect of using social media. When you strip away the technological features, social media is simply people communicating with each other electronically. If you can learn how to communicate better, identify who the people are that you're trying to communicate with, and understand the tools that are at your disposal to create and distribute that communication, then there's every reason to think you will be able to master social media usage in sports.

Let's get started!

Acknowledgments

Projects of this size are always an indescribable mix of thrilling, satisfying, and frustrating, both for the writer and the people who know the writer. With that as a backdrop, I am indebted to several people who helped to make the writing of this book possible.

First and foremost, my family have been tremendous throughout the process. My wife, Katie, has been a beacon of understanding and patience as I dealt with the biggest project of my career, giving me feedback, encouragement, and parenting breaks throughout. I love you, honey.

I want to thank my mom, Laura, for her thoughts and encouragement throughout, and my sister, Olivia, for always reminding me that I'm not a lawyer.

This project wouldn't have happened without the efforts of Drew Tyler, who came to me with the original idea for a textbook on the topic, helped me work through the structural elements of how such a book might look, and provided editorial guidance throughout. I appreciate his ideas, feedback, and flexibility.

Amanda Ewing has been a wonderful editor from the start, answering questions, asking for more details, and nudging me to provide context.

My sincere thanks to Human Kinetics, which has always been willing to publish in new and innovative areas of sports and media pedagogy.

Thank you to Bloomington Bagel Company's Dunn Street location, which served as my unofficial office for large parts of this writing.

Thanks to my research collaborators and doctoral students over the years. There are too many of you to list, but your collegiality and willingness to work on previously unresearched aspects of sports communication helped to pave the way for this book.

Finally, a thank-you to my former students, particularly the ones who had to forge careers in sports and media as the industry was changing over to something driven by social media. Your resourcefulness, intelligence, and willingness to adapt in the face of change is a constant inspiration, and I thank you for your insights into the professional journeys you are on.

Social Media and the Sports World

Effectively using social media requires a working knowledge of how the field operates, and using social media within sports requires a working knowledge of that environment. This chapter helps you to do the following:

- Comprehend the good and bad parts of the sports world.
- Examine the social media world and understand what things are likely to change (or not) in the future.
- Evaluate how sports and social media interact with one another.

The intersection of sports and social media is a fascinating place, largely because both sports and social media are independently fascinating. The popularity of sports spans the globe, and increasing numbers of sports are popular across multiple cultures and societies. The bonds of sports connect generations and communities and can serve as important touchstones for groups of people.

Meanwhile, social media offers distant populations a chance to connect in a new way. Textual, aural, and visual communication now instantly extend past national borders, providing the people of Earth with a common medium for interaction. And while local and regional interests still dominate areas such as politics, certain sports can act as an almost universal mode of connection and commonality. The global popularity of sports such as football, basketball, cricket, and esports help demonstrate that humans can coexist and coalesce around shared experiences when properly motivated.

The Sports World

Sports occupy a fascinating place in society. Plenty of people claim to not care for sports at all, and yet broadcasts of live sporting events are consistently the most watched television and video events in many countries around the world (Crupi, 2017; Crupi, 2018; Shazi, 2018). Cultures and societies watch a sport for diversion and entertainment, and sporting events have also served as the venue for political protests and complaints about human rights violations. Popular sports occupy a wide spectrum of forms and functions, from the finesse of golf to the brutality of combat sports.

If you're reading this book, you're probably a fan of certain sports or athletes. Maybe you have a favorite team, or perhaps you follow a league closely. Perhaps you have a rooting interest based on where you're going to college or with a team located close to where you grew up. Or perhaps you are a fan of a certain athlete because of her accomplishments or what she stands for.

Jacek Kozyra/fotolia.com

Sports play an important role in almost every society across the globe.

It is important for sports social media professionals to remember that the sports world is both global and intimate, interconnected and isolated. Whatever your interests are in sports, you should do whatever you can to expand your knowledge beyond those parameters. The more you know about different sports and athletes, the easier it will be for you to grasp what makes those sports appealing to fans and learn about how those elements are communicated effectively.

In an increasingly globalized culture, the historical separations between sports cultures continue to vanish. The most popular figure on social media worldwide is a football (or soccer) player (Fenton, 2018), and many sporting events are viewable via video streams regardless of what country you live in. Broadcasts of English Premier League football have become a major source of ratings growth on American television (Yoder, 2018), and the most popular professional sport organization in the United States, the National Football League, is hoping to place an American football franchise in the United Kingdom by 2022 (Hamilton, 2018).

With all these barriers disappearing and the traditional sociocultural fences between countries and sports starting to be torn down, what does the future hold for the industry? We're likely looking at a future where sports leagues, teams, and athletes are attracting and managing a multinational roster of fans, business partners, and stakeholders. Local popularity may sell tickets, but international popularity will become the new measuring stick for a wide variety of sports entities. The best way to tap into that international popularity and interact with those fans and stakeholders across the globe will be through social media.

The Social Media World

Why is social media so important to the future communication needs of a global sports world? It's mostly because unlike traditional media forms such as television and newspapers, social media networks are largely borderless. With the notable exception of China, the average sports fan anywhere around the globe can log on to Facebook, Twitter, and many other social networks and see the same thing as another fan in a completely different country. A television viewer in the United States is likely to have a much different sports media experience than a television viewer in Germany, but a Twitter user will have nearly identical access to messages and experiences in either country.

One of the most remarkable things about social media is how quickly it has connected the globe in a short time. Understanding the history of social media development and how we got to where we are is important.

The Beginnings of Social Media

We could have an endless debate about when modern social media officially started. Some claim the beginnings go all the way back to GeoCities, the tech startup from the mid-1990s that was eventually purchased by Silicon Valley giant Yahoo for US$3.9 billion (Kaplan & Piller, 1999). Some point to the late 1990s with the launch of the SixDegrees.com network website (Hendricks, 2013). But realistically, the launch of social media as we know it occurred with two major events over a six-month period in 2003 and 2004:

1. The August 2003 launch of Myspace (Jackson & Madrigal, 2011)
2. The February 2004 launch of Facebook by students at Harvard University (Hall, n.d.)

To some degree, Myspace and Facebook were in the right place at the right time. While the World Wide Web was birthed in late 1992, the world didn't start to become truly mobile and Internet-focused until the first decade of the 21st century. In 2000, the number of global Internet users stood at 361 million. A decade later in 2010, that number had increased nearly sixfold to 1.96 billion (Pingdom, 2010). Online life was primed to explode, and these two companies made the most of it.

What made Myspace and Facebook so initially popular? Much of it had to do with providing avenues for self-expression and socialization, something that was sorely lacking in the early versions of the Internet experience.

Key Point @ DoctorGC ⌄
Social media as we know it started in the early 2000s with the launch of Myspace and Facebook. #SocialMediaAndSports

The "Old" Internet

Before the early 2000s, the Internet didn't feel like a particularly friendly or personal place. The World Wide Web was based around so-called Web 1.0 content. Web 1.0 was basic, undynamic content that had little or no interactive capacity (Madurai,

2018). Sites during this era were focused mostly on conveying information to audiences in a one-way setting, and audiences were not provided the ability to interact with that information in any way other than simply consuming it. This was largely due to slow Internet connectivity that made it difficult to transfer high-resolution images or large video files as well as the lack of Internet-enabled mobile devices (such as cell phones and tablets), forcing almost all Internet users to use desktop computers or laptops.

Myspace

While Facebook would eventually become the dominant global social network, Myspace first captured the attention of the burgeoning Internet marketplace. Founded in August 2003 by a marketing company named eUniverse (Douglas, 2006), Myspace presented itself as a place where people, musical groups, and businesses could create an online profile that was free to register. The site's architecture encouraged users to make connections to other profiles, presenting it as adding "friends" (Douglas, 2006). These profiles were relatively easy to set up and generally only required a picture and a few lines of text. Users had the ability to customize their profiles visually as well as with audio.

Myspace appealed to many people very quickly, surpassing a million unique visitors per month within a year of launching and attracting musical artists with mass appeal like Hilary Duff and R.E.M. (Jackson & Madrigal, 2011). Within two years of launching, Fox News parent company News Corporation purchased the site for over half a billion U.S. dollars and claimed to have 22 million members (Jackson & Madrigal, 2011).

There were questions raised about the true nature of Myspace, with writer Trent Lapinski penning a detailed investigative piece about the site's founders and claiming that the entire experience was little more than a vehicle for email spam (Douglas, 2006). However, regardless of whether the site was a truly organic social experience or just a method of intrusive marketing, the public showed that there was a market for the kind of online experience that Myspace offered. The site gave people the ability to connect to other people online in a far more personal way than most had known existed.

The early successes of Myspace made the future of the site look bright, which made it even more surprising when the bottom fell out instead. Competition from emerging social networks such as Facebook and Twitter led to a mass exodus of

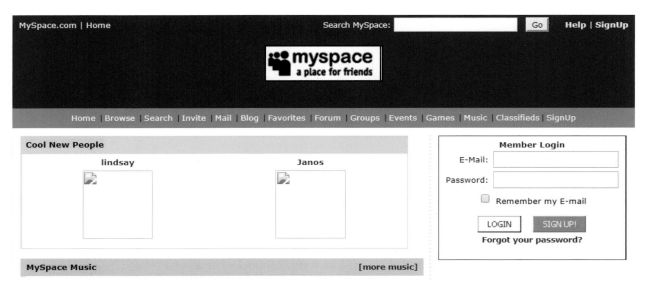

Though largely forgotten to time, Myspace was an important network for social media growth and popularization.

users, and Myspace would lose over half of their 66 percent social network market share between 2008 and 2009 (Garrahan, 2009). Consumers disliked the lack of innovation and clunky graphical interface on Myspace, and the company's lack of innovation in the face of competition led directly to its falling popularity (Moreau, 2018).

While Myspace survived to the end of the 2010s as a social network under new ownership and with a smaller userbase (Moreau, 2018) and a focus on a cleaner interface (Solon, 2018), it embodies a cautionary tale, showing that social media requires consistently engaging the audience, maintaining a coolness factor, and having a consistent vision that extends beyond advertising.

Facebook

On its surface, Facebook has one of the classic origin stories within social media. Created by a group of college students at a prestigious American university, pulled into the burgeoning Silicon Valley scene, and experiencing explosive, almost exponential growth during its first decade, Facebook's story was so compelling that a major motion picture was made about the site's founders. But while *The Social Network* focused primarily on the personalities of Mark Zuckerberg, Eduardo Saverin, and the Winklevoss twins, the tremendous success of Facebook has far more to do with the people who use it than the people who made it.

The early versions of Facebook and Myspace shared many common features. At the center of the user experience for both was a profile that a user would fill with information. The user would then make a connection to other users, known as "friending" on Facebook, allowing the user to create and grow a network of connections.

However, Facebook's early popularity was helped along by presenting itself as the anti-Myspace in several key areas. Facebook sported a clean, well-organized, and easy-to-read profile page, while Myspace profiles tended to be messy and confusing (Herrman, 2018). Facebook was initially open only to people with a college or university-based email address, while Myspace was open to anyone. Facebook's terms of service required that people use their real names on the site, while Myspace allowed fake names and pseudonyms (Herrman, 2018).

Once Facebook overtook Myspace in total users in late 2008 (Jackson & Madrigal, 2011), the company started a remarkable period of growth, eventually dwarfing all other social media networks. Less than a decade later there were over 180 million daily users of Facebook in the United States and Canada alone (Herrman, 2018), and the Facebook name had become synonymous with social networking among large portions of the globe.

YouTube

While Myspace and Facebook made it possible for people to connect with each other directly, the development of YouTube in the mid-2000s laid the groundwork for people to connect to common pieces of culture. Founded by Steve Chen, Chad Hurley, and Jawed Karim in 2005, YouTube gave the Internet world a common space to upload and

The 2007 release of the iPhone helped to mobilize social media, allowing people to take the Internet with them wherever they went.

stream videos, two actions that were not easy to do in the early days of the online experience (Wasserman, 2015). After being purchased by Google in late 2006, YouTube quickly became the cultural center of video sharing, used by everyone from users wanting to upload cooking videos to major motion picture studios looking for ways to rent movies to consumers. In the words of YouTube director of product management Hunter Walk, "YouTube . . . accelerated online video in some major ways. YouTube removed gatekeepers, let new voices amass millions of subscribers" (Wasserman, 2015, p. 31).

The iPhone and Other Smart Phones

Every social media company talked about so far in this chapter started during an era in which Internet traffic was coming almost entirely from desktop and laptop computers. However, the introduction of a revolutionary technological device in 2007 would forever alter the trajectory of social media.

Apple's release of the iPhone changed the way people thought about online social connectivity. The Internet was now in your pocket, wherever you went, and you could access networks simply by pressing on a screen and opening a network-specific application, known as an app. There was no need for cumbersomely typing "www.facebook.com" into a tiny browser address field when you could just click on the inviting blue icon on the screen and immediately load your profile and see your friends.

The iPhone, along with other smartphone editions such as Samsung's Galaxy series, would have a tremendous impact on many areas of Internet access and social media sharing. For instance, smartphones went from being the source of 50 percent of all digital photos taken in 2011 to 85 percent of all digital photos taken in 2017, while mobile Internet consumption grew into the second-largest type of media consumption by 2017, exceeded only by television, though it was rapidly eating into television's consumption share (Molla, 2017).

Twitter

Even though Twitter was technically a product of the era before smartphones, you could argue that it was the first social network to truly capitalize on the networking capabilities that smartphone connectivity provided. Founded in 2006, Twitter would quickly find a place as a sort of global public conversation venue, a place where celebrities, newsmakers, and ordinary people were all communicating on the same level.

While Facebook was focused on delivering a broad variety of rich media types, Twitter's early incarnations were all about brevity (Clavio, 2015). Tweets were limited to 140 characters and did not include photos or videos, which allowed the network to flourish on smartphones running on a cellular data network that was still relatively slow.

Despite being tailor-made for the smartphone era, Twitter has failed to come close to Facebook in terms of adoption and popularity. Nearly 70 percent of adults in the United States say they use Facebook, while only 24 percent say they use Twitter (Smith & Anderson, 2018). However, Twitter has become quite popular among journalists, and the network's capacity to break and share news rapidly is unparalleled among social media.

Instagram

The growth of Instagram in the 2010s has shown how important visual media have become in the

TONY AVELAR/AFP via Getty Images

lives of Internet consumers. The photo- and video-sharing app was cofounded by Kevin Systrom and Mike Krieger in 2010, growing from a small startup with a low install base to a network owned by Facebook that would trail only YouTube and Facebook in number of users by the end of the decade.

Although the rise of smartphones had given every Internet user the ability to take and share digital photos, it was difficult to take good photos on the devices (Jarvey, 2016). The cameras included with early smartphones were of relatively low quality, and most consumers didn't have access to expensive software to make their photos look professional. Instagram helped to democratize Internet photography by introducing uniform photo sizes as well as built-in filters that let users add their own artistic flairs to what they posted. Facebook's acquisition of Instagram in 2012 was initially seen as a risky move, but built-in access to Facebook's immense user base, combined with the addition of new features to the Instagram app, led to Instagram's incredible level of popularity among social networks (Hempel, 2018).

Snapchat

The social networks that have been discussed so far in this chapter have all had a common approach to their content: Users upload information and store it on a central site, and then other members of the network access that stored content. Whether you are creating a profile on Facebook, uploading a photo to Instagram, or sending a message on Twitter, the formula is the same.

Snapchat, however, brought a different paradigm to the social media party. Instead of uploading and storing content, what if you could send something that would disappear after it was seen?

The idea probably seemed ridiculous to older Internet users. After all, why would you waste time uploading something to the Internet if it was going to vanish? But for a key demographic of the Internet, teenagers, it immediately presented what they were looking for: a place to communicate freely among themselves, away from the prying eyes of adults and employers.

Snapchat not only introduced disappearing photos to the social media game but also created a unique platform for major content producers such as ESPN, CNN, and the NFL to reach the coveted under-25 demographic (Vaynerchuk, 2016). Snapchat also created one of the most in-the-moment social media experiences, with 49 percent of users saying that they access the network several times a day, second among social networks only to Facebook in that category (Smith & Anderson, 2018).

Advertising and Social Media

The early popularity of Myspace helped to open a new front for advertisers to reach audiences. Following News Corporation's purchase of Myspace, tech giant Google agreed to a three-year, US$900 million advertising contract with the network (Garrahan, 2009). This would become a critical recurring theme in social media: the connection between social networks, audiences, and advertisers.

The rise of social media presented a new scenario for advertisers. Historically, advertising in media has been an inexact science, with companies focusing advertisements and commercials around the types of content that target consumers were likely to consume. Companies relied on audience surveys and market research companies such as Nielsen and Arbitron to tell them what type of people were watching a show and then would purchase commercials in the hopes that their product was appealing. Unfortunately, this type of marketing tended to be too broad and general to effectively target key influencers that could truly help a product or service to generate sales and brand loyalty (Wright et al., 2010).

However, the realities of social media and how its architectures are constructed allowed advertisers to avoid much of the guesswork that had dominated the profession. Instead of guessing at the consumption patterns and personal preferences of those watching a television show, social media companies could collect both direct and indirect information about each user and then pass that information along to advertisers.

While many consumers have expressed disdain for these practices, they are part of the social media experience. As social media journalist Alexis C. Madrigal noted in *The Atlantic*, "This detailed information about people constitutes Facebook's

 Key Point @ DoctorGC
Social media platforms allow advertisers to directly target audience members. This ability comes from the information that platforms gather, both directly and indirectly, about a user's demographic information, interests, and other aspects that are obvious from their Internet usage. #SocialMediaAndSports

Simonkr/E+/Getty Images

Social media networks regularly track a large amount of usage and demographic data about the people who use them.

competitive advantage: If it knows what people like, it can put ads in front of them that are likely to result in purchases" (Madrigal, 2019, p. 2).

What Social Media Can Tell Advertisers

Social media provides both direct and indirect information. Direct information includes things like a user's name, age, location, and personal preferences. Sites like Myspace and Facebook were able to make providing this information feel like a fun part of "filling out your profile," with Facebook giving users from its early days prompts to enter their favorite books, music, movies, and more. Indirect information includes the ability of sites to provide advertisers with users' web browsing history, purchasing patterns, and in-network click history. While those items may not seem as important as direct information, they may be more important because they often tell advertisers a more complete story of a user than direct information (Duhigg, 2012).

One example that made waves in 2012 demonstrates the power of this type of information (Hill, 2012). U.S. retail outlet Target hired a statistician named Andrew Pole to map out certain aspects of purchase behavior among shoppers, and a group from the Target marketing team worked with Pole to develop an algorithm to predict when female consumers were pregnant. The company wanted to send targeted advertisements to pregnant women as early as their second trimester to capture their business before the child was born and secure the woman's business before other companies inundated her with advertisements and commercial enticements (Duhigg, 2012).

Pole's predictive model was put into action, and soon after, a Target manager received an angry visit from a father who was furious at Target for having sent his teenage daughter coupons for baby-related materials. The manager was uncertain why this had happened and apologized. In a follow-up phone call, the manager discovered that the teenager was indeed pregnant, a fact that her father had only just learned. Something as simple as a purchasing pattern had identified a key element of a consumer that even a household member did not know (Duhigg, 2012).

Social Media Advertising Growth

The targeted nature of social media advertising and the growing popularity of social networks have led to social networks becoming a huge part of all advertising in the United States. As of 2018, advertising on social media represented US$1 of every US$10

PROFESSIONAL INSIGHTS

The Ever-Changing World of Social Media

Dr. Jimmy Sanderson

Twitter: @Jimmy_Sanderson
LinkedIn: www.linkedin.com/in/jimmy-sanderson-16202625

Courtesy of Jimmy Sanderson

Dr. Jimmy Sanderson, an assistant professor at Texas Tech University, is one of the foremost experts on social media usage by sports teams and athletes in higher education. Sanderson wrote one of the first books on the topic and has published many scholarly articles about the nature of social media usage among athletes, teams, and fans. He has researched social media usage for over a decade and notes that sport organizations didn't take social media seriously when it first emerged in the mid-2000s.

"In the early days, social media was seen as just a fad, something 'these crazy kids' are using that will eventually go away," says Sanderson. "Then people realized it wasn't going away."

Sanderson notes several key elements to social media usage among sport organizations today, which the smart teams seem to grasp but many others do not.

"It's not just about communicating to fans or whether your account has the craziest video or GIF," he says. "Teams need people who know how to design things and use software and hardware that looks attractive as part of their social media content."

He says that the biggest shift in social media usage over the last decade has been the way athletes use the platforms.

"Athletes are starting to figure out how to monetize their presence. For example, Trevor May, who pitches for the Minnesota Twins, has a whole YouTube channel where he just plays *Fortnite*," says Sanderson. "Big stars like Kevin Durant have a deal with YouTube. Athletes keep finding ways to harness social media more and more."

Much of that harnessing of social media has taken place on Twitter and Instagram, but the nature of the communication approach from athletes has changed.

"We still see the traditional engagements and interaction approaches at times from athletes, but we see those more on Instagram or Snapchat," says Sanderson, "whereas Twitter is for the masses. For most athletes, it's viewed as how they tell their story and get their narrative out there. It's a place for athletes to have social and political takes. It skews more for the mass audience. We've talked about this in the research for years, and we're finally seeing athletes using social media as a bona fide media channel."

As social media networks have become more ingrained in the day-to-day lives of consumers, Sanderson notes that it has changed people's attitudes toward media consumption overall.

"People now want stuff on demand," he says. "The podcasting market is a good example. People want the content, but they want to be able to access it when they want it, on demand. So you have to find ways to get people social or semisocial content on demand. That's what the sports fan expects from professional accounts today."

Sanderson has some words of wisdom for aspiring social media professionals about what areas of skill growth to focus on.

"My advice to young people is to learn software, particularly the Adobe products. If you want to work in social (media) in any capacity, you need to learn the Adobe production suite and how to edit video. If you can learn those things, you can write your ticket to most jobs."

He also recommends not being shy about contacting the working professionals in the sports and social media scene.

"So many people in the sports social media industry are on Twitter or LinkedIn," says Sanderson. "Take some initiative and reach out to those people. They will give you their time. Find out who the people are in different social media jobs, follow their content, and follow the content their teams put out. And remember that if you're in college, every athletic department has a digital and social media department."

spent on advertising across all platforms and media types, both digital and nondigital (eMarketer, 2018).

Of all the social networks, Facebook has been the most successful at building a robust advertising revenue stream. The first time that Facebook's net advertising revenues exceeded the whole amount of money spent on print advertising was 2019 (Marketing Charts, 2019; Sloan, 2019). While other social networks have attracted their share of advertising dollars, the numbers are highly disproportionate. Facebook's 2018 advertising revenue was forecasted to be over US$21 billion, while Snapchat and Twitter (US$1.1 billion each) were far behind (eMarketer, 2018).

Sports and Social Media

Sports and media have had longstanding mutually beneficial relationships with each other (Beck & Bosshart, 2003). The mass media era was good for sports due to the nature of the media–audience relationship. Sports leagues used media to broadcast their games, publicize their stories, and lionize their athletes as leaders of men. Media got something important out of that exchange as well: money from advertisers looking to capitalize on sports audiences.

The social media era has introduced new and confusing elements to the sports and media mix, and those elements have upset the traditional system by which sports media operated. As you can see in figure 1.1, the dark shaded processes at the top represent how sports media worked for most of the mass media era. Teams and leagues would rely on media outlets as intermediaries to get the word out about news and information, and then consumers would use media outlets to learn about what was going on with their favorite sports. There was a limited amount of space available for information, so media organizations wielded a great amount of power in choosing which teams and leagues were covered and which ones were not.

The light shaded processes in figure 1.1 showcase how the media landscape has changed in sports during the social media era. The traditional dark-shaded processes still exist, but the light-shaded processes have entered the picture as well. Instead of having to rely on media outlets to carry their messages, teams and leagues can now communicate directly with consumers and fans—and consumers can communicate directly to teams and leagues, making the communication process far more interactive in nature. Notably, athletes have found a much greater voice via social media than they enjoyed

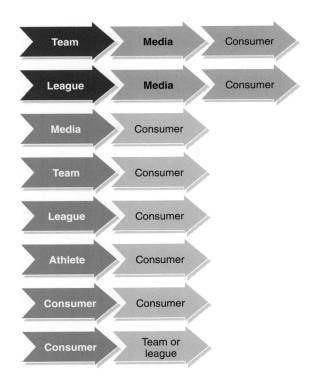

FIGURE 1.1 Information flow in sports media.

Key Point @ DoctorGC

Social media has changed how information flows in sports. Traditional media entities used to be a required go-between for information about sports to reach the public, but social media now allows teams, leagues, and athletes to communicate directly to consumers—and for consumers to communicate back. #SocialMediaAndSports

through traditional media, cultivating their own images outside of their team or sport.

The Sports Media Cycle

Social media networks have become an integral part of the overall media cycle when it comes to sports. SportsCenter and other sports television programs regularly integrate tweets and Instagram posts from athletes, coaches, and fans into their broadcasts. Sports journalists, particularly those at traditional media outlets such as newspapers, are now hired with the expectation that they will post regularly on social media outlets and interact with audiences, ostensibly because it attracts and retains audiences (Moritz, 2018). Meanwhile, social media–driven accounts such as House of Highlights, which provides short clips of NBA games on YouTube, have

Paul Chesne/Michael Ochs Archives/Getty Images

Some athletes, like former NFL quarterback Colin Kaepernick, have leveraged traditional and social media platforms to argue for societal or cultural change.

grown tremendously in popularity, taking advantage of unique aspects of social media and its audiences.

Political and cultural controversies have also gained more traction thanks in part to social media. Former ESPN anchor and personality Jemele Hill found herself at the center of controversy in 2017 after tweeting controversial statements about Donald Trump (Demby, 2018). Former NFL quarterback Colin Kaepernick, who was alleged to be blackballed from the league because he kneeled during the U.S. national anthem as a form of political protest, was featured in a commercial of sporting apparel giant Nike that focused on sacrificing one's career for one's beliefs. While the commercial was first seen on television, it reached widespread audiences via social media, with Nike uploading an extended version to YouTube. Some fans reacted in protest to the commercial, burning their Nike apparel and posting video of the destruction to social media (Abad-Santos, 2018).

Athletes and Social Media

Social media networks have also given a voice and a public face to athletes and other sports personnel who otherwise would not have direct contact with large numbers of consumers. Athletes have used all major social media platforms to communicate with fans, extend their brands, and establish their personae. Many in branding and advertising view athletes as excellent social media influencers, people who can move opinion and sell products (Murphy, 2018). In fact, researchers have studied deliberate patterns of message control, branding, and framing on social media by athletes as young as in high school (Frederick & Clavio, 2015).

Unsurprisingly, there are also negative aspects to athlete social media usage. Many athletes are untrained in how to communicate effectively on social media, and negative public relations events have taken place consistently throughout social media history. College athletic departments often struggle to balance the athletes' rights to free speech with the potential negative public relations consequences of what athletes post on social media (Hale, 2018). One incident involving prospective top NFL draft pick Josh Allen, who was found to have tweeted racially insensitive items during his high school days, may have caused his draft stock to fall (Leccesi, 2018).

Audiences and Reach

Sports touch all aspects of social media and vice versa. From athletes tweeting and posting on Snapchat to athletic departments posting stories on Instagram to journalists hosting live chats on Facebook, sports media content can be found everywhere on almost every platform.

Social media serves as both a primary and a secondary source of sports content. Journalists, athletes, and fans all post on social media, and some of that content is original in nature, existing outside the realm of games. For instance, discussions about events relating to free agency, player drafts, college recruiting, and the hiring and firing of coaches receive a much broader discussion than before the social media era.

However, the largest audiences in sports social media are generally reserved for discussion of live sporting events as they happen. Fans congregate on services with real-time interaction such as Twitter and Facebook, or in chats on services such as Twitch, and converse about what is happening in games as they take place.

The FIFA World Cup final, the single most-watched sporting event on the planet, is a prime example of an event where global audiences choose to congregate on social media. The 2018 World Cup tournament generated 115 billion views on Twitter, with the highest rates of messages coming after major goals or the end of surprising matches (Bavishi & Filadelfo, 2018). March Madness, the NCAA Men's Basketball Tournament, has drawn large numbers of audience members as well, with a relatively unimportant 2017 midround tournament game drawing almost three million unique interactions on Facebook and Twitter (Umstead, 2017). Marketers have been able to use social media analysis to generate real-time sentiment evaluation of commercials aired during the Super Bowl, quickly relaying what audiences found engaging or negative (Marketing Dive Team, 2019).

Social media popularity in sports is not limited to teams and events. Individual athletes have built immense global fan populations on sites such as Facebook and Twitter, and in some cases the social media followings of individual athletes have exceeded those of the teams they play for. For example, as of 2018, Portuguese football star Cristiano Ronaldo had 122 million likes on Facebook, while his then employer, Spanish soccer club Real Madrid, had only 106 million likes on Facebook (Fenton, 2018).

 Check out the web resource for more information on how to effectively reach sports audiences via the major social media channels.

Sport Business and Social Media

While sports journalists and media outlets are using social media as a new avenue to distribute content that used to reach audiences through traditional mass media forms, sport organizations are leveraging social media to form direct out-of-arena connections with audiences for the first time ever. Sport organizations can provide fans and potential fans with written and video content that lets them know about games, special events, and opportunities to interact with athletes, coaches, and staff members. Teams and leagues can craft their own messages and put them on the social media feeds of their audiences, versus the traditional methods of buying advertising space in newspapers or relying on journalists to include news and information in stories about the teams.

Facebook and Instagram have many tools to assist sport business initiatives. Students who want to work in almost any aspect of sport business need a comprehensive understanding of how social media works, what audiences exist in what places, and how to use the tools provided by the services to better do their jobs. As social media and digital communication continue to alter the traditional methods of interaction between businesses and consumers, sport organizations and their employees will rely on social media platforms more to conduct their daily tasks.

Social Media and the Globalization of Sports

Those follower numbers for Ronaldo and Real Madrid highlight an important aspect of social media that has already helped to change the sports world: the promise of greater globalization and the ability to extend the audience of athletes, teams,

Valerio Pennicino - UEFA/UEFA via Getty Images

Social media has helped sports figures like Cristiano Ronaldo grow into truly global icons.

leagues, and media outlets outside of the national borders that have historically defined and segregated them. Ronaldo's Facebook followers, LeBron James' Twitter followers, and Neymar's Instagram followers don't just hail from one country—they hail from across the globe.

The array of social media networks is the most likely conduit for the continued globalization of sports. Sharing game news, stories, personalities, and fandom through sites like Facebook, Twitter, and YouTube bring the world of sports closer together. Rather than relying on each country's sports television networks or newspapers to produce individual coverage of each athlete or league, those athletes and leagues can produce their own social media content and deliver it to interested audience members regardless of most national borders.

The emerging world of esports is a prime example of this philosophical shift brought on by social media and Internet connectivity. The 2018 finals for *League of Legends* were reported to have had an international streaming audience of nearly 100 million viewers (Goslin, 2018), while the Overwatch League, an international league of teams featuring

teams from several different continents, already had 14 teams with over 100,000 social media followers as of the start of its second year of existence (Cord, 2019). One of the primary social networks responsible for the growth and popularization of esports is Twitch, a platform dedicated to streaming video games and other content. It has a built-in social chat and many other aspects of traditional social networks.

As the NFL ponders a franchise in London, the NBA considers international expansion, and major European soccer clubs spend their preseasons on barnstorming tours of the United States and Asia, the global growth of sports will continue to be a major commercial consideration. Due to its universal nature, social media will continue to play a key element in the globalizing process.

 Key Point @ DoctorGC ⌄
The borderless nature of social media networks has allowed for the globalization of sports news, information, and fandom. #SocialMediaAndSports

PROFESSIONAL INSIGHTS

The Changing Nature of Sports and Social Media

Dr. Ryan Vooris

Twitter: @ryanvooris

LinkedIn: www.linkedin.com/in/ryan-vooris

Academia.edu: https://cortland.academia.edu/RyanVooris

Courtesy of Ryan Vooris

Dr. Ryan Vooris has focused his career on research at the intersection of sports and social media. His research papers have included investigations into various areas, including why people follow Major League Baseball on social media and how sports fans conduct themselves online. Currently an associate professor at SUNY Cortland, Vooris talked with me about his perspectives on the changing nature of sports and social media.

Q: You've been studying social media for several years now. What would you say is the biggest difference in the sports social media environment from when you started to the present day?

RV: The biggest difference I see is how the major social media sites have expanded their use of multimedia. Everyone does video streaming now, everyone supports embedded video, and everyone allows pictures and graphics. That's a big change from when social started, and it was mostly text-based.

Q: What kind of effect do you think that shift to multimedia and visual content has on the experience for sports social media consumers?

RV: It's an ideal shift for sports consumers because consuming sports is all about seeing the action. It's also made for a marketplace where many people create their own kinds of visual content for social media.

But I wonder if it also pushes more eyes away from traditional viewing. For example, I don't watch very many National Hockey League games live these days, but that's okay because I'll see the important highlights on Instagram.

Q: Do you see sports leagues changing their approaches to move more of their "traditional viewing" to social media? Would that process work?

RV: I think we've seen some of that already, with leagues streaming games on Twitter and YouTube, but I'm not sure how successful the process is.

I suspect we will see a streaming service jump in the sports rights game in the near future. I think the NFL and NBA already do a solid job of making sure highlights go out quickly on their official accounts.

Q: I wonder sometimes if it's an audience-based issue or a media structure issue. Esports doesn't seem to have any trouble finding audiences to watch streams online, but that's because they've had to, due to a lack of willing TV partners.

RV: That's a valid point, and I suspect that the esports audience is well-versed in the online world so they can make it happen with ease.

Q: What do you think aspiring social media professionals need to learn to be competitive for jobs in this industry over the next decade?

RV: Know what's new but also be good at the basics.

Aspiring professionals in this area need to know graphic design and video editing while also understanding the basics of lead and headline writing.

Writing is still at the core of social media content. It's just that sometimes the writing has to be accompanied by the right combination of emojis.

(continued)

Professional Insights *(continued)*

Q: Your research has looked at what motivates people to consume social media in sports. What are the most interesting, worthwhile, and surprising things you've learned from that line of inquiry?

RV: The most surprising thing is that the anonymity of social media empowers some people to be a different person online, rarely to positive ends.

I also continue to be surprised by how many people are just passive consumers. They check Facebook, Instagram, Reddit, and so on but rarely post. They are consumers of news and status updates but don't share much.

On the worthwhile front, it's great to learn how social helps people gather the information they want in a timely matter. I also am fascinated by the communities that sprout up, like the NBA on Reddit or certain Facebook groups.

Q: What is it about those communities that you find to be so fascinating?

RV: How much fun people have in them, along with the creation of inside jokes, and the development of the kind of verbal shorthand normally present among a small group of friends.

It's also fascinating to see how Internet conversation spreads. For example, a small group of passionate fans on the NBA subreddit can help spread a video or meme. Something gets shared to their community, and then they share that content around the world on their own social accounts.

Q: What do you think is the reason for the large numbers of passive consumers? And do you think they are latent content creators just waiting to be "activated," or are they likely to remain passive consumers indefinitely?

RV: I'm not sure. I suspect it's related to personality and would like to test that idea someday. I don't think most of them will change, but I'd like to learn more about how personality affects our relationships with social media. I wonder if most people are just passive consumers of media.

Q: Do you think we will see a new social media platform to compete directly with the established hierarchy, or are the existing platforms too difficult to unseat now?

RV: That's a big question. If I was a betting man, I would say no because I think all the avenues are filled in terms of what could be provided from a social media network.

But someone could take what Twitter or Instagram does and do it better. They provide a cleaner interface, or subject you to fewer ads, or give you more features.

The computer revolution of the early 1980s is a good comparison. Compaq changed the PC game and dominated the market for a long time, but then others came along and did what Compaq did, only better and cheaper. That's probably the most realistic comparison for what could happen to the big social media players.

On the other hand, the market saturation for Facebook—around 80 percent of online adults in the United States—is simply amazing. It would take a lot to threaten that. Other networks have 20 percent of online adults, which is still a huge number.

I think there's a small chance some of these companies get broken up by governments, although that's very dependent on who is in power.

Q: Do you think online sports audiences are getting nicer or nastier?

RV: Social media networks, particularly Facebook and Twitter, are doing a lot to improve conversation. The YouTube algorithm and comment section has changed a lot, and it noticeably improved overall interaction. I suspect we'll always have a mix of both nice and nasty, just like we have a mix of both in real life.

In 50 years, I'm sure some sociologist and neurologist will write the definitive account about how online communication changed our brains and our interpersonal communication skills. Hopefully we'll be alive to read it.

The Nature of Social Media

As we enter the 2020s, social media stands at perhaps its biggest crossroads since the launch of Twitter in 2006. While social media popularity continues to grow, the traditional social networks that brands and media organizations have built their approaches on appear to be experiencing struggles in retaining and expanding influence, particularly among youth.

Facebook appears to have lost its hold on younger audiences and still struggles to gain trust and market share in Europe. Twitter continues to struggle for relevance outside of media and business professionals, and Snapchat faces an uncertain future due to superior competition and a struggle to provide effective monetization options. Instagram appears to be in the best shape of the "major" existing social networks, but it still trails Facebook by a significant margin in terms of overall user numbers.

These apparent struggles within social media do not mean its impending end, however. Rather, they indicate the very natural process of mutation that is bound to take place within a converged media environment. As technology continues to advance and as audiences become more capable, social media is guaranteed to change and mutate.

As a student trying to learn social media, this can be a daunting environment for you. After all, how are you supposed to learn how to do something when it keeps changing?

Well, the social media world is never going to stop changing. New technology, and better versions of existing technology, are as much a part of the social media experience as the words and images that we use to communicate.

Early social media was dominated by the paradigm of people connecting with other people. That period was superseded by the second phase of social media, where the networks became vehicles for brands, businesses, and other entities to connect with people, using demographic data and users' self-identified interests to subdivide the audience to target messaging. This has largely supplanted the direct person-to-person communication that the networks had been built on, moving person-to-person interaction into other modes of online communication, such as direct messages and chats.

IU Women's Water Polo
41 mins · ⚙

It's Friday and that means it's almost game day!!!
#IUWP ⚪ ⚫

INDIANA WATER POLO

UP NEXT

HOOSIER INVITE · MARCH 7-8

MERCYHURST
3.7.20 // 10:30 AM

CAL LUTHERAN
3.7.20 // 5:30 PM

MCKENDREE
3.8.20 // 9:00 AM

👍 6   1 Comment

Courtesy of Indiana University Athletic Department

Social media can be used as a news source by sports teams, informing media members and the public about upcoming games and matches. The same graphics and information can be used across different social networks.

There will likely be a next social media phase that may end up looking completely different from the first and second phases. As we proceed in this book through the various aspects of social media and sports, keep in mind that change is part of this environment. Your ability to anticipate those changes and properly adapt your skill set to them will be a major factor in how successful you are.

Summary

The evolution of social media has led to a vibrant ecosystem of networks, each of which provide unique communication elements to audiences. The gradual changes that have been seen in the transition from early Facebook and Myspace through Snapchat have revealed an industry that continues to innovate, feeding human beings' insatiable appetite for communication and using data from that communication to market and advertise products to those same people based on their revealed interests.

Social media has significantly changed the sports landscape, allowing athletes, teams, leagues, and fans to communicate on the same level as journalists and traditional media entities. Social networks such as Twitter and Facebook allow sporting events to be at the center of global conversations, and international audiences can now follow sports that were previously inaccessible.

Review Questions

1. What were two of the reasons Facebook overtook Myspace as the most popular social media platform of the early 2000s?
2. In what major ways has social media changed information flow in sports?
3. Why are athletes considered to be natural social media influencers?
4. According to Dr. Vooris, what is the biggest change in how social media works now versus when it started?

Tools of the Trade

Producing social media content requires an understanding of the hardware and software tools used for it. These tools constantly change, but the effective social media creator has to stay current with methods and approaches. This chapter focuses on the technical side of social media creation, including the following:

- Explaining software and physical devices that allow for efficient social media use
- Identifying training programs and opportunities available to social media users
- Discussing market research that allows for greater insights into social media audiences and trends

As you begin your journey into the world of social media content creation, you will need to develop skills to maximize your potential. Whether you are aiming for a career as a dedicated social media worker in sports or just plan on using it as part of your career path as a sports journalist, your social media skill set must grow from its current level if you are going to take full advantage of the opportunities that the field offers.

This chapter focuses on the core technical skills that you need to best prepare yourself for success. In many cases, these technical skills aren't strictly focused on social media content creation but stretch through most of what we would consider sports media content, including audio, photo, and video editing, graphic design, and social media interfaces. Because all media forms converge in the online environment, the effective social media creator is generally using the same tools as the effective sports media creator.

The chapter also focuses on some of the important training and informational opportunities that are available to young social media creators. By using a combination of hands-on training and various online training opportunities available to creators, you can set yourself apart in the internship and job markets by learning how to effectively handle software, hardware options, and market research reports on your own. The earlier you can start to master these areas, the more likely you are to get opportunities before your schoolmates who haven't yet taken the time to do so. These types of skills make it easy for sports and media organizations to integrate you directly into their operations, and proficiency in these areas is often a deciding factor in hiring one person over another. Many sports and media employers are going to assume you know how to use these tools already—and aren't likely to pay for your training.

Software and Hardware

As media content has converged, the software and hardware that create that content have advanced and improved, largely through a process of digitization. During much of the mass media era, the tools for creating media were analog. As recently as the 1990s, newspapers were still being laid out by hand in many places, and video was being edited by using multiple tape machines to assemble shots in a linear fashion.

The dawn of the social media era coincided with an explosion in digital technologies. Nonlinear video editing using digital camera footage replaced tape-based machines, while web design and layout software changed the way written media was created. Meanwhile, photography and videography were altered by cameras capable of digitally storing thousands of pictures, and software equipped with animation and filters put editing effects previously only available to professionals with expensive machines in the hands of most content creators. In many ways, the digitization of software and hardware has enabled the social media era to thrive, providing people and organizations with the ability to produce media quickly and distribute that media cheaply.

Software Tools

Jobs across the social media industry require employees to have a functional knowledge of software to achieve the content goals of organizations. Even if you're a solo journalist trying to use social media to build your brand and make yourself better, you still need to learn how media software works and how to apply it effectively to your social content.

Some software tools are standalone products, allowing users to edit content and then output an improved version. Other software tools are connected to one another as **software suites** and integrate various programs.

For instance, Adobe Systems, headquartered in San Jose, California, has assembled a suite of media production software that allows the user to edit various aspects of media in each. A user might use Adobe's Premiere Pro **video editing** software to edit a video, Adobe Audition to modify the audio tracks, and Adobe's After Effects **visual effects** software to add interesting motion graphics or other items to the content. Similarly, Apple Inc. offers a range of integrated software in media production, with the ability to use the video editing program Final Cut Pro in tandem with **digital audio workstation** software such as Logic Pro.

 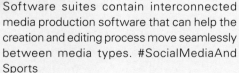

Key Point @DoctorGC

Software suites contain interconnected media production software that can help the creation and editing process move seamlessly between media types. #SocialMediaAnd Sports

Image Editing and Design

Manipulating images has become a key component of social media usage in sports. **Image editing** takes on various forms, from the simple application of filters and color correction to wholesale alteration of images for news, promotion, and entertainment purposes.

Most computer-based image editing software programs cost money to use. Adobe Photoshop and its reduced-feature version, Adobe Photoshop Elements, have long been popular in the realm of image editing, but there are a variety of other stand-alone software programs, including Affinity Photo, Phase One Capture One Pro, and DxO PhotoLab. Increasingly, image and photo editing has moved toward online or app-based solutions, and that is covered later in this chapter.

Image editing is a core skill that everyone in social media content production and management needs to possess. Given social media's continued move toward visual communication and image-based messaging, you need a solid grasp on the fundamentals of cropping, filtering, and altering images. As with most of the skills-based items mentioned in this chapter, the best way to learn how to edit images is to just start doing it. Taking your own photos with a smartphone and then putting those photos into a basic editing program and playing around with the parameters helps you to gain both visual and haptic understanding of what the various filters and effects do.

While image editing focuses on altering a single image at a time, **graphic design** often involves manipulating several images at once, along with other visual elements, to create a single image. Social media platforms that focus primarily on visuals, such as Instagram, have seen a significant increase in the publication of complex graphically designed images. Graphic design often involves integrating photographs, text, colors, and shapes into something easy to read and visually appealing. Software for this runs the gamut from free, open-source titles like GIMP to more expensive and professionally oriented Adobe InDesign.

Audio and Video Editing

While image editing is an obvious core technical skill for social media content creators, **audio editing** may not be immediately recognized as such. However, the increase in podcasting popularity has led to more audio-only materials being used for both news and marketing purposes. Video editing is

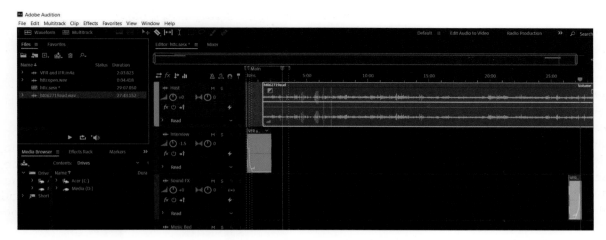

The Adobe production suite allows for cross-editing of different type of media and includes programs like Adobe Audition, which focuses on sound editing.

obviously quite important in social media content production and has become a core component of many organizations' social media strategies.

Digital audio and video editing is done in a non-linear fashion: Clips are assembled in a multitrack environment and arranged in a logical order, and then various filters, transitions, and other effects are applied. Beyond the basic technical skills of assembly and application of effects, stylistic skills are also involved in audio and video editing. Certain types of audio and video call for certain production approaches, and it is important to learn and know what is appropriate for the type of content you are editing. For instance, video from the 1990s tended to be filled with effects and transitions that were interesting at the time, but now the video would be considered cheesy and unappealing.

Visual Effects Editing

Another layer of editing that has become more important in social media is visual effects editing. This process involves taking existing edited video and adding special graphical effects to it, such as motion graphics, animations, and 3D visual aspects. Social media–based programs like ESPN's SportsCenter Snapchat use these effects on a regular basis in their shows, providing a different look from traditional broadcast video. Software for these effects include free titles such as Blender and premium titles such as Adobe After Effects.

Web and App Interfaces

While the above skill areas include references to several standalone programs, the increasingly inte-grated nature of computing means that many of the best and most-used skills-based programs rely on cloud computing rather than traditional desktop computing. Social media apps often contain built-in tools that allow basic image and video editing, and standalone apps give phone and tablet users tremendous creative control and flexibility.

Native Interfaces

As Facebook, Twitter, Instagram, and Snapchat evolve, they continue to adjust the tools and capabilities of their apps. Users now have far more control over visual elements than they did even five years ago, and as visual communication continues to become the preeminent mode of social media interaction, you can expect the user interface of each social media platform's app to become more feature-rich when it comes to editing images and video.

For example, it used to be that Twitter did not even allow posting photos on its service; you had to put a link to the photo in the tweet, and that photo had to be hosted somewhere else. Now, Twitter's phone app includes the ability to take a picture within the app itself, add emojis to the picture, apply photo filters, crop and rotate the image, and post the image directly to your feed. Facebook and Instagram allow similar editing controls within their platforms without having to rely on any third-party apps.

For most professional social media users, it is important to stay abreast of the full slate of capabilities for each of the social media platforms you're planning on using. In many cases, it is more important to publish something quickly that has acceptable design elements than it is to delay publishing so that you can go back and use your desktop software and make something perfect. Speed and efficiency with social media editing and design are often key in reaching your audience and connecting them with important moments from a game or event, and if you can learn how to use the native interface of platform apps in a mobile setting, you can give your organization's content a leg up on potential competitors.

Remember also that the social media user interface can change over time, and you may have to reevaluate how you use an interface, depending on the design changes that the platform makes. Snapchat users found this out the hard way in 2018, when a redesign of the user interface caused many Snapchat users to react negatively, ending up in some users deciding to migrate to a different platform entirely (Angulo, 2018).

Third-Party Apps

Numerous apps for image editing expand the user's ability to edit and design social media content. Many **third-party apps** have a basic free version and a premium version that includes unlocked functionality and more publishing options. Phone and browser apps like Canva provide design templates and ease of use for beginners, plus the ability to customize the branding, look, and overall feel of images. Video editing apps like Quik allow you to add music and visual effects on the go, using media stored in your device's photo or video library.

The app versions of many popular computer software titles allow you to do mobile editing of images, audio, and video. These versions tend to be smaller and much less expansive in terms of effects or features but can still allow for some interesting mobile editing experiences.

Since most of these apps have a free version, I would advise you to download them all and test them out to see how their functionality works and what makes the most sense for your social media situation. Keep in mind that different employers may already have working relationships or practices that mandate the use of certain software or apps. It is important to learn the basic functionality of different software and apps, and the versatility of knowing how to use multiple software programs will increase your employability.

Dashboards and Aggregators

Social media content for a popular team or media organization can be difficult to create and manage

Third-party apps like Canva allow you access to quick graphic design tools for social media uses.

if you're only using the native apps or web interfaces. Fortunately for professionals, **social media dashboards** provide tools for professional content creators to monitor social media channels, manage content, schedule posts, and analyze traffic and engagement patterns.

For the beginning social media manager, it is best to start with free or free-plus-premium web software solutions such as TweetDeck or Hootsuite. TweetDeck is probably the easiest one to learn on because it focuses its attention on the usage of one social media platform. TweetDeck was originally designed and maintained by British programmer Iain Dodsworth as an independent application but was eventually bought by Twitter in 2011 (Halliday, 2011).

TweetDeck is usable on either mobile app or via a computer browser, and it allows Twitter users to manage one or multiple Twitter accounts by organizing a dashboard into different columns. Each column contains different aspects of the account(s), including the home feed, the account's notifications, a list of trending Twitter topics, and more. TweetDeck also allows tweets to be scheduled, which can be tremendously useful for organizations that want to plan when content is released to the public.

Key Point @DoctorGC ⌄

Social media dashboards allow quick and integrated management of content and interaction across multiple platforms. #SocialMediaAndSports

Hootsuite takes the social media dashboard concept a step further by allowing people to manage different social media platforms—Facebook, Instagram, Twitter, YouTube, and others—from the same dashboard, and access can also be shared between different users. As of this writing, most of these functions require a monthly subscription, but the cost may be worth it to you or your organization if you are interested in more precise management and analysis of your social media activity.

More advanced options are available to organizations engaged in social media content, such as those offered by Sprout Social. However, much of the core functionality of social media dashboards and management software can be found in the free options, and since this book is aimed at students who are just getting started in the social media world, I would recommend learning those first because that will arm you with many of the skills needed to effectively use the more complex and expensive social media dashboard options that you may encounter.

A section of the web resource is devoted to social media dashboards. Be sure to visit the web resource for more information on how to get started in this area and what the possible applications are within these environments.

Hardware

Social media may exist primarily in software, but much of it is created using hardware. From phones to tablets to computers, and from DSL-R cameras to GoPros to broadcast video cameras, the quality of hardware can have a serious impact on the quality of content you can produce.

Hardware is often the most difficult financial barrier to entry that you will find in social media content creation. Some people and schools have access to modern technology that is among the best and most feature-rich available, while others simply do not.

Fortunately, you can still learn the basics of media creation even with equipment that isn't state-of-the-art. Most iPhones and Android phones made since 2016 have cameras and processor speed that is more than sufficient for effective social media access, photography, and video. Computer processing power and memory generally gets less expensive each year, and plenty of computers are entirely functional for social media content uses and don't have huge price tags.

Phones and Handheld Devices

Smartphone technology continues to advance at an impressive rate. Processing speed, software capacity, and camera technology have all improved greatly since the first smartphone was released in 2007. Smartphones have become content creation machines, allowing the pairing of hardware and software to make media that would've required expensive studio and production lab time just a couple decades ago.

High-end smartphones like the latest versions of products from Apple and Samsung will allow you to capture effective images and record acceptable video for content that is social media bound. The resolution on the phone cameras will be sufficient for many of your uses, even without peripheral items. However, there are specialty lenses and rigs that can be purchased to enhance the quality and zoom of your smartphone video. These items are often used when filming commercials and films using a smartphone.

It is important to remember that once the target media channel becomes larger than a phone screen, the limitations of smartphones will start to show. Smartphones are wonderful tools for capturing certain types of media content on the go, including pictures taken in daylight of broad scenes, close-ups of people and small groups, b-roll–style video, and interviews with people. They are less than ideal at capturing sports highlight footage, low-light images and video, and close-up scenes that require a lot of camera movement. While using a smartphone in those situations is better than having no media hardware at all, you should try to get more appropriate technology if you have it at your disposal and can plan to do so.

Most modern smartphones can capture pictures and video at very high resolution. For instance, on the iPhone you can go to the Settings app, scroll down to Camera, and view the recording settings that your phone currently has. The iPhone X has a range of video recording settings from 720p at 30 frames per second all the way up to 4K resolution at 60 frames per second. These settings can have a sizeable impact on your recordings and photos, so be

Key Point @DoctorGC

Smartphone hardware has improved tremendously every year and is often good enough for publication-quality images and video on social media. #SocialMediaAndSports

sure to experiment with them in different settings and learn what each of them does.

Similarly, smartphone software can allow you to work quickly and produce quality media for field publication. Image and video editing apps provide the flexibility to craft effective social media posts, and many of those apps offer an impressive array of features. However, the tiny screen and touch-only interfaces of smartphone screens can be very frustrating to use. You may be able to work more efficiently if you use your smartphone primarily as a media-gathering device, then import the files into a portable computer or tablet with a more work-friendly interface.

Computers and Tablets

The laptop computer has become a mainstay in social media content creation, largely due to the same increases in processing power and memory that have propelled smartphone advances. The advantages that traditional laptops have include full-feature media editing software, computer-based browsers (as opposed to their mobile cousins, which have fewer functions), and plentiful storage capacity.

Contrary to popular belief (at least among my students), you do not need a MacBook to make social media. While MacBooks are wonderful devices, they are often severely overpriced and underpowered compared with PCs at similar price points. I would never try to talk somebody out of a MacBook if he liked the features and could afford one, but I have used mid-level PC laptops for years to run a whole suite of media editing software without any issues.

If you do purchase a computer, please be sure it exceeds the minimum specifications for running the media editing software you plan to use. Be cautious of computer–tablet hybrids or Chromebook-style computers because they are often underpowered and lack enough memory or storage space to do much at all with video editing. Always understand what you want to use a computer for, and then be sure to purchase a computer that can do the things you want it to do.

Tablets are a mixed bag when it comes to social media creation. They are excellent tools for things like podcasts and audio recordings and make good video editing platforms in a pinch. They can also be paired with peripherals to increase their functionality as media editing devices. But often the price tag for a good tablet and the required peripherals ends up exceeding the cost of a good laptop computer, and generally the computer will be a better overall purchase in terms of creating and editing media.

Professional Media Hardware

Quality sports content often relies on camera technology that smartphones just can't reproduce (at least, not yet). The kinds of images that capture fans' passions and attentions are generally taken using expensive DSL-R cameras, and the high-quality video footage of important plays normally must be shot with broadcast-quality cameras. If you have access to that type of equipment through your university, find a way to access it and learn how to use it.

However, if you don't have access to that kind of technology, don't be concerned. Very few employers are going to expect you to know how to use that type of hardware, and fewer still are going to expect a demo reel full of material shot on such hardware. Employers are cognizant of the equipment limitations that many beginning content creators face and are more likely to look for signs of creativity shown within those limitations than anything else.

Evaluating Your Needs

With all the choices listed above for software and hardware, it can feel overwhelming trying to pick which items are right for you and your media needs. Many students get caught up in believing that they need the newest and best of everything, and unfortunately they often neglect to fully learn the tools already at their disposal.

Master the basic tools before deciding to move on to something more advanced. An experienced social media creator can still make something that looks good in a free video editing program, while a novice social media creator can be given an expensive piece of equipment and produce something that looks awful.

An exception to this rule is if your school provides you with access to advanced software or equipment. For example, my university has provided students with complimentary access to the Adobe production suite for years, and I regularly urge my students to take advantage of this opportunity, download the software, and learn how to use it.

But for most basic social media content needs, you can do what you need to with a decent smartphone and a desire to work at creating content. You can create wonderful Instagram posts without a professional camera as long as you understand the boundaries of both Instagram and your smartphone's camera and stay within those lines.

If you're trying to figure out where to begin, check out table 2.1. It will help you to ascertain your needs and understand what things will help you succeed. For these content creation avenues, there are training options, but remember that the best training for any of these areas is hands-on practice.

Training Programs

If you are lucky, you go to a school that provides some type of coordinated instruction into software, social media, or both. This training may take place within a course, or it may be part of a standalone class, or it may be non-course training offered through your university's media technology department. Always seek out the possibility of this kind of training and take advantage of it if it is available.

Evaluating Training Needs

From the moment you decide to pursue a career in social media, you need to know about the required software and hardware experience in your area of the industry and work toward building competency in those areas as early as you can. Your job prospects will increase considerably if you can truthfully put on a résumé that you are proficient in several programs, particularly if those match up with what your potential employer wants applicants to know how to use. Software proficiency demonstrates a seriousness toward wanting to work in the field, which is something you need to be trying to demonstrate anyway.

Some employers will provide training on the software they use. However, most will not, and you will still be required to learn and use the required software regularly. For instance, I have had former students get jobs where they were required to use Adobe After Effects, but they had never even opened the program before. That didn't keep the students

TABLE 2.1   Hardware and Software Choices for Social Media Content Production

If you are . . .	Beginning hardware	Beginning software	Beginning training
Writing for digital	A smartphone, tablet, or lightweight computer	Native apps such as Twitter or social media dashboards such as TweetDeck	Writing drills and observation, followed by certification training such as Hootsuite Academy
Taking still photos	Most modern smartphones are capable; DSL-R camera	Free apps like Snapseed; paid software like Adobe Photoshop or Lightroom	Learning the basics of the "rule of thirds" and how to avoid backlighting subjects
Taking action photos	DSL-R camera with zoom lens	Free apps like Snapseed; paid software like Adobe Photoshop or Lightroom	On-the-job practice; training through courses
Recording podcasts	Standalone microphone with USB plug-in	Free software such as Audacity or GarageBand; Also consider podcast-focused apps like Anchor	Basic audio editing training often can be found for free via YouTube
Recording video	Modern smartphone or standalone video camera	No special software needed for recording	Still photo training applies to video as well
Editing photos and graphics	A smartphone, tablet, or lightweight computer	Canva, Photoshop, or equivalent	Free YouTube training videos; paid training videos
Editing podcasts	A smartphone, tablet, or computer	Computer software like Adobe Audition or Garage-Band; apps like Anchor	Free YouTube training videos; paid training videos
Editing video	A smartphone, tablet, or computer	Computer software like Final Cut Pro or Adobe Premiere Pro; apps like Splice or Quik	Free YouTube training videos; paid training videos

PROFESSIONAL INSIGHTS

Applied Social Media Skills

Blake Zimmerman

Twitter: @BlakeZ1908

LinkedIn: www.linkedin.com/in/blake-zimmerman-43b19341/

Courtesy of Blake Zimmerman

Blake Zimmerman's role as the director of social media for Texas Tech University Athletics has placed him at the epicenter of some tremendously exciting sports media moments since he started the job in 2017. In his role, he oversees social media operations for all 17 of Texas Tech's varsity athletics programs, including the Texas Tech men's basketball team that made the National Championship game in April 2019.

I spoke with Blake about his perspective on skill development for aspiring social media professionals and got a chance to talk with him about the hands-on experiences that a Final Four trip helped to provide.

Q: Blake, let's start off with your own skill development. What did you do as a student at Oklahoma State University that helped to prepare you for this career?

BZ: I worked for the student newspaper for a year and a half and covered various things, from women's basketball to the (NBA's) Oklahoma City Thunder. At one point while covering a soccer game at Oklahoma State, I met a sports information director (SID) from the school and said "What are you doing? That looks like an interesting job." I started working in the sports information office as a student for my first sport, which was track and field and cross country at Oklahoma State.

Q: You went from that role to working at Texas Tech, first as a SID and communications specialist. What did you learn along the way to make you effective at social media?

BZ: I was always writing while a SID, and all the writing I had to do was helpful. I still write every day in my social media position, so that's always been a huge help.

The other area was connecting with coaches and athletes. That's always been very beneficial. If you can create relationships with your coaching staff and your student-athletes, that's going to make your access better, which will in turn make your content better.

My original sports information role at Texas Tech was splitting the primary football duties. My coworker was handling daily media requests, and I was handling social media and web content. We started to see the need in the department for a specific social media role, so it was a natural transition.

Q: What sorts of skill development do you think college students interested in sports and social media need to be undertaking?

BZ: Make yourself as versatile as possible. Writing is an important part of this business. But the way the business is going, you won't hurt yourself by mastering other areas, like shooting video, editing video, taking photos, and designing pages. Being able to do as many of those things as you can will only help you and make you more of an asset to a potential employer.

Q: What's it been like working with Texas Tech men's basketball, a team that's suddenly at the center of attention for its sport?

BZ: It's incredible. Much of the experience has been about adapting to different scenarios. None of us knew what to expect because none of us had ever been to a Final Four before. (Texas Tech men's basketball) had gone to the Elite 8 the year before, and that was a great experience, so we knew what to expect right up to the end of the 2019 Elite 8 game against Gonzaga. When the buzzer sounded and we had more points than the other team, we just kind of flew right into it. We had amazing people in place creating content for us who had been in similar situations. And they just banked on that experience to do awesome things for us.

The experience we got was incredible, and we can incorporate that into everything we do. The Texas Tech baseball team turned around two months later and went to the College World Series, so our social media team was able to draw on the Final Four experience when covering that.

We learned how to capitalize on moments. Texas Tech became the darling of the Final Four very quickly, and we were able to use that to our advantage. We had more interactions on Twitter for the duration of the tournament than Duke did, which is crazy considering they had two million more followers than we did and (eventual number-one NBA draft pick) Zion Williamson. The main thing we took away from it is learning how to be in the moment and capitalize on it for your audience. Make the audience feel like a part of it, on the biggest stage.

Q: How do you do that?

BZ: We focused on having things "in the moment" for engagement purposes. For instance, we had two photographers on-site. One would take photos and the other would run memory cards back and forth and edit images so that we have things ready to post, sometimes five minutes after something happens.

If you let too much time pass, maybe you've lost that moment and maybe you don't get as much engagement as you might have because the audience has seen the highlight online 15 times already. You want to be the account that people are going to at the time things are happening.

It's the same thing with video. Our philosophy was "Let's not worry about a two-minute video recap of the game right now . . . let's focus on a 12-second clip of a big block or a big three-pointer with a celebration." Everybody's already watching the game on TV, so how can we enhance what they're seeing? How can we give them something different?

Q: Do you have a methodology for working with your photographers and other content creators?

BZ: It's a mix of planning and freelancing in the moment. For instance, we went into the Elite 8 game against Gonzaga with a plan of "If we win, I think we're going to be on the court and cut down nets and then follow the team to the locker room." So Person A should be here; Person B should be there.

Then the final gun sounded, and the security staff wasn't letting our team photographers or videographers anywhere close to the basketball team while they were on the court, receiving the trophy. So, we were having to adjust on the fly with what we were doing. We were lucky to have extremely talented people who could adjust on the fly.

from getting the job, but they were still expected to learn how to use it—on their own time. They were able to bridge the gap using free training videos and a lot of practice during their off-work hours. The earlier you can gain those types of skills, the less likely you'll need to put in extra time later in your career on those skills.

Software Program Training

Most software companies offer training modules and videos for their programs . . . at a price. These training courses are quite comprehensive and can help you to understand how programs work at a deep level. If you are working for an organization that will pay for you to take these courses, then you should take advantage of the opportunity.

Online services also offer paid training modules for various aspects of software. LinkedIn Learning, which previously went by the name of Lynda.com, is an example of such a company, and they offer extensive training for software titles, social media platforms, and online social media business practices (LinkedIn Learning, n.d.). These programs can be taken online and provide certifications that you can display on your LinkedIn page, indicating to potential employers that you have achieved expertise in the area. However, much like the company-sponsored training opportunities mentioned above, these programs cost money to use.

Free Training Resources

Several free training opportunities are available for the software used in social media. The popularity of social media content creation, combined with how widely available the programs often are, means that an army of users have taken the time to post videos and write tutorials about various features and aspects of the software.

On sites such as YouTube, there are literally thousands of free training videos for software.

It is entirely possible for an interested student to learn most of the features of image editing or video editing software through training videos posted on YouTube. I use this method myself whenever I've got an interesting video effect in my head but am unable to figure out how to make it happen through editing. I am normally able to find a YouTube video that explains how to achieve that effect, and I've managed to amass several dozen cool tricks and ideas for photo and video editing just through random videos that I have come across. Many of these are produced by the same user and are organized in easily accessible playlists, such as Justin Odisho's 180-plus video playlist of Adobe Premiere Pro tutorials (Odisho, n.d.).

Similarly, sites such as Reddit have **user communities** dedicated to answering questions from fellow users about how to achieve certain software effects. An example is the Reddit community dedicated to Final Cut Pro (/r/FinalCutPro, n.d.). These communities often feature users posting their own work, and other users querying them about the processes used.

Additionally, many schools offer free software training to students through their technology or computer departments, and you should take advantage of those opportunities if they are there. These training courses are often extracurricular in nature and can span experience levels from beginner to advanced.

Academies and Other Training

Several organizations have started to offer online academies that walk users through important aspects of software, use of social media platforms, and other aspects of the social media environment. Many of these online academies have a free component for students, and some of them are completely free.

- The Hootsuite Academy (n.d.) offers a free training module in using the Hootsuite management platform as well as a free training module in social marketing. There is also a more extensive training module in social selling that requires a subscription.
- The Poynter Institute, an organization that trains and supports journalists and their missions, launched a series of training modules to help journalists and others learn how to effectively use Facebook for content creation

and interaction purposes (Facebook Journalism Project, n.d.). This includes a whole suite of journalist training resources that can be integrated into newsrooms or classes or taken as standalone courses that focus on different journalistic Facebook applications.

- HubSpot Academy (n.d.) focuses on marketing and business-focused social media use.

Market Research

Social media market research has become a popular field in recent years. As the online population continues to grow and mutate, and as businesses and media companies grow more dependent on attracting and maintaining a core online audience, the business of metricizing and analyzing those audiences has grown.

Market research can be a tremendous tool for anyone working in the social media field and can provide fascinating insights into who your audience is, how that audience differs across various social media platforms, and what social media content your audience regularly engages with. Market research is not an all-encompassing enterprise because much of the data is collected passively and lacks direct contact with the actual people visiting your content. But the broad quantitative data that market research can provide will make your understanding of the audience much richer and can help you grasp why things happen the way they do on each social media platform.

Professional Market Research

When it comes to learning about broader trends in social media, particularly in the United States, few public resources are better starting points than the Pew Research Center. Pew regularly publishes demographic information about social media users as a whole and provides revealing breakdowns on users of various platforms. For a beginner in social media work, this is valuable information that can

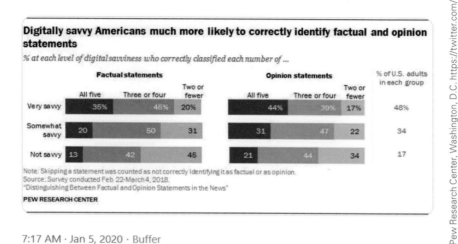

Pew Research Center, Washington, D.C. https://twitter.com/pewinternet/status/1213796544178249728

Pew regularly puts out publicly available reports on social media and digital trends.

aid your understanding of who the audiences are on each social network, what primary characteristics those audiences possess, and how those audiences have changed over time.

Pew research tends to be consistent, scientifically valid, and willing to change scope as social media and the Internet change. For instance, in 2018, Pew started considering YouTube and Reddit in their social media audience calculations due to the growing popularity and broadening definition of social media.

Many other companies do regular social media research that can be insightful at times. Much of the research on social media is done by businesses that have access to the social media platform application programming interface (**API**) data or other metrics, and those companies will provide reports on social media traffic and audiences, often for a fee. It is important to be cautious about this type of research. While it may contain valuable insights and access to data that's not available elsewhere, often it lacks statistical reliability or scientific validity, which means that its conclusions may not be reliably generalized to a larger audience.

Academic research is often an excellent reference point for understanding social media and its audiences. Your university may have access to scholarly journal articles that focus specifically on social media users, sport organizations that use social media, and other aspects of the field. Journals like *Communication & Sport*, the *International Journal of Sport Communication*, and *Sport Marketing Quarterly* often contain articles specifically focusing on social media and sport, and the results of those articles can be of real use to your understanding of how social media works within the field of sports.

Using Research Intelligently

Whatever research you end up using, you need to make sure that you are using it in an intelligent and appropriate manner. As a trained social scientist, one of my biggest irritations is when people look at data and don't consider whether the numbers have achieved a level of statistical significance. Many surveys produce data where 56 percent of a group prefers one type of content and 44 percent of the same group prefers a different type of content. But if there's not a statistically significant difference in the content they prefer, then the difference between the two is worthless from an analytical standpoint.

 Key Point @DoctorGC

Not all research is the same. Good research takes statistical significance and margin of error into account, rather than simply reporting percentages. Be careful about putting too much faith in numbers without a clear understanding of their basis. #SocialMediaAndSports

Many misconceptions exist about social media and its audiences, so it is important to use research to understand who the audiences are and what they generally want. Later in this book, we will look specifically at audiences and their overall impact on the social media scene as well as the architecture of social media networks and how that affects the audiences that use those networks. Intelligent use of research can help you to grasp what is going on in social media and how to best use your content to reach the audiences that you or your organization are interested in engaging with.

Summary

Social media creation involves tools, and many of them can appear overly difficult to learn or overly expensive to acquire. But by understanding what goes into content creation and how social media content is produced, you can better prepare yourself for a career in the field by picking the right tools for the type of content you're looking to create.

Different platforms require different types of media, and it's likely that you'll be called on to do a bit of everything in your role as a social media content creator. Learning the process of creating images, shooting and editing videos, developing visual effects, and using social media dashboards to efficiently send things out to the world are all likely to be part of what you do.

Fortunately, help exists in the form of training for much of the software you will use, and market research will provide you with regularly updated insights into how and why things happen in your corner of the sports social media world. Knowing that these resources exist is half the battle. The other half is using them effectively to further your knowledge base and ability levels.

Review Questions

1. How did the process of digitization alter the way media was created and assembled?
2. Why is image editing a core skill that everyone in social media needs to possess?
3. Why are third-party apps important for creating media content?
4. Where can you find free training for software?
5. Why should you read market research about social media?

Creative Sparks

Creativity is a key aspect of social media, but many people are scared by the prospect of having to produce original creative content. This chapter delves into the following:

- Using vocabulary to improve your creative approach
- Evaluating and understanding the sports media industry and incorporating that knowledge into your messages
- Applying cultural and societal knowledge to the creative process

Some people seem to be born as creative geniuses. We've all seen them in class or at a job. These are the folks who can write impressive, witty content; edit videos together in mind-blowing ways; or quickly sketch amazing artwork. Seeing that kind of creative ability can make you feel like those people are on a different planet, one you'll never have a chance of reaching.

But you shouldn't think that way. With almost no exceptions, those "creative geniuses" have spent countless hours honing their craft, developing their knowledge base, and synthesizing the world around them into the kind of creative impulses that you are seeing. Creativity is far more likely to be made than born, and in the social media world, it's a product of hours of knowledge development, consumption, and repetition. This chapter walks you through some recommended steps for sharpening your creative skills and applying those skills to the world of sports social media.

Core Creativity Elements

The path to being effective in any creative pursuit starts with a solid base of knowledge. Throughout nearly 15 years of teaching communications and media, I have found that students who are more knowledgeable about their areas of media focus are more confident, more productive, and almost universally have better job prospects than those whose knowledge levels are lacking. This may sound like simple advice, but it is consistently surprising how many people neglect to build their knowledge bases, particularly within the worlds of sports and social media.

Many students mistake knowing a lot about a small segment of the field for being truly knowledgeable about that field. This is largely due to students' interests initially developing out of fandom, rather than professional interest. In other words, most students develop a casual knowledge about a sport, such as a fan in high school learning about the roster of their favorite Major League Baseball team and perhaps a few of the leading players elsewhere in the league. While that level of knowledge is more than sufficient to effectively demonstrate fandom to members of their peer groups or on a message board, it falls well short of what is needed to be successful working in a communication-oriented job within sports. The earlier that students understand that a knowledge base must expand considerably to be effective, the better chance they have of succeeding.

Specific areas that students should strive to work on, regardless of what aspect of sports social media they are interested in, are vocabulary, industry literacy, cultural knowledge, and grammar and writing conventions. Each are detailed below.

Vocabulary

The building block for nearly every aspect of social media communication is vocabulary. In some cases, this means the actual words that are written or spoken as part of the social media message. In other cases, it refers to the visual imagery or editing patterns used to produce photos or videos.

Regardless of the content being created, the person doing the creation must possess a broad and ever-growing vocabulary of words and ideas to choose from. See Tips for Improving Vocabulary for some ways that aspiring social media specialists in sports can improve this part of their approach.

Vocabulary improvement is a lifelong pursuit, requiring mental flexibility and a willingness to change one's perception of how concepts fit together. The most effective method of improving vocabulary within the context of a job is to study the way that content providers already employed in that field use words and images. Consume their content on a regular basis, taking notes on what approaches are used and seeing what kind of audience feedback they receive.

Grammar and Writing Conventions

Most written sports media content requires the writer to adhere to traditional norms of professional writing. The **AP Stylebook** and proper grammar and punctuation are still expected to be adhered to by most sports media content producers. However, it's not always an ironclad requirement when it comes to social media posts, particularly when you're trying to be creative and fit into the existing cultural landscape.

Some of the best and most recognizable memes, both graphics and with only text, rely on purposefully poor grammar, spelling, or punctuation. This is due to the nature of memetic media and the online cultural habit of laughing over mistakes. Traditionally published media tries to anticipate and correct mistakes. Effective social media sometimes relies on purposely making mistakes and doing so for comedic effect.

Your role as a social media professional requires you to understand the differences between the two and to know when to appropriately use both. Understanding the expectations of your employer and the general cultural atmosphere of the area of sports that you are creating social media for are important elements of effectively using language conventions, or lack thereof, in your creative content.

 Key Point @DoctorGC
Proper grammar is important, but social media culture and effective communication practices within sports can change the situational definition of "proper."
#SocialMediaAndSports

Industry Literacy

Understanding the sports industry is an important aspect of creative development within social media. It's not enough to have a good grasp of social media within many aspects of the sports world. You have to comprehend how audiences view the sport, what kinds of outlets lend themselves best to the portrayal

TIPS FOR IMPROVING VOCABULARY

- Pick a random word a day from the dictionary and figure out how to integrate it into a social media post. Using new words can force you to consider new contexts and structures for social media messages.
- Read things from outside the sports world on a regular basis and keep your source material varied: science journals, poetry, fiction, technical manuals—anything that includes words and word combinations that are different than what you are used to seeing.
- Use Internet sites that harness the power of stored dictionaries and random number generators to learn new ways of putting words together. Sites like the Random Word Generator (WordCounter. net, n.d.) or TextFixer's (n.d.) Word Generator can present words and word combinations that you wouldn't have thought of on your own.
- Keep a notepad page on your phone open so that you can jot down words, concepts, and ideas that you see or think of throughout the day, and constantly add new things to it. When it is time to post on social media, go back and look at what you've jotted down and see if any words or ideas fit your content for the day.

of the sport, and how others have communicated the sport.

A good way to start the process of developing your industry literacy is to evaluate where your interest in sports comes from. Consider the following questions.

- Are you a fan of a team?
- How deep is your knowledge of that team?
- Would you win a trivia contest about the team's history, or are you mostly focused on current players and the last few years' worth of results?
- How much do you know about the non-sports aspects of your team's business, such as their sponsorship deals, community relations involvement, and philanthropic efforts?

- What is your team's philosophy when it comes to their social media messages?
- How is your team portrayed in the media outlets that cover it, and who are the reporters and commentators who provide most of the coverage?

If you don't know the answers to those questions, you have a nice place to start in terms of building your literacy levels.

The same sorts of questions should be applied to leagues and players across the sports world. The more that you can understand about how the sports industry works and how it gets communicated about, the greater chance you have to become an effective sports media communicator. Publications that focus specifically on the sports industry, such as

© Human Kinetics

Increasing your level of industry literacy will help you cover sports on social media more effectively.

Key Point @DoctorGC

Keeping up with important cultural and business trends within sports and media is key to understanding how things work within this industry and how to most effectively communicate to the public. #SocialMediaAndSports

Sports Business Journal, should be required reading for those working in any aspect of sport business, including media. Internet publications such as *Awful Announcing* are also an excellent resource that focus more specifically on the world of sports media.

You can also channel your fandom of sports or teams into your social media work. Almost everyone involved in sports social media is a fan of sports in one way or another. However, it is important to remember that there are differences in how you should approach expressions of fandom via social media professionally.

Journalists, including writers and broadcasters for independent media, will generally want to remain objective and impartial in how they use social media. This means you can show positive or negative things about the teams or leagues you cover, but you should not be expressing personal enjoyment or disgust at what you are seeing or covering. These rules of objectivity are strong in the United States, and less so in other countries, so just be aware of what the cultural expectations are of the country's media industry you are working in.

Some media members serve as opinion leaders, which may lead them to express fandom and more partisan thoughts and feelings on social media than traditional media members. This can include talk radio hosts, columnists, and sites that are fully or partially run by fans and part-time journalists.

People who work for sport organizations generally have much freer rein to express fandom and positive opinions on the team they work for. Conversely, working for a team or league also means that no negative opinions will be permitted on social media, and employers will monitor your social media output for things that could be construed as negative. Be sure to check with your employers to see what the expectation of expression is within your organization so that you have a better sense of what to do on your social media feed.

The separation within social media usage between journalists and team personnel is discussed in greater detail in chapters 8 and 9. Be sure to check there for more information.

Cultural Knowledge

As important as it is to understand what's going on within a sport, effective communication often rests on being equally knowledgeable about what's occurring outside of that sport and having the ability to harness broader cultural trends in your social media communication. In a social media world where your brand's messages are going to be constantly compared with the other communication types in the same online spaces, a working knowledge of pop culture can be the difference between engaging your audience and being ignored or disregarded.

Consuming media from different sources can help your creative abilities. Reading articles, viewing art and photographs, watching movies—all these pursuits add to your cultural knowledge levels bit by bit, and the more sources and topics that you open yourself up to, the more material you provide your brain to draw from during the creative process. Within social media, this process becomes even more important. You are creating media that exists in a converged state, with writing sitting alongside video, artwork, and sound in most social networks. Consider a Twitter feed, where a simple scroll down the timeline can reveal words, pictures, animated GIFs, autoplay videos, and other forms of media.

Pop Culture

Certain media creations are more widespread and popular than others within given cultures, and the mix of these creations is often referred to as pop culture, a term short for *popular culture*. The concept of pop culture is an important one to understand for those looking to create social media messages because it encompasses public aspects of social life that are affected by media, particularly mass media (Delaney, 2007). Pop culture has historically been viewed as youth-oriented, mass culture oriented, and aimed at the lower and middle classes of society.

Pop culture on social media tends to be a hybrid of content and messages from both outside and inside social media culture. External content includes traditional trendsetting cultural artifacts such as celebrities, music, and movies. The late 2010s saw pop culture focus on celebrities such as the Kardashians, television shows such as *Game of Thrones*, and musical artists such as Ariana Grande and Cardi B.

Internal social media pop culture content can emanate from traditional mass media personalities, such as Ariana Grande getting into or settling Twitter feuds (Nelson, 2019), or from people or content

Scott Legato/Getty Images for Live Nation

Understanding social and cultural elements outside of the sport you cover—such as the popularity of Cardi B—will make your social media usage more effective.

that originates from within the digital realm of social media itself. An example of this is esports personality Ninja, who rose from relative obscurity to appearing on the cover of *ESPN The Magazine* in 2018 after his success playing the online video game *Fortnite* made him a near-overnight celebrity (Teng, 2018).

As a rule, pop culture bends and shifts through time, discarding certain elements when they fall out of vogue and adding new people and influences. The rise of social media has added an extra layer to pop culture because people can use media platforms to create and distribute content themselves. Whereas pop culture in the mass media era tended to feature professionally generated content that focused on pop culture phenomena or personalities, pop culture in social media can also include personalities that are directly communicating with audiences.

Social media managers who are engaged in creative pursuits need to keep in touch with pop culture trends for many reasons. Because pop culture is a kind of communication currency among young people, correctly identifying and using pop culture-influenced messaging can make the brand appear witty and attractive to consumers. Paying attention to what is popular in the mass culture becomes just another part of being a conscientious creator of content, allowing you to place your social media messaging within an easily accessible context. At the same time, using outdated or inappropriate pop culture messaging can create messaging problems for your organization.

Memes

Within social media, pop culture becomes its own form of capital. The most recognizable form of pop

 Key Point @DoctorGC

Don't limit yourself to keeping up with only sports. Staying in touch with pop culture allows you to incorporate that into your social media usage and reach larger audiences. #SocialMediaAndSports

culture exchange on social media is the **meme**, a shortened version of the term "memetic media." The social media content producer who understands how to effectively use memes is at a great advantage in the field. The concept of the meme, first identified by evolutionary biologist Richard Dawkins in his book, *The Selfish Gene* (Solon, 2013), refers to a "virally transmitted cultural symbol or social idea" (Gil, 2019, ¶1). Within the social media world, the term generally refers to still images or animated **GIF** files that retain a vague central meaning but can be recast within several different contexts. Memes can also be text or text-character based, such as the "leaning around the wall" meme that is often used on sports Twitter.

Social media memes largely originate outside of the sports world on discussion forums and message boards often dedicated to political or cultural discussions (Emerging Technology from the arXiv, 2018). Memes that are considered fun tend to be shared more by users on Reddit and Twitter (Cole, 2018), and while the origins of these memes are often from what would be widely considered as fringe or toxic online communities (Cole, 2018), by the time they are circulated broadly on social media, they have lost most or all of the original context and now exist as little more than shared cultural currency.

Sports social media has seen its share of memes sourced from sports content. An informative example of meme generation and flow is the infamous "Crying Jordan" meme (Downer, 2018). A picture of a crying Michael Jordan, originally sourced from a video of the NBA legend's induction ceremony into the Basketball Hall of Fame in 2009, began to circulate a few years later on a meme creation website. As Downer (2018) highlights, the image of Jordan crying slowly began to work its way into the popular press, often being photoshopped onto still images and animated GIF files in ways that were intended to be humorous. The phenomenon reached its traffic peak in the spring of 2016 according to Google web search statistics (Downer, 2018) and was notably used by the social media team of the NBA's Atlanta Hawks to poke fun at their team's defensive struggles in a playoff game versus the Cleveland Cavaliers (Ingrassia, 2016; McGuire, 2016). The "Crying Jordan" meme started to die down in popularity shortly thereafter and faded into obscurity again within a year of its peak. However, it made enough of an impression on Jordan himself that he mentioned it nearly four years later during a memorial service for the late Kobe Bryant.

Issues have sometimes been raised about the legality of memes and GIFs, particularly those that use video clips or images of popular people. As of this writing, there has been no definitive legal precedent set regarding these types of creative content. Within the United States, social media companies like Twitter and YouTube are generally protected from legal responsibility for the things that users post. Using images of public figures likely falls under the doctrine of **fair use**, although the constantly evolving nature of both social media and judicial attitudes toward online content could change that in the future. The European Union has attempted to pass controversial copyright laws that could make both content creators and online platforms more liable for using these types of materials (Rosati, 2018). If you are a content creator, I would urge you to learn both the laws and norms of the country you plan to produce media in and adjust your approach accordingly.

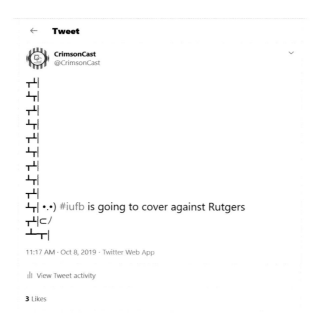

An example of a Twitter meme that doesn't use an image or GIF.

 Be sure to check out the web resource for the appropriate social media platform for more information on best practices for including memes and similar materials.

Social Media Consumption

The media world outside of social media is important to keep track of, but for the aspiring social media professional, keeping track of what's going on within social media is a key part of the creative process. This section details the importance of feeding yourself a steady diet of social media content, learning how to evaluate that content, and incorporating the lessons from that evaluation into your own approach to social media messaging.

You Are What You Eat

You've already learned that developing creativity relies in part on consuming media from sources outside of sports social media. The same principle applies to consuming content from within sports social media. The more content you consume, the more sources you can draw from when you are creating content.

The idea that consuming content helps you to learn how to create your own content more effectively is not something unique to social media. Bill Simmons, former ESPN writer and podcaster and founder of *The Ringer*, spoke about this on an episode of his podcast:

> This is the question that I get the most: "How do I do what you do? Give me some advice. How do I get in to (sports writing)?" And one of the things I always say . . . if you want to be a writer and you want to write about sports . . . read! It sounds stupid and clichéd, but it's not. We have 60, 70 years of great sports books at this point, including some of the all-time classics that have been written in the past 40-plus years. Sometimes you tell somebody under 25, "Have you read all the books?" and they kind of look at you sometimes like, "Oh, really? I should do that?" (Simmons, 2019)

In any creative pursuit, the consumption of the type of media that is to be created is as important as anything—and perhaps more important than anything else. Expert Instagrammers aren't born that way. They may possess a keen eye for photography and visual effects, but learning how to apply those talents to a successful series of Instagram posts requires studying what other people are doing on Instagram, taking notes on what looks the best and gets the best audience reactions, then internalizing that information into their future efforts. That process, combined with creating posts and learning from mistakes, is what helps to generate success.

The first step in improving your social media consumption habits is to significantly increase your consumption levels. Most college-age students have cultivated their social networks with a focus on following two primary groups of people: their friends and the people and things that are in their own narrow field of interest.

I advise students to stop thinking of their social media accounts as portals for personal communication and start thinking about them as tools for professional growth and expansion. In sports and social media, this involves significantly increasing the number of accounts that they follow, reading those accounts regularly, and taking notes on what they see.

I have gone through this same process myself. In the early days of Twitter, I felt like I was getting very little of importance out of the network. After consulting with others who study it, I realized it was because I follow too few accounts. Even though I was following an above-average number of accounts at the time (roughly 700), I wasn't getting exposed to nearly enough messages or content approaches. So, I went through the process of adding hundreds of accounts from across the sports world: teams, people who created social media, reporters, prominent fan accounts, and athletes. Now I follow over 3,000 accounts on my Twitter feed, and I look to add more every day, both through Twitter's recommendations and through content that gets retweeted or favorited into my timeline by others that I already follow.

That isn't to say that I enjoy every account that I follow or that I think all the accounts I follow generate good content that deserves emulation. Quite the contrary! Following that many accounts has only reinforced that there are both high-quality and low-quality social media accounts within sports. But exposure to both types of accounts, and the ones in between, is crucial to the development of your own creative process. By following as many accounts as you can in the professional areas you are interested in, you give yourself a chance to see a much broader set of ideas and approaches to doing social media.

  Key Point @DoctorGC

If you're going to work in social media, you need to consume a lot more social media content than what you would as someone who just uses it for fun. #SocialMediaAndSports

You see bad ideas executed incredibly well and great ideas executed poorly.

Analysis of Successful Accounts

Simply expanding your social media follow lists to include accounts from across the spectrum of sports is not enough. You must also be willing to analyze those accounts to see which ones are successful and why.

Here are some key concepts and ideas to apply to your social media analysis:

- *Don't focus solely on engagement numbers.* A message isn't necessarily great just because it receives many likes, comments, or retweets. Sometimes the engagement numbers a social media post receives are simply proportional to the number of people who were already following the account, and that may have more to do with the overall popularity of the team than the effectiveness of its social media messaging.
- *Read more than one message.* No single social media post encapsulates the mentality or approach taken by an organization or person. To evaluate successful accounts and understand what makes them work, you need to look at a cross section of their posts.
- *Are they changing focus?* As we have already established, consistency of message does not have to equate to consistency of content. Most of the best social media organizations modify their approaches based on the network they are using and will focus their content and attention on the demographics most likely to be reading on those individual networks.

You do not have to look at every post from every account that you follow. Instead, view messages as they come through the algorithm that defines your social media feeds and look for the posts that stand out, good and bad. Take the time to delve into those accounts and see what they are doing across multiple posts and multiple networks.

There are several important elements to look at when evaluating social media accounts:

- How often do they post?
- What types of content do they post?
- What tone do the posts have?

- Does the account engage in a lot of interaction on social media, and if so, with whom?

To some degree, social media success is subjective. What one person deems a successful account might be viewed as sophomoric or unserious by another person. Social media is a bit like stand-up comedy: The best comedians all have different approaches and what they each do "works" for them but might not necessarily work for someone else—or be seen as funny by everyone who hears it. There is no one-size-fits-all approach when it comes to social media success, and your analysis of existing accounts should try to keep that in mind. The more messages you see on social media, the more you will develop your own opinion of what you like, what you don't like, and what you might want to emulate.

Additionally, remember that your employer will almost certainly have its own opinion about what good content looks like on social media and will expect its social media creators to share that vision. By taking the time to evaluate many social media accounts and better understand what kinds of approaches exist, you give yourself a much better chance at being able to adapt your approach for future employment situations.

Informational Interviews

In a world of social media accounts that exist with team branding and logos, it can be easy to forget that a person is responsible for posting messages on those accounts. If you are interested in working in this field, one of the most important things you can do to further your career ambitions is to reach out to that person and politely ask if you can do an informational interview.

Like most other aspects of sports media communication, social media is a very small world where most of the people involved know each other. Approaching active professionals in the field and asking to interview them in an informal environment can be beneficial in several ways. You get a chance to introduce yourself, and this can lead to a professional rapport that you can use in your own professional development. Learning about the way those professionals approach their jobs allows you to ask questions about their methods and actions.

When you get an informational interview, you should never go into it expecting anything from the person you're interviewing, but if you conduct yourself professionally and exhibit genuine curiosity about the job and the way the person approaches it,

Key Point @DoctorGC ∨

Informational interviews with professionals in the social media field are a great way to expand your network while learning important parts of the business. #SocialMediaAnd Sports

you will often find that these professionals will react quite positively. While everyone is different, most people working in sports media fields are happy to "give back" by talking with aspiring young professionals. Reaching out to multiple professionals in the field and asking them questions about their jobs and careers is a good way of learning key things about the field in which you are interested and can also help you to form lasting professional relationships with those people that can pay dividends down the road.

Support Groups

As you try to find your way through the social media world, you'll quickly realize that other students just like you are trying to do the same thing. Rather than look at those people as competitors or rivals, you should look at them as potential friends and allies from whom you can learn a lot—and vice versa. You will also find a mostly friendly and engaged set of professionals in social media willing to give you advice and support as you attempt to learn the ropes of this profession.

Twitter has long been the best online place to interact with other social media workers on a professional level. Hashtags such as #smsports and #sportsbiz have been around for over a decade and are used by both veterans and newcomers to establish a central place of conversation and sharing. The #smsports hashtag has been the site of a series of regular weekly chats for years, and many social media professionals still contribute to it. Getting involved with that conversation early on can be a tremendous educational benefit to you.

If you are working on social media for your student media outlet, look at what other schools' student media are doing and consider reaching out to those accounts to see who is behind the messages. It can be tremendously helpful to have a conversation with someone in a similar position to you at a different institution.

Finally, look for other people on your own campus who share a passion for social media. If your campus maintains a Public Relations Student Society of America (PRSSA) chapter, consider going to a meeting and talking about your interests. If your school has marketing or advertising clubs, you might find other students who are currently doing professional social media or at least have an interest in it.

The Importance of Repetition

You've upgraded your vocabulary, you've followed a bunch of social media accounts and analyzed them, and you've reached out to some social media professionals to ask them questions. Now what?

The answer is to start creating content on social media—a lot of it, consistently and over time and ideally on multiple types of social media. It's a cliché to say practice makes perfect, but it's also true, and it applies to any form of creative media.

One of the primary benefits of working in social media as a young person is that you can start doing it on your own with limited resources and not have it cost you anything extra. If you have a smartphone, you've got a broad array of technological tools at your disposal to start creating social media posts, and all the platforms you will be creating on are free to use.

There is no substitute for repetition in developing one's skill in social media, and the unique thing about sports social media is that even young creators of social media messages are liable to find an audience by using hashtags on Instagram and Twitter. These hashtags can provide an instant audience— and instant feedback, both positive and negative.

As you begin to create your own social media content, there are several different items to consider, including the importance of active analysis, the need for consistency, and ways to handle feedback.

Question Everything

Look around the social media landscape that you are working in and ask yourself why certain messages are succeeding or failing. Is a social media brand having success with messages because the quality of the messages is genuinely high, or is the brand enjoying the benefits of a large built-in audience on social media channels? Are there brands with messages that you find to be enjoyable that aren't receiving the same levels of likes or comments? If so, what do you think the problem is?

Social media analysis tends to focus on the already-popular messages, and there are certainly lessons to be learned from what those messages are doing. But there may be just as much to learn from

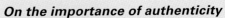

PROFESSIONAL INSIGHTS

The Approach of a Social Media Pro

Josh Handszer

Twitter: @joshhandszer

LinkedIn: www.linkedin.com/in/joshhandszer/

Courtesy of Josh Handszer

Josh Handszer works as a social marketing specialist for Draft-Kings and has seen the social media industry change significantly over the past few years. He gives us some insights into his approach to social media work.

On the current landscape of social media marketing

Social media has become a much more content- and influencer-driven space. Everyone these days is doing content. The goal here is to find out how to stick out and be unique, and that's something we're still working on figuring out. How do we put together a graphic that looks different from one that Bleacher Report has created about the same topic?

On the influencer side, influencer marketing is all the rage right now and definitely something we are working on at DraftKings. You see influencer marketing all over the social space, most notably on Instagram. If you're able to partner with high-ranking influencers and have them create content for your brand that's going to relate to their followers and get you new customers, that's key.

You also need the right influencers. I'd be much more likely to sign up for DraftKings if I saw a famous player posting a video on Instagram about it than if some supermodel or YouTube personality did it. Make sure influencers and brands match. It's got to feel natural.

On the importance of authenticity

One thing I say all the time to people is don't try to win the Internet. The Internet can tell when you're trying too hard to relate a meme to a certain topic. It can tell when you put out a piece of creative media that's off-brand and that they're not used to seeing. It can tell when you're making a huge stretch to get a point across.

I've often found that the tweets that go viral are the ones I've thought the least about. If you're thinking too hard about a tweet, it's going to come off that way. You don't always have to try to swing for the fences. Sometimes singles, doubles, and triples are just as important to your success. It's all about getting your batting average—in this case, your engagement—up because that helps to tell the whole picture of your all-around game. Brands need to be authentic. If forcing ad language or doing things so off-brand is obvious to you as the publisher, it's obvious to your users.

On his day-to-day approach to the job

I'm a sports fan, and I'm a social media junkie. I just make and share things I think other people with the same mindset would find interesting, and it's worked. I always try to spin it back to DraftKings somehow, and if I can't, I post anyway because we're sports fans too, not just fantasy fans.

One example of this is "narrative street," a phrase coined in the DFS (daily fantasy sports community). It's self-explanatory: You draft certain players based on a narrative. For example, you could put together a graphic on a player right after a trade who is facing his former team in a big game. You know that the player is a popular topic from a narrative street already. So you capitalize on it and make content for it, and you could end up getting some very high engagement numbers. It shows the community that we're not just a brand—we are sports fans who know what we're talking about.

messages that aren't enjoying widespread success. Is the actual content not as good, or would it be more successful in front of a wider audience? Do the less successful messages hit the mark on content but miss on timing? Is there something off about the tone of the less successful messages?

How to Handle Feedback (Good and Bad)

Feedback is a natural aspect of the creative process, and many successful creators can take important lessons from the various sources of feedback they receive without allowing it to affect their personal feelings or their faith in their own creative processes. Unfortunately, feedback can also be incredibly challenging to deal with because creative people often struggle to separate the professional and personal aspects of the feedback they receive.

There are several different sources of feedback in relation to social media content, and each of them can present its own challenges to the creative person. The most public form of content feedback is built directly into the interface for most social networks, and that is the ability of users to comment on or reply to social media messages. Facebook, Instagram, and Twitter all provide users with the ability to publicly respond to content, and many users are not shy about expressing their feelings, positive or negative, regarding the content that they see.

Social media creators should take all types of feedback with a grain of salt. Don't let yourself become overconfident due to praise you receive or feel bad about yourself because of criticism you receive.

Feedback from nonprofessionals on the Internet may not be worth caring about in the first place. Much of the positive feedback on social media comes from audiences who are excited that a piece of content is focusing on their favorite players or teams, rather than being excited about the quality of the content itself. Much of the negative feedback on social media comes from people who don't care that much about the content, but they will leave negative responses anyway because they know it causes discomfort to the creator of the message.

© Human Kinetics

Consistently using social media is the best way to succeed at it.

There's a fascinating phenomenon called the online disinhibition effect (Suler, 2004) that explains this behavior. In short, people behave differently online than they would in person, and a person might be motivated by the lack of face-to-face interaction or repercussions to say or do things online that wouldn't be said or done in person.

Early Adoption

Social media is an ever-changing environment, as has been detailed earlier in this book. Social networks change over time, and as a creator, it is vitally important that you jump on those adaptations and additions as they take place.

We do not know what direction social media will take next. The backlash against Facebook could lead to another site with a greater emphasis on privacy and user control entering the picture. The increasing popularity of chat-based interactions could lead to the rise of a site like Discord. A network such as Twitter might continue to add base features that are less text-based. There's little sense in trying to

 Key Point @DoctorGC
Feedback on social media can be amazing! It can also be brutal. Don't take any of it personally, and don't let it change how you approach your job. #SocialMediaAndSports

predict the direction of things because the growth and change of communication technologies is rarely predictable or linear.

With that said, as things do change during your college and professional years, jump on those changes as early as you can and try to learn how to work with them. The earlier you can become comfortable with a new technology or method of connecting with people on social media, the better off you will be.

For example, early social media focused primarily on written messages and sometimes threw in still images, but video, animated GIFs, and sequential storytelling weren't part of the equation. When Snapchat launched, some social media creators ignored it, assuming that the large base of Twitter and Facebook would keep Snapchat inconsequential. But Snapchat's importance among young audiences eventually created an enormous demand for people who knew how to use Snapchat effectively, and that meant that the folks who took the time to learn how to effectively use Snapchat were suddenly a lot more valuable in the job market.

 Key Point @DoctorGC
Staying ahead of the curve on social media is important. Keep an eye on emerging trends in content creation, try them out, and be conscious of what is out there. #SocialMediaAndSports

Take Notes When It Happens

Your odyssey of content creation on social media is bound to have a series of highs and lows. There are going to be moments when your content just isn't landing with audiences and where nobody seems to be clicking on your stuff (let alone reacting to it). There will also be moments where extremely exciting things happen, like your first tweet going viral or your first Instagram post getting serious attention.

A key factor in developing your creative impulse on social media is to take notes throughout this whole process, and then periodically go back and examine those notes for ideas on how to improve your output moving forward. When something big lands, what were the factors that led to it? Did you feel like you were on a creative hot streak leading into that moment? Were there other things in your

area of sports or social media that influenced you at the time? By taking **reflective notes** on important things as they happen, you provide yourself with context for those moments that can be easily forgotten over time.

Consistency

Building an appreciative audience on social media is the same regardless of whether it's your own account or a huge sports entity's account. It's all about consistency—in posting, tone, and message. Audiences appreciate consistency. Most audience members have likely followed your social media accounts because they like what they have seen before, and they would like to see more of the same thing in the future.

From a timing perspective, consistency in sports media can be a bit tricky. You're going to be posting messages around games, but what about outside of that? In most cases, it is advisable to come up with a logical and consistent posting schedule during times when your team or athlete is not engaged in athletic competition.

A consistent **posting schedule** helps your creative approach because it forces you into a posting pattern where content has to be regularly generated. Some might look at this as a negative, but the pressure of having to come up with new material every day, rather than just when inspiration strikes, will lead you toward a more disciplined and sustainable level of creativity. You can use automated tools in social media management software to help come up with a regular posting schedule.

Generally, social media platforms have their highest engagement numbers between 9:00 a.m. and 4:00 p.m. on weekdays, but media-specific engagement tends to be at its highest just before and after those periods, which is normally when people are commuting to and from work (Arens, 2019). There are differences between platforms, such as Instagram tending to feature more media and business engagement in the late mornings, and Twitter featuring more engagement on Thursday evenings. Nevertheless, a good basic rule for content is to keep your regular posts happening during the periods that people are traveling to work, are at work, or are traveling home. Sports teams and sports media organizations will want to maintain a regular content posting schedule during those times, while also maintaining irregular posting schedules around games and other team events.

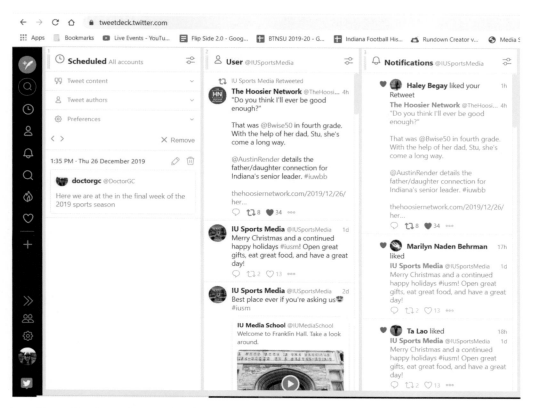

Tools such as TweetDeck can be used to help establish and maintain a posting schedule.

 Be sure to check out the web resource for more information on social media management software.

Instinct

Ultimately, what you want to create in yourself is an instinctive response to stimuli. When you see something that warrants a social media post, you don't want to spend forever thinking about it, then slowly craft a message around that thought process. Your onboarding of culture, content, and technical ability should eventually create the ability to react on instinct to things that occur.

Why is instinct so important? In the social media world, speed is among the most important forms of currency that exists, particularly when you can combine speed with appropriateness and accuracy. Social media content creators rightfully get criticized for hastily created messages that miss the mark or lack accuracy. But brands and their social media teams that instinctively read situations and react in ways that generate positive reaction and response are recognized as being good at using social media.

Much of instinct comes down to repetition. You have to be in the moment on social media, and you get there by continually posting in response to things that are happening while also observing the things that other accounts post. This is where following many accounts on social media comes in handy because it allows you to pattern your response instincts based on the things that you see that you feel have the greatest impact or do the best job of communicating what you want to communicate about a situation.

When you start out on social media, you may find yourself constantly overthinking what you're about to post. That generally leads to either not posting anything at all or posting something well after the moment has passed. Building instinct on social media has to include the process of going through with the posts you are considering. Don't try to be perfect every time you post on social media, especially early in your career. Avoid saying something that will get you fired, but don't be so paralyzed by trying to find the exact right words or phrase that you end up posting nothing at all. And as I've mentioned, take notes about how the process went, move on to the next moment, and incorporate what you've learned.

Mentality

When you combine all the elements in this chapter, you should develop a creative mentality when it comes to your social media work. Creativity isn't some magical formula that only exists in the brains of a select few. Instead, creativity is the product of consuming a great deal of information, evaluating that information effectively, and using that evaluative process to change the way you think to better use that information to produce content that audiences enjoy, appreciate, and want to share with others.

Having a creative mentality means that you are rewiring your brain to do more than just passively consume content, which is the default approach for most people who follow social media accounts as fans. You must become an **active consumer of content**, constantly thinking about how the content you see and hear affects you and others. Instead of thinking solely about the sport that's being mentioned in the content that you see, you have to think about the way the content works (or doesn't work) and what the content and its creator are trying to say or do. Once active consumption of content is central to your mentality, you'll find that applying the lessons that you learn to your own created content will work more naturally.

Summary

Creativity in social media is the same as creativity in any other media field. Some of it is inherent but most of it is learned, and that learning process involves familiarizing yourself with the important aspects of the field in which you are working. Social media creativity requires you to expand your vocabulary, cultural knowledge, and industry literacy to better understand both the field of sports social media and the tools you can use to increase the effectiveness of that communication.

Once you have established those building blocks of creativity outside of social media, the process continues within social media. Increasing the number of accounts you follow, observing those accounts, and taking notes on what is and is not successful are all key elements of the process. Talking to people within the sports social media world is important, both for the knowledge they can impart to you and for the networking connections those contacts provide.

Finally, increase your ability to be creative by actively engaging in social media creation on a consistent basis. Repeated posting on social media and a properly inquisitive approach to understanding why your posts succeed or fail will provide a much clearer sense of how to measure your own creativity on social media. Through that process, you put your mind in a position to develop creative responses organically, through repetition and development of instinct.

Review Questions

1. What is "industry literacy" and how does it apply to working in sports social media?
2. How does pop culture influence social media content creation?
3. Why is it important to increase your social media consumption if you are working in the business?
4. When are good times to schedule social media posts?

Audiences and Networks

CHAPTER OBJECTIVES

Not all social media networks are the same and neither are the audiences that use those networks. This chapter focuses on the following:

- Tracing the historical development of social media networks
- Helping you understand the demographic characteristics of major social media networks
- Highlighting how network infrastructure affects audience usage and growth

Professional social media usage relies on leveraging two connected elements: the audiences that form and use social media networks and the technological infrastructure of social media platforms. Both elements have consistently changed over the lifespan of what we now call social media, and it is important for professional social media users to understand the evolution of audiences and underlying social media platform infrastructures.

In my experience working with students and professionals regarding social media use in sports, there is a lot of attention paid to audiences but not that much attention to social media platform infrastructure. That is unfortunate because the platform infrastructures dictate a huge amount of the content that can be effectively used on a given social media platform as well as how audiences can or cannot effectively access and interact with that content.

This chapter takes a deeper look at how Internet audiences have used social media since the turn of the century. We trace the development of social media platforms and the types of audiences they attracted or allowed. We then talk about the infrastructure of present-day social media platforms and how the technological decisions that companies have made about the platforms affects audiences, messaging, and suitability for usage in sports social media.

Historical Development of Social Media Audiences

As we discussed in chapter 1, social media audiences slowly started to develop in the early 2000s along with the social networks that they would come to occupy. It's important to remember that during that time, not as many people were online. In 2000, only 50 percent of American adults used the Internet (Perrin & Duggan, 2015)—not "used social media" but used the whole Internet! That included mundane tasks such as checking your email. In the days before social media, being online still didn't have a tremendous amount of cache among the general population.

There is still a sizeable split in the age of people who use the Internet, and we will be talking about the differences in age groups throughout the chapter. But in 2000, the split in Internet usage based on age was even more pronounced than it is today. About 70 percent of young adults were using the Internet in that year, while under 50 percent of people aged 50 to 64 were online, and only 14 percent of people aged 65 and older were online (Perrin & Duggan, 2015).

There was also a rather pronounced separation in Internet usage based on one's level of education and household income. Of American adults with a college degree, 78 percent used the Internet during that time, compared with only 40 percent of those with just a high school diploma and less than 20 percent of those without a high school diploma (Perrin & Duggan, 2015). In terms of income, 81 percent of households making US$75,000 or more in 2000 were online, compared with 34 percent of households making less than US$30,000.

Understanding the online audience origin is important because these patterns end up setting the scene for much of what was to follow in terms of social media audience development. The core audiences for social media would track very closely to the Internet audience before social media: young, educated, and middle-to-upper class.

Table 4.1 illustrates some of the more popular social media platforms, their broad market demographics as of 2020, and the types of messages that work the best within the platform architecture.

Myspace

It was into this Internet world that Myspace entered, showcasing a profile-based, connection-centered infrastructure that was discussed in chapter 1. By Myspace's third year of existence, its demographic profile skewed older than one might expect. Of the network's nearly 56 million users, 51.7 percent of them were aged 35 or older, and only 30 percent were under the age of 25 (Comscore, n.d.).

In hindsight, there should have been alarms and warning bells going off in Myspace offices around this time. Despite network accounts being available to everyone (as opposed to Facebook's college-email-only approach at the time), Myspace was not only failing to expand its percentage of younger audiences but also actively watching them shrink. From 2005 to 2006, Myspace lost nearly 13 percent of its age 12 to 17 audience, and 1.4 percent of its age 18 to 24 audience (Comscore, n.d.). Some at the time viewed these demographic shifts as evidence that social media was maturing and becoming more appealing to older audiences. True, social media was about to do that, but not on Myspace, which would start hemorrhaging users, money, and market share within a few years due to poor design and management decisions (Lee, 2011).

Were young users the canary in the coal mine for Myspace, figuring out earlier than others that the social network wasn't delivering on a long-lasting product? It certainly seems that way, and it would be the start of a pattern that would repeat itself more than once in social media development.

Facebook

If social media has anything close to a ubiquitous network, it would unquestionably be Facebook, with over 2 billion global users as of 2020. But Facebook

TABLE 4.1 Important Social Media Platforms

Platform	Demographics	Types of media	Best uses
Facebook	Largest percentage of overall users; greatest popularity among people 40+	Video, images, written pieces, stories	Major events posting, live video, community interaction
YouTube	Audience nearly as large as Facebook, all ages	Preproduced video, live-streaming video	Produced shows, exciting visual content
Instagram	Most popular among 18-34 demographic	Stories, images, candid video	Compelling visuals, graphics with information
Snapchat	Dominated by ages 12-23	Stories, video	Behind-the-scenes, youth-oriented content
Twitter	Used by opinion leaders, brands, and journalists; use lower among "average" user; not popular in Europe	Short messages, links to other platforms	Breaking news, live game updates
Pinterest	Demographics vary, popular among women in USA	Images	Merchandise, visuals
WhatsApp / Facebook Messenger	Popular messaging app outside of USA	Links to content	Direct-to-fans messaging

didn't start out this way, and it's important to trace the development of the Facebook audience for clues as to why it succeeded on a scale that few other social networks have been able to approach.

Early Facebook

The approach that Facebook took with its early audiences guaranteed that the bulk of users would be in the sweet spot of the primary Internet demographics: young, educated, and affluent. From the moment of launch, Facebook kept a tight hold on admission to the network at first by only allowing new users from Harvard University, where Mark Zuckerberg and his cofounders were students. Within a month, over 50 percent of Harvard's undergraduate population had signed up for a profile on the site (Phillips, 2007). The site gradually expanded to other elite East Coast schools, then to schools across North America (Phillips, 2007), and then to anyone with a .edu email address.

Facebook for All

Facebook gradually expanded its user base beyond just college students but in doing so chose to initially focus on the groups sitting at either end of the college experience. High school students in the United States could start signing up for accounts in late 2005 (Phillips, 2007), and then people with email addresses of large corporations were allowed to sign up (Hansell, 2006), largely to help recently graduated college students maintain a presence on the network. By September 2006, Facebook was ready to open its membership doors to everyone, with Zuckerberg explaining in 2006, "We have two years of alums already, and more than one-third of the people using the site are not in college anymore . . . If we make it so other young people can use the site, it strengthens the experience for everybody" (Hansell, 2006).

Facebook Today

The growth and expansion of Facebook after the network started letting everyone sign up for an account led to a dominance in the social media marketplace that no networks have been able to challenge. By 2012, the number of U.S. adults who had used Facebook was triple the amount of the nearest competitor and represented more than half of all adults in the country (Gramlich, 2019). Almost a decade later, Facebook still held a nearly 2-to-1 audience lead over all other traditional social networks, with 69 percent of U.S. users having used

Key Point @DoctorGC
Facebook still has a huge size advantage over every other traditional social network, with users outnumbering other sites by an almost 2-to-1 margin. #SocialMediaAndSports

Facebook compared with only 37 percent for Instagram and 22 percent for Twitter (Gramlich, 2019).

Facebook achieved more than mere market penetration during this time. At the end of the 2010s, Facebook still led all social networks in U.S. adults who visited the site at least once a day. The network also became a primary portal for news, with 43 percent of Americans receiving their news from Facebook, compared with 21 percent for YouTube and 12 percent for Twitter (Gramlich, 2019).

Facebook's total **daily active user (DAU)** numbers across the globe exceed its numbers in the USA and Canada. As of 2019, there were 186 million DAUs in the USA and Canada, 286 million DAUs in Europe, 600 million DAUs in the Asia-Pacific region, and 490 million DAUs across the rest of the world (Schulze, 2019).

Signs of Trouble

However, the end of the 2010s signaled some of the same warnings for Facebook that Myspace encountered more than a decade earlier. While still the top social network in the United States, Facebook use had declined from 67 percent to 61 percent between 2017 and 2019 (Webster, 2019).

The news related to young users and Facebook started to look dire as well. A Pew study in 2018 showed that Facebook's popularity among teen users had dropped precipitously from its early days, with only 51 percent of teens saying they used Facebook at all, and only 10 percent saying that they used Facebook the most often of any social network, far behind the numbers of Snapchat (35 percent) and YouTube (32 percent) and even trailing corporate stablemate Instagram (15 percent) (Anderson & Jiang, 2018). From 2017 to 2019, there was a 22 percent decrease in Facebook usage among Americans 12 to 34, dropping the total percentage for that demographic down to 62 percent.

What has been the cause of Facebook's decline in popularity among young people? A large part of it has been the perception of Facebook as an older person's network, which has both reduced the coolness factor of Facebook and given rise to legitimate fears from teens and young adults that monitoring from elders keeps them from being able to express themselves in culturally significant ways among their peers.

The perceived lack of effective privacy controls on Facebook as well as the practical reality that you probably can't unfriend your mom without repercussions have led young people to divert time and attention to sites such as Snapchat and Instagram, where their content feeds can be freer and more personal, and their friend lists can be more carefully curated. Research into social media platform penetration of the age 12 to 34 demographic (Webster, 2019) indicates that while Facebook's numbers have dropped in that area, so have several other social media platforms during the same time. This includes Twitter (7 percent drop), Pinterest (5 percent drop), and LinkedIn (2 percent drop).

Facebook has also faced a growing amount of criticism in the press for its role in the dissemination of fake news and misinformation, an issue compounded by the number of people who receive news through Facebook. The European Union enacted the General Data Protection Regulation (GDPR) in 2018, stricter privacy laws targeted at social media in general and Facebook in particular, that led to a temporary drop in Facebook users (Schulze, 2019), although those numbers did recover relatively quickly. Furthermore, many users expressed confusion over how Facebook's newsfeed and advertising algorithm worked (Gramlich, 2019).

Smartphones and Mobile Facebook Access

A key component in Facebook's continued growth and cultural acceptance was the release of the original iPhone in 2007. Smartphones, and eventually tablets, would revolutionize the way in which most people interacted with online platforms. Adaptation of smartphones grew consistently over time. The Pew Research Center first surveyed smartphone ownership numbers in 2011 and found that 35 percent of American consumers owned one. By 2018, that number had more than doubled to 77 percent, exceeding the percentage of Americans who owned a desktop or laptop computer (Pew Internet, 2018).

Aurora Samperio/NurPhoto via Getty Images

Facebook has come under significant scrutiny due to privacy concerns and issues with message veracity, compelling Mark Zuckerberg to testify before Congress in 2019.

From an **audience access** perspective, the introduction of smartphones was important because most early adopters of smartphones were young adults and teens, demographic groups whose ability to access Facebook and other social media in a mobile setting ensured that those networks had a steady supply of active young users just as older demographics were fully adapting to online access via traditional computer-based means.

Twitter

While Facebook's audience development started with college-aged users and then gradually expanded, Twitter's audience initially developed within the business climate of Silicon Valley and the cultural sensibilities of people in their immediate post-college years. Twitter was introduced at popular media festival *South by Southwest (SXSW)*, gained acceptance in the San Francisco Bay Area as a network used extensively by tech professionals, and gradually rounded into shape as a site very popular with journalists, celebrities, and business leaders.

The attraction of Twitter to those audiences was its clean, no-nonsense **design**, which made it perfect for rapid dissemination of news, demonstrations of wit and intelligence, and the possibility of having near real-time discussions with people across the country (or around the world) about important things going on in culture and society. Someone who is not a celebrity could get a Twitter account and possibly have a discussion with a celebrity, well-known journalist, or other public figure.

While this led to significant early growth for Twitter, the problem for the network was that its user numbers stopped well short of catching Facebook and then slowly started receding in popularity versus other social networks introduced in the mid-2010s. Instagram, Snapchat, Pinterest, and LinkedIn would all eventually become more widely used among social media platforms than would Twitter.

A collection of different problems caused Twitter many issues in terms of growth. New users struggled to understand how to find people with whom to interact, and while Twitter tried to address that by providing **suggested accounts**, most of the accounts suggested were media or celebrities. Once new users did find their way onto the network, they struggled with understanding exactly what they were supposed to do—write tweets? Respond to other people's tweets? Simply follow and observe what others were saying? For a celebrity looking for an audience or a media member trying to publicize their content, Twitter provided much value. But for a teenager looking to communicate with friends, or a middle-aged person wanting to interact with peers, it fell short.

Twitter excels as a **broadcast channel**, allowing brands and influencers to communicate with each other and with the small part of the online population that uses the site daily. However, Twitter isn't nearly as successful as a social network because its users generally aren't extending existing **personal connections** on the platform and make relatively small numbers of new personal connections, especially when compared with Facebook, Instagram, or Snapchat.

Instagram

The growth of Instagram's popularity over the late 2010s makes it hard to believe that the platform hasn't been around since the dawn of social media. The photo-sharing (and editing) network has become the platonic ideal of a social media network: enough freedom to express yourself and showcase your world, enough privacy to avoid revealing more about yourself than you want to, the ability to follow celebrities and brands without their messaging becoming overwhelming, and the ability to combine moments into curated stories that are shared with connections.

When it launched, Instagram provided a different sort of **social media experience** than the existing crop of Facebook, Twitter, and Myspace. Its experience centered around abstraction, creativity, and images in place of words. As one early Instagram user noted, "Usually people are sharing beautiful images, so I feel like it's more positive emotions, rather than people who bitch on Facebook or complain that it's Monday or something like that" (Ashpari, 2012).

Instagram offered users glimpses into enticing worlds that would not normally be accessible. These glimpses came both via friends' feeds and through feeds from celebrities and brands (Bolt, 2011). While photo sharing existed on other social networks,

 Key Point @DoctorGC
The original design of Twitter was focused on quick dissemination of small amounts of data, which made it perfect for the rapid spread of news and information across the globe. #SocialMediaAndSports

SOCIAL MEDIA SUCCESSES IN SPORT: TEXAS TECH

Within the United States, many athletic departments have been able to foster a high level of national popularity through their teams' successes. Institutions such as the University of Alabama, Duke University, and the University of Southern California have enjoyed nationwide and worldwide visibility and media attention due to their football or basketball programs.

Texas Tech University would be unlikely to make any list of best-known universities. A relatively small public school in west Texas, its athletic successes have been overshadowed by regional powers like Oklahoma and Texas A&M.

However, an unexpected run to the men's basketball Final Four in the spring of 2019 gave the university a chance to gain a broader national audience. The power of social media allowed Texas Tech to capitalize on that opportunity, promoting a synergy between

Texas Tech Basketball ✓
@TexasTechMBB

🔟 straight Big 1️⃣ 2️⃣ wins.

⚫#4To1 | #WreckEm⚫

RECAP: No. 22 Red Raiders 85, Oklahoma State 50
Jahmi'us Ramsey scored 18 points, TJ Holyfield went for 17 and seven rebounds and Chris Clarke added double-digit rebounds for the sixth time this season to ...
🔗 texastech.com

6:28 PM · Jan 4, 2020 · Twitter Web App

Courtesy of Texas Tech

Texas Tech's social media presence includes both brand-based tweets such as this and athlete-based posts where players serve as brand ambassadors.

the athletic department, a star basketball player, the department's social media team, and social media industry consultants.

Texas Tech star Jarrett Culver was used as one aspect of the team's approach to social media connection with fans, with the athletic department's social media team producing highlights, graphics, and other content that provided fans a platform for connecting with Culver on a more significant level (Yasak, 2019).

While many college athletic departments discourage social media use among athletes, Texas Tech took a different approach. The social media department spent the season crafting messages for Culver and other players, allowing them to grow their own brands while also connecting those brands directly to Texas Tech. This pattern of athlete-driven content allowed the athletes to serve as both their own brands and brand ambassadors for the university.

The approach yielded significant popularity for Texas Tech athletics while also providing Culver's social media audience and overall brand with a significant boost. His combined Twitter and Instagram follower counts exploded during the season, rising 1,100 percent from the start of the year to the end (Yasak, 2019).

Texas Tech's success highlights some key lessons for sports teams when it comes to social media:

- *Don't be locked into traditional approaches.* Just because you haven't leveraged athletes through media in the past doesn't mean you can't change your ways.
- *Social media can be a great equalizer.* Even if your brand is not historically expansive, a good strategy on social media can level the playing field.
- *Audiences love engaging content.* Think about what your audience wants and then figure out a way to give it to them.

it was not a central part of the experience. At the time of Instagram's launch, Twitter images still had to be hosted off-site, and Facebook had yet to fully transition to a network that revolved around photo and video sharing.

One of Instagram's most attractive features since its launch has been the suite of options it offers to smartphone users in terms of making their photographs look more professional and aesthetically pleasing. As industry expert Nate Bolt observed shortly after Instagram launched:

> The quality of camera phone images and filters . . . is now relatively high. Instagram came along and offered the same quality and visual appeal as other phone apps but added a simple and well-designed interface to let you choose filters after the photo was taken . . . Even if you compare Instagram photos to . . . all the tricks and desktop software that photographers use, Instagram photos have a decent quality. The Instagram images are certainly not *comparable* in terms of quality or resolution, duh, but the images are at least interesting. (Bolt, 2011, ¶3)

Initially, Instagram kept the viewing experience simple, with only one photo displayed at a time in a feed format that allowed you to see as many or as few photos as you wanted within a single session. The later addition of Instagram **stories** had the dual effect of cutting the heart out of a business rival in Snapchat by lifting its most appealing network feature while also expanding the "access to other worlds" effect at the center of Instagram's user experience.

Unlike Twitter's struggles with youth popularity and audience growth, Instagram has excelled in both areas since its 2010 launch. In 2019, Instagram firmly established itself as the most popular social network not named Facebook, with 37 percent of U.S. adults using it, including 75 percent of U.S adults aged 18 to 24 (Perrin & Anderson, 2018). Instagram also fielded the second-largest net daily usage among all social networks, with 63 percent of users accessing the app at least once a day and 42 percent accessing it several times a day (Perrin

& Anderson, 2018). And among 12- to 34-year-olds in the United States, Instagram was the third most-used social media platform in 2019 (Webster, 2019), with 26 percent of users in that demographic identifying it as such, barely trailing Facebook (29 percent) and Snapchat (28 percent).

 Instagram's popularity makes it a crucial part of sports social media. Learn more about how to effectively use it in the web resource.

Snapchat

The development and maturation of Snapchat has been fascinating to watch from an audience perspective. While Facebook, Instagram, Twitter, and other platforms all ultimately live in the same ecosystem, Snapchat largely occupies its own space. Users communicate directly with each other or in small groups, there is no **native functionality** for sharing Snapchat content to other platforms, and there's no traditional home screen for the user's account.

Snapchat's big advantage in terms of audience attraction and retention has been its lack of public, shareable content infrastructure. Teens and college students feel more comfortable posting on Snapchat than other social media, and the lack of public performance required on Snapchat versus other social media platforms is a key element for many younger people. As one teen noted, Snapchat "feels more like communication than like exhibition. More like I'm talking to somebody" (Harrison, 2019).

While Snapchat was projected in 2019 to lose users for the first time (Wang, 2019), the overall share of 12- to 34-year-olds who identified Snapchat as their most-used social media brand was 28 percent, a number only eclipsed by Facebook (29 percent), and just barely (Webster, 2019). Despite direct attempts by Facebook and Facebook-owned Instagram to copy Snapchat's most popular features, young users appear unlikely to give up their Snapchat use anytime soon.

As the turn of the decade approached, Snapchat continued to diversify its feature set, adding **gaming** and **augmented reality (AR)** features (Harrison, 2019). One popular AR feature was a gender-swap filter released in the spring of 2019 that allowed users to make themselves look like their opposite sex, leading some former users who had deleted Snapchat from their phones to reinstall the app (Barron, 2019).

 Key Point @DoctorGC ⌄

Instagram's focus on visual storytelling and simple yet effective controls have made it very popular among younger audiences. #SocialMediaAndSports

YouTube

While Facebook, Instagram, Snapchat, and Twitter are very obviously social media networks, other important online environments should be mentioned in any discussion of audiences and social media. First among those is YouTube, the video content platform that launched in 2005.

Those who argue that YouTube isn't a social media network point to how it exists primarily as a place where people go for content rather than for interaction with other accounts. This is a worthwhile point to make, since most active social media users are consumers of YouTube content, not creators. Furthermore, while most Internet users have YouTube accounts if they have a Google account, most do not use the social aspects of the network, avoiding commenting and messaging with others.

However, YouTube's robust worldwide user base, the ease of creating and uploading visual content, and the ability to easily embed that content across sites like Facebook and Twitter make YouTube an important part of the social media firmament. The increasingly visual orientation of social media continues to increase the importance of YouTube, and its global reach makes it one of the few truly worldwide media environments. As of 2019, over 40,000 YouTube channels had at least 250,000 subscribers, and those channels produced nearly 50,000 hours of content in just one week (Van Kessel, Toor, & Smith, 2019). Only 17 percent of the content was posted with English as the sole language used, highlighting the global reach of the network (Van Kessel et al., 2019).

For many years, social media trafficking sites did not consider YouTube a social media network, and therefore did not track its users in comparison to more traditional platforms. Pew Research Center started doing so among users in the United States in 2018 and found that YouTube was used more than any other platform (73 percent), even more than Facebook (69 percent) and more than double any other social network (Pew Research Center, 2019). YouTube also ranked as the social media platform with the most active users in countries as distinct as Great Britain and India (Iqbal, 2019).

YouTube's network infrastructure is primarily focused on curation and delivery of content. Viewers can create playlists of videos, search the extensive YouTube library for videos, or use YouTube's algorithm for identifying videos to watch. YouTube also features pay-per-view movies and content as well as livestreaming videos. Of all the social media platforms mentioned in this chapter, YouTube is the only major one to offer a subscription version of its service as of 2019. This service allows users to avoid advertisements and commercials being inserted into videos while they are watching.

For video content creators, YouTube offers an increasingly robust set of features, including online video editing, the ability to embed messages and advertisements on top of videos, and the opportunity to link videos to each other in a series format. Content creators also have monetization options on their videos, most of which are reserved for accounts that exceed 1,000 subscribers.

Pinterest

When the CEO comes out in the press and says that the service he runs is not a social media network (Bonnington, 2018), you should take him at his word, right? And yet Pinterest, which debuted at roughly the same time as Instagram, shares a lot in common with its social media cousins. Its audience popularity in the United States exceeds that of Snapchat and Twitter, and while its overall user base in Europe is relatively low (8.3 percent), it is still more popular than Twitter and Instagram in that region (Statcounter, 2019).

Pinterest's infrastructure differs from the other social media platforms discussed in this chapter. Users create visual interest boards and pin items to those boards, allowing the user to collect ideas, thoughts, or links. Pinterest gains significant exposure to women, particularly in the United States, with the site reaching 83 percent of women aged 25 to 54 (Cooper, 2019). Much of Pinterest's attractiveness to audiences may lie in two of the aspects of social media that other networks have enjoyed: It is primarily visual, much like Instagram, and it is less performative and public, similar to Snapchat.

Reddit

Of all the networks and platforms discussed in this chapter, Reddit is the least-used among audiences in the United States, with only 11 percent of online users on the site (Pew Research Center, 2019). However, Reddit is an important and emerging social media network, one that warrants close observation as social media enters its third decade.

Reddit's infrastructure centers on forums, called subreddits, that focus on areas of shared interest among users. The users on Reddit can opt for anonymity, an interesting distinction from Facebook. Reddit users post messages within subreddits, and then those messages are interacted with by other users through two primary methods: commenting and upvoting/downvoting. Both interactions affect how the Reddit algorithm evaluates the message, with popular, controversial, or hot topics moving up the display order of the subreddit, and poorly regarded material sliding down the display order.

Many subreddits feature thriving communities of interested and engaged people who post and comment regularly about the topics at hand, with most of the best-trafficked subreddits featuring unpaid moderators that police the content and interactions posted by users. Sports subreddits can be quite active. For instance, the NBA subreddit had 2.7 million members as of late 2019, with over 50,000 active users online during peak hours. The soccer subreddit had similarly large numbers, with 1.7 million users, over 20,000 of them online during peak hours.

Reddit has struggled with issues relating to user harassment, moderator protests, and distasteful content being posted on its subreddits (Isaac, 2015). However, Reddit continues to grow in popularity, and many of the sports communities on the site contain highly identified fans who are interested in quality content.

WhatsApp

Although WhatsApp does not get regularly mentioned in the United States as a social media network, it would be foolish to ignore the power of this platform when it comes to connecting people and, increasingly, brands. The simplicity of the platform, its built-in encryption, and its focus on person-to-person and small group communication has made it tremendously popular among people worldwide (Manjoo, 2016).

This messaging service, purchased by Facebook in 2014, is unquestionably one of the biggest global communication services that currently exists. As of 2019, WhatsApp had 1.5 billion users across 180 countries, with one billion active users sending 65 billion messages a day (Iqbal, 2019). It ranked as the top social messaging service in most countries around the world, including nearly all of Western and Central Europe, Russia, India, Indonesia, Brazil, and Canada (Iqbal, 2019). And yet WhatsApp has struggled to gain audience share in the United States, where its user base was only 23 million at the turn of the decade. It has fewer users than Twitter.

There are important reasons for this discrepancy, largely due to communication infrastructure in the United States. Most United States smartphone plans included either free text messaging or Apple's iMessage system from an early point in the smartphone's release history, whereas many cellular

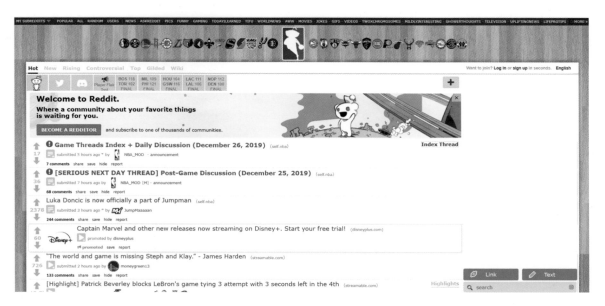

Reddit's forum system includes subreddits like /r/NBA, a popular place for fans of the association to converse about their favorite teams.

carriers in other countries started off by charging users per message. While many of those plans have changed since then, the free communication offered by WhatsApp allowed it to establish a strong user base. Other messaging apps and services filled in the gaps for users in the United States, with Facebook Messenger and the popularity of apps like Instagram allowing users to connect to their friends on these platforms instead of WhatsApp.

WhatsApp's sizeable global user base will cause it to remain a key element of online social communication well into the future. Facebook has already attempted to monetize WhatsApp through the introduction of business controls and its own Facebook News Feed tie-in (Gesenhues, 2018).

Network Infrastructure and the Effects on Audiences

From a technological perspective, social media networks are more alike than they are different. They all rely on a graphical user interface that connects each user to the back end of their own account. This allows the user to connect to accounts controlled by other people and entities, create media that is distributed into the network, and limit access by selected accounts to the created media. But once you get past that shared core functionality, the difference in infrastructure starts to affect everything, from the type and number of people who use the social media platform to the kinds of content that people consider appropriate for posting on the platform.

For most brands and people using social media networks, content creators have two primary things they must do to achieve their goals:

1. Maintain social media accounts that audiences actively choose to follow
2. Create social media messages that audiences want to see

Given those two goals, how do each of the social media platforms help you achieve them? The earlier details supplied in this chapter about the audience composition and basic infrastructure of social media networks is a good start.

 You can keep up-to-date with the latest information and tips on leveraging these platforms effectively through this book's web resource.

Figure 4.1 shows a basic process of message creation on social media. This process highlights three important aspects of the process:

1. Understanding the concept of the message you want to create and filtering that concept through your brand's identity
2. Understanding the constraints of the platform you want to publish on and the target audiences on those platforms
3. Reaching existing followers of your social media channels and expanding your audience to capture new followers

The result is a message that should capture new audience members and retain existing audience members on that platform.

As you consider your posting options for social media content, always keep in mind the way that your content will be affected by the network infrastructure and the likely audiences that your content will be encountered by on that network. You will have to create variations in your content creation strategy based on what network you plan to post the content. That's a good thing because content posted with no regard for the network it is on or the audience that is viewing it is not very good content.

The following sections provide tips to help better understand how infrastructure affects content and audiences.

FIGURE 4.1 Network infrastructure and message creation.

PROFESSIONAL INSIGHTS

Social Media Networks

Danielle Kilgo

Twitter: @danikathleen

LinkedIn: www.linkedin.com/in/daniellekilgo/

Academia.edu: https://indiana.academia.edu/DanielleKilgo

Scholarly research on social media provides us with a chance to see broader societal and cultural trends in how networks are used, how users interact, and how social media fits within society. Assistant Professor Danielle Kilgo of Indiana University is an expert in social media research, and she gives us insight on several different aspects of the social media world in this Q&A.

Q: How do you define "social network," and do you think it's a good or bad idea to try to create a rigid definition?

DK: The emphasis on only one definition or perspective of social networking is so limiting in academic scholarship. To me, social networks are the connection of people—one node connecting to another node. If that's happening through a specific platform like Twitter, then that's one venue for thinking about a social network. But if we just say, "Twitter is a social network and Reddit is not," then we're really blocking out the ways that networks can be made and the parallel conversations that can be taking place within different groups.

Q: With the various issues it has faced over the last few years, many people have vowed to leave Facebook. Do you think it's still possible for a single social network to be the central location for everyone to interact online?

DK: I think when you get 2.7 billion people on a social media site, you can expect that somebody's going to get annoyed about something and find a niche somewhere else (or make it themselves).

And why would you want there to only be one location for interaction? People will always need something different. It's not just the network and the site affordances; it includes considerations like the people who are already in a network and people's willingness to adapt to changes and cultures. For example, we know that we typically adopt technologies at a much slower rate as we age, and we're less likely to change to a new technology. So to achieve a central site, the young people would go where all the older people are, and that's what's driven younger people away from sites like Facebook already. So no, I don't think a single social network can be universal at this stage.

Q: Facebook seems to be losing its youth demographic. Does that raise concerns that Facebook could die in the same way that some other social networks have in the past?

DK: We've seen a rotation of sites for a while. Myspace was one of those sites that died. I don't see Facebook dying, but I do think it will face challenges. Facebook has gotten so big that it isn't able to cater to all the individual interests of people. And, of course, it's also wrapped up in scandal and controversy.

Facebook and Twitter, I don't think these sites are dying. But I do anticipate we're just going to have more diversity in the sites people like to use, especially as technology develops, and Facebook and Twitter won't always be the essential players.

[Losing the youth demographic] could change Facebook's culture long term. I think it is going to be a space young people connect with but avoid until they are older. But to this day, I ask my students, "Do you have Facebook?" and most of them still do. They just don't use it because their moms are on there. I think those students will recapture wanting to use it later in life, especially as more companies start using Facebook groups and because more classes use Facebook as a means of classroom collaboration. We've introduced its relevance into all kinds of different places in our lives. I don't see people completely losing interest in Facebook because it's so integrated.

(continued)

Professional Insights *(continued)*

Q: Twitter sees a lot of usage by politicians and media and businesses. Do you see Twitter getting to a point where it can appeal to a larger public audience?

DK: Well, Twitter does appeal to some large demographic groups. "Black Twitter" is made up of about 25 percent of black adults that use the Internet. So Twitter does appeal to major publics that are powerful and separate from elites.

As for the general public, a lot of [the lack of larger public audience] is a result of the media's fascination with Twitter. News media have a somewhat unhealthy obsession with it, and the general public doesn't even have to have a Twitter account or network to be able to access what they need from those spaces. From a social network perspective, Twitter doesn't need the general public to make accounts because the information is communicated beyond the site already.

Q: What is it about Instagram that people find so appealing to use?

DK: Generally speaking, for young people, their parents weren't there before they were. That's a bonus. For users generally, Instagram forced you to talk in pictures. There's a big push overall on social media to talk in pictures, to talk in GIFs and emojis, to use pictures to communicate thoughts and feelings.

There appear to be fewer risks in posting things on Instagram than on Twitter or Facebook because of the network structures and because it is mostly apolitical. I did a study on the Women's March, thinking I would find a ton of influencers that were constantly talking about women's rights. But Instagram is more of a self-presentation or selfie network. This was a place where users took selfies and showed their participation in the march but didn't constantly become vocal advocates or engage in debates. Instagram is not necessarily a place where you fight other people all the time about political issues, as is the case with other social network sites. That might change in the future, especially as news organizations try to engage audiences in that space. But I don't see Instagram becoming the go-to location for conversations about politics or news anytime soon.

Q: A social network that doesn't get talked about as much is Reddit. What's your perspective on how Reddit is used and what its network allows?

DK: Reddit has evolved quite a bit since its early days. It's got just about as many users as Twitter, and it's a place where many people read but don't engage, so there are likely more redditors. They just don't have accounts. It has been one of the most visited websites for years and years. We used to think of it as a previral network because the conversations that users had there were so robust and topic-centric. Reddit was a hub for finding content and memes that could potentially go viral.

One of Reddit's biggest advantages is that you don't have to identify yourself, which some people have always said would breed incivility. That's fair. But what it also allows for is the negotiation of identity politics and network politics that are more present or visible on other social media sites.

Reddit's also organized in mini groups or subreddits, where users engage with each other because they are interested or invested in the same topic or share a common interest, not because they know each other. People join networks with intention and can have conversations about what they want to have conversations about, and all the other social media functions are somewhat secondary. Plus, Reddit has a system of upvoting and downvoting, which is effective and helps the site balance out its algorithms. Reddit is structured very differently [than other social media sites], and I think it has many advantages.

The disadvantage to Reddit is its reputation: It has a history of being a hub for extremists, racists, and sex offenders, and the site may never be able to overcome those obstacles in the arena of public perception. However, Reddit's design doesn't necessarily mean that you have to like the website itself. Many users simply go to a specific subreddit and become part of that community. It's more about identifying with a community in that subreddit than it is about liking Reddit.

Twitter's System

The network infrastructure of Twitter is straightforward and a good place to start any discussion of how social network infrastructure helps to define both the network and its audience, for better or worse. Twitter's infrastructure relies on a simple concept, where each account is uniform in importance. A teenager's account has the same basic place in the Twitter network infrastructure as a celebrity, and a Twitter "egg" account with zero followers has the same basic place as a multinational corporation's account.

Modifying variables help users distinguish which accounts are more important to them. Early in the network's lifespan, Twitter launched **verified accounts**, which placed a blue check mark next to the accounts of celebrities and public officials to help users know that they were following that actual person, rather than a fake account purporting to be that person (Cashmore, 2009).

Twitter also gives search preference to accounts that have accrued large number of followers and to accounts that match the user's geographic location and language preference, among other variables. Twitter also allows account owners, including businesses, to purchase advertising space via **promoted tweets** so that their messages appear in the timelines of targeted audiences, regardless of whether the audience member was following that account.

Twitter's system works largely because the standardization of the Twitter newsfeed compresses all messages sent on the service. Since every post is limited to a short number of characters, the newsfeed avoids becoming visually unwieldy for users and is largely reliant on what accounts the user chooses to follow. Users can therefore customize their newsfeeds by creating a mix of personal, professional, and other accounts to follow and can simply mute or unfollow accounts that are no longer wanted.

This compression process also means that effective messaging on Twitter is dependent on how effectively the account uses the limited number of characters and space that each message provides.

 Key Point @DoctorGC
Twitter has changed aspects of its network to improve the user experience and make the service more attractive to advertisers. #SocialMediaAndSports

The concept of effectiveness on Twitter is subjective and often depends on the goals of the account doing the tweeting. For many brands, effective tweeting may be to generate engagement with the audience or to generate an intent to purchase on the part of the consumer. For a journalist, effectiveness may involve developing a long-term rapport with the audience or being able to clearly communicate observations and opinions on a news story.

Facebook's System

Facebook's decision to allow anyone to sign up for an account certainly opened the floodgates for the network in terms of audience numbers, but that wasn't the only major change that it made during the late 2000s. From a commercial perspective, I would argue that Facebook's decision to diverge from the "one person, one profile" approach it had taken throughout the first five years was even more significant and set up much of what was to come for the company commercially over the next decade.

Facebook's initial network infrastructure was similar to Twitter, with all profiles being equal. However, the nature of Facebook's profiles made this arrangement problematic for privacy-minded users. Whereas Twitter's profiles don't require any private information to be made public about a user, the entire purpose of Facebook profiles was for users to display as much private information about themselves as possible. Facebook users were generally fine sharing that private information with friends and other users but were not happy about providing businesses with Facebook profiles access to that information. Additionally, "friending" people on Facebook required that both users mutually follow each other, whereas on Twitter (and later, Instagram) it was possible for only one account to follow another, without reciprocity.

Facebook introduced a major change to its approach in 2007 with the development of Facebook Pages. Business could now create something that looked like a Facebook profile but allowed private users to follow the business without giving the business direct access to photos, wall posts, and other personal items that the user did not wish to divulge.

The new Pages also gave business owners much greater control over their Facebook presence through a suite of features. This included the ability to create events that Facebook users could indicate interest in, the ability to pay for certain posts to appear in users' Facebook feeds, and the ability to

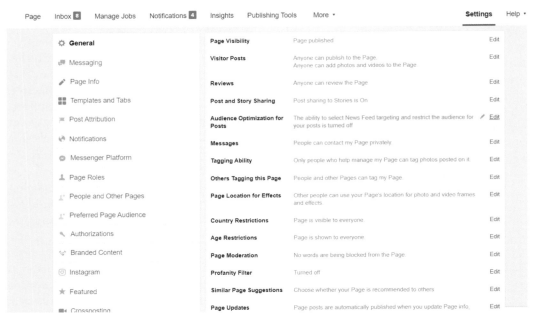

An example of the back end of Facebook for businesses.

directly sell products and merchandise to users. It also allowed business owners the ability to create posts that users could comment on and share to their own profiles.

That change, and the subsequent ability of businesses and brands to connect directly to users and provide them with an array of services, allowed Facebook to monetize itself in a way that no other social media platform has been able to achieve. A business page on Facebook has many tools to help with posts, traffic, and interactions with audience members, and learning how to use those tools can maximize your time spent on the network.

Even with a separate class of business-oriented pages, it can still be a challenge to cultivate a new audience on Facebook. The platform seems oriented toward making businesses purchase advertising that appears in targeted users' feeds, and it can be difficult to break through the Facebook algorithm in other ways to reach the people you're trying to reach. Getting users to engage with your content,

Key Point @DoctorGC ⌄

Facebook provides businesses with a suite of back-end services that allow them to better isolate and target certain members of the audience. #SocialMediaAndSports

through likes, comments, and shares, can have a positive effect on traffic, but the success of that may be limited by the nature of the audience you're aiming for.

The fake account problem on Facebook made this situation worse. As of May 2019, Facebook had reportedly already removed 2.2 billion fake accounts since the start of that calendar year (Stewart, 2019). While Facebook has claimed that it catches most fake accounts as they are created, the sheer number of fake accounts being created means that at least five percent of all Facebook accounts are fake, perhaps many more (Stewart, 2019).

Instagram Infrastructure

The way Instagram is set up allows for a relatively straightforward approach to posting content. The platform offers a business account option, which provides the ability to post, tag, and cross-post across other platforms while also providing the ability to edit in the platform itself, import images from elsewhere on your mobile device, or use a computer browser to upload images or videos.

Direct brand-to-user contact on Instagram can also be difficult unless your brand is already relevant to the users you are aiming for. Similar to Facebook's system, there are incentives to use paid promotion of content to break through the algorithm and reach targeted users. However, the relative youth of Instagram's audience makes paid advertisement less desirable, so these promoted pieces often must correspond to the aesthetic sensibilities of Instagram users and feeds. Facebook and Instagram both use an algorithm-based system that uses various elements to show users potentially interesting advertisements. The elements used include an evaluation of the accounts that the user follows, the user's prior search and browsing history, and their geographical location.

As Instagram has continued to mature, it has made some interesting choices in how the audience interacts with its content. The late 2010s saw Instagram become highly identified with influencer culture, where individual accounts are run by people who have a large number of followers and therefore can leverage those followers to purchase or use certain products, normally with a financial kickback from the maker(s) of those products. Instagram influence was largely driven by the number of likes and comments that an account's posts received on the service rather than necessarily being derived from the actual purchasing of products.

In 2019, Instagram announced that it was testing a new format that would hide the number of likes a post got to create "a less pressurized environment" (Graham, 2019) for users on the site. The potential for changes such as this should be a reminder that social media content needs to be high quality and contain relevant messaging rather than chasing after vanity metrics such as likes, retweets, or comments.

TikTok and the Rise of AI

One of the social media platforms that ran out of steam and disappeared in the mid-2010s was Vine, a service that allowed creators to produce looping six-second videos. Largely replaced in importance and necessity by animated GIFs, Vine wasn't missed when it disappeared. However, within a few years, the social media world would see the rise of a service with similar properties when the China-based platform TikTok would start to enter the social media consciousness.

TikTok's arrival and early success raised concerns among industry observers due to a number of factors, including aggressive advertising on other social media platforms, adaptive AI that relies on user data to provide users with uncannily accurate recommendations of videos they are likely to enjoy, and concerns over user surveillance and intrusion of privacy (Holmes, 2019). Regardless of these concerns, adaptive AI will be key in the further development of audience and brand interaction on social media, with sites such as YouTube, Facebook, and Pinterest also using AI to pair users directly with desired content.

Summary

Social media audiences continue to grow and change based on various factors. The network infrastructure plays a significant role in both the interactions of audiences and message creation to reach those audiences.

Social media audiences have adapted over time to the way the various networks set up their architectures. Certain networks serve segments of the audience better and more effectively based on the needs of each segment. For example, young people who crave privacy and social status have gravitated toward visually oriented platforms like Instagram and Snapchat.

Understanding how social media networks operate, what their infrastructure allows and doesn't allow, and how audiences react to those elements is key to effective social media usage in sports. Your ability to fit your messages to the proper platforms allows you to both reach your intended audience and increase the spread of your message by exposing other potential audience members to what you are communicating. Remember, platforms and audiences both change over time, and you stand a greater chance of capitalizing on social media messages by keeping abreast of those changes.

Review Questions

1. How did smartphones play a role in the adoption of Facebook by younger audiences?
2. Why is WhatsApp more popular in Europe and Asia than it is in the United States?
3. How do the infrastructures for Facebook and Twitter differ?
4. What are influencers on Instagram?

The Online Community

CHAPTER OBJECTIVES

Learning about social media networks ultimately requires learning about the people who use those networks. This chapter helps you to do the following:

- Learn how singular and group psychological tendencies can be used to predict and direct audience activities
- Find out why the Internet can be a very mean place
- Understand the difficulties that women face in the online sports media environment

So far, we've learned about the beginnings of social media, the tools that you can use to make social media messages, the methods that people use to develop creativity in the social space, and how network architecture affects the way audiences interact with social media. Now it's time to take a close look at the tendencies and behaviors of audiences themselves.

Social media audiences are often talked about in monocultural terms, as if all the people on social media are somehow the same. But as we've already seen through some of the examples in this book and the web resource, social media audiences are quite diverse, even within a network. There is no singular audience characteristic that social media content should be focused on attracting.

Instead, people and businesses who use social media need to evaluate what audience members they are hoping to reach, understand what those people are doing online and what they hope to get out of the experience, and develop a plan of action to cultivate the awareness, attention, and action of those audience members. This chapter focuses on the characteristics of online audiences, the patterns of online audience migration, and the psychological elements that often govern online behavior.

Audience Adoption and Migration

I have been observing online audiences for a long time, well before I was ever paid to do it. When I was in middle school in the early 1990s, I got my first chance to go online on a service called CompuServe. This was before the World Wide Web, so there weren't any websites to visit. Services like CompuServe, Prodigy, and AOL offered a series of meeting places, called **forums**, where people could log in, interact, upload and download files, and write messages to each other.

My early experience with CompuServe was interesting. I had never interacted with people online before, and it was exciting to chat with people from all over the United States about the topics I was most interested in—primarily sports and video games. Functionally, the experience wasn't much different from the websites and social networks that would follow in the next few decades.

One thing that stuck out to me when I started interacting with people on CompuServe was how the nature of the interactions changed over time. The people I interacted with early on were generally good people to talk with, helpful when I had questions, and friendly. As my experience with the

Patrick Durand/Sygma via Getty Images

Online audiences have moved from platform to platform for years, based on various factors.

service continued over the next few years, however, the quality of many of the interactions changed. Many of the earlier people who I'd interacted with started to disappear and were gradually supplanted by newer users who didn't fit well with the online communities I'd come to enjoy. The new users seemed to me to be ruder, less interested in maintaining conversation, and overall just not a good fit for the community.

This pattern has been mirrored in modern social media networks and their ever-changing audiences. In turn, the pattern has been augmented by the technology that social media platforms use and the gradual adoption of technology by different demographic groups.

Audiences online are basically just large groups of people bound together by technology or common interests. They tend to be influenced by different types of psychological impulses, ones that rely on feedback from other group members or feedback (or lack thereof) from the technology they are using to facilitate their actions. For social media managers in sports, it becomes important to understand some of the ways that online audiences are influenced psychologically and how to incorporate that

understanding into day-to-day interactions with the audience.

Most people join a social media network because of the promise of something positive for them coming out of the exchange. Perhaps it is an opportunity to connect with old friends or make new friends. Perhaps there is social capital inherent in joining the social media network due to a peer group using it or a large amount of news coverage. Regardless of the incentive, people join social media networks for a reason, and they stay on them for a reason.

As we discussed in chapters 1 and 4, there have been plenty of changes over the years to both the social networks themselves and the people who participate in them. But how do people make a decision about what technology to use in the first place, and what could lead them to change their minds over time?

Theory of Planned Behavior

Perhaps the most appropriate psychological theory to consider when looking at social network adoption is the theory of planned behavior (Ajzen, 1991). The basics of this theory are that a person's intention of doing something can be predicted by looking at their attitudes toward that behavior or action, the "subjective norms" of their community or peer group, and the person's perceived level of behavioral control. Figure 5.1 shows a diagram of the influence and decision chain in the theory of planned behavior.

Key Point @DoctorGC ⌄

Social media audiences change over time for a variety of reasons. Audiences migrate to new platforms based on what those platforms do for them socially. #SocialMediaAndSports

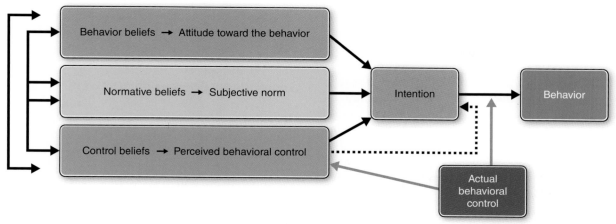

FIGURE 5.1 The theory of planned behavior.

If that sounds confusing, it's not. In plain language, the theory states that a person's intention of doing something is affected by three primary factors:

1. How they feel about the activity or behavior
2. How they think the behavior is perceived by others in their social environment
3. How easy they feel it will be to perform the behavior

These factors fit quite well into the social media realm because they get at many of the elements of online behavior that we are most curious about.

Look at the above points and think about how they apply to social media usage based on what we've learned so far. Facebook's early success in capturing college students relied on a combination of these factors. For Facebook to be something that college students wanted to use, it needed to

1. present itself as an attractive and entertaining activity for that group,
2. there needed to be buy-in from people who could influence the actions of others, and
3. it needed to be simple enough that people without much computing skill would still want to use it.

In this light, Facebook's strategy of rolling out enrollment first to elite universities, then to large public schools, then to high schools, and then to the general population was quite clever. The process created a constant buzz around the idea of using Facebook that propelled each successive wave of users, it created an established class of influencers that kept a positive subjective feeling about using

Facebook, and it made it easy for older users to accept the idea of getting accounts because there were already people on the network that those older users would want to connect with: their children. Once parents were connected to their children on Facebook, those parents would soon invite their friends and relatives, who would again be more likely to have a positive attitude toward Facebook use because people they knew were already on the network.

Applying Theory to Practice

The above section shows you how the theory of planned behavior helps to describe the audience movement across various social media networks. You can also apply this line of thinking to how audiences approach your social media channels, both in comparison to other organizations and across the various platforms you use.

The approach that you take toward a prospective or actual audience should be grounded in observation and analysis for the following items:

- Your brand's target audience
- How much of a demographic spread can be found in your audience
- What type(s) of social media you want to use
- What type of content you want to deliver
- What factors will affect your audience's ability to consume that content

Your Brand's Target Audience Identifying the audience should be the first thing you think about when deciding to create and share content on social media. Without knowing the audience you want to target, you run the risk of creating messages that are either too broadly constructed or lack appeal to any single group. If you are working for a brand or organization, you should be able to draw from market research and past media content creation experiences. If you are building your own brand as a journalist or commentator, think about who is most likely to consume and enjoy the content you are creating. For instance, if you are an aspiring NBA writer, your audience is logically going to consist of NBA fans. But think about who those people are and what their demographic makeup is as well as the geographical region of the country (or world) that you wish to aim for.

Demographic Spread That last element feeds into understanding how broad or narrow your audience happens to be. When one examines the Twitter feed of the popular English American soccer podcast *Men in Blazers*, one finds a specific consumer is being addressed. The intended audience appears to be educated American soccer fans between 18 and 49 who root for both an English Premier League team and the United States men's and women's national teams and who appreciate pop culture references, soccer-specific jokes, and inside jokes that relate back to the podcast.

While the focus of this account is specific, the account's content choices and the podcast's overall popularity have led it to over 200,000 Twitter followers as of late 2019. Your audience may be this specific or broader, depending on the factors governing your brand or organization. Be conscious of how wide or narrow a net you wish to cast, letting your audience spread be a guide.

Social Media Content and Delivery The type of social media and type of content should generally be considered together. Think about what content you want to generate, such as writing, images, pre-produced video, live video, podcasts, or something else. Then think about what social media platforms are most effective at serving that type of content to an audience, keeping in mind what your target audience happens to be.

Audience Consumption This leads to the factors that affect the audience's ability to consume your content. As we covered in chapter 4, the way that social media platforms and networks are constructed can have a big effect on the willingness of certain audience segments to spend time there.

Audience Normative Beliefs

Understanding your audience's attitudes when it comes to social media usage is important. As we saw in chapter 4, those attitudes are affected by various things, including social norms and network infrastructure. If you know that your younger audience isn't likely to log on to Twitter, or that your older audience isn't using Instagram to connect with your organization, don't put that kind of content on there. You are unlikely to force a change in your audience's

The *Men in Blazers* podcast has a social media presence across several platforms and successfully capitalizes on a specific consumer type.

social media usage habits, so don't expect segments of your audience to alter their consumption patterns just because you ask them to.

This concept also applies to the broader audience. For instance, let's say you want to open a new front on social media by expanding your organization's postings on a subreddit. The likelihood that your existing audience not already on Reddit is going to migrate there simply because you have started posting is low. You may gain new audience members, and that is important. But don't expect the rest of your social media audience to change their social media diets simply because of your strategic decision.

 Key Point @DoctorGC
You can't make people use a social media platform that they don't want to use. Learn the social media tendencies of your target audience and structure your approaches accordingly. #SocialMediaAndSports

Audience Control Beliefs

Similarly, understanding your audience's control beliefs is important. For example, older audiences may be hindered by their own doubts about technological use when it comes to social media content. If you produce content intended for that audience and the content is perceived as difficult to access, consume, or interact with, you risk that audience segment avoiding the content altogether. Always consider ease of use and accessibility with the content you generate, and understand that on broad, demographically diverse sites such as Facebook, simpler is generally better.

Audience Behavioral Intention

The goal is to understand why your audience chooses to consume or interact with your content on social media. The approach that you or your organization take to creating or posting content can affect the intent of audiences to participate as content consumers, responders, or creators within the environment. The NBA Twitter sidebar included in this chapter is an excellent case study in how a league's messaging decisions can help change its audience's behavioral intentions.

As you take audience intention into account, remember that your goal isn't to force people to change their consumption habits but to make it easier and more attractive for them to do so. You might not be able to make people follow you or engage with your content, but you can increase the likelihood of them doing so. Here are some ways to do that:

- Be consistent with the quality of your content, allowing the audience to know what to expect from you.
- Be consistent with the quantity of your content, allowing the audience to know when to expect it from you.
- Make it easy for users to access the content you are providing.
- Help the audience to understand why consuming new content types or accessing new platforms for content would be in their best interest.
- Understand that you're probably not going to be able to do some things, like make older adults regularly watch Snapchat.

The Darker Side of Online Audiences

Much of the book so far has focused on the positive aspects of social media audiences, from their attitudes and behaviors to the types of content to which they positively respond. It is important to realize, however, that the social media experience is not always a pleasant thing. In fact, the online experience often is defined by its worst aspects. Twitter has a reputation for its audience brutally criticizing public figures, the Facebook experience is increasingly defined by anger and disagreement in comments, and sites like Reddit often must rely on moderators to keep subreddits from descending into chaos.

Most social media users are good people who are interested in legitimate conversation and interaction with others. But in an area like sports social media, you are going to run into audience members whose intentions aren't that pure, and you will have to deal with situations where it feels like the entire Internet has decided that it's angry at you. This section focuses on some of the key elements to consider when dealing with the darker side of social media.

The Internet Outrage Machine

Social media audiences engage in many enjoyable and positive interactions, but many of the networks also play host to a seemingly unending cycle of outrage. *Slate* devoted an entire 2014 interactive

NBA TWITTER

Rob Perez ✓
@WorldWideWob

while we wait this thing out ... would you guys be interested in re-watching the NBA's best games together? director's cut style live on Periscope? what time works best?

11:15 AM · Mar 13, 2020 · Twitter Web App

1K Retweets   **20.3K** Likes

The NBA's usage of social media, especially Twitter, has helped to foster a community of fans, journalists, and worldwide observers invested in the game.

"We believe that greater fan engagement through social media helps drive television ratings" (Maese, 2018). Those words, spoken by NBA commissioner Adam Silver, represent something unique among major sports entities when it comes to social media: a straightforward plan and desire to fully use social media as a tool for growth.

The concept of NBA Twitter extends far beyond just a league mandate to leverage a communication platform. Twitter has allowed the NBA to establish an ecosystem online where players, fans, team accounts, and sports media journalists can all participate and feel like they belong to something unique (Maese, 2018). Rather than continue to use the boring and conservative messages that dominated much of the Twitter environment in the first several years of the network, NBA Twitter started regularly using video clips, memes, emojis, and excitable language to project an aura of coolness and youth that no other sport collectively achieves in the space.

Many sports leagues might try to tamp down on language or messaging that strayed too far from the brand that they are trying to project. Part of the brilliance of NBA Twitter is that it takes the opposite approach, allowing audience members to create their own content, giving players agency to communicate how they want, and letting teams cut loose with their approaches.

Events like the DeAndre Jordan saga, where the popular free agent's decision to back out of a free agent contract with the Dallas Mavericks and re-sign with the Los Angeles Clippers, played out in a fascinatingly bizarre, emoji-filled series of tweets by current and former teammates (Favale, 2017). It highlights just how unique and accessible the NBA has made itself via its collective attitude toward Twitter. The ability of a former outsider like Rob Perez to channel his love of the NBA and his creativity with media into a Twitter feed that has become a must-follow for NBA fans and media alike (Front Office Sports, 2018) is largely due to the association's commitment to leveraging social media to its own benefit.

By creating a sense of community and engagement that focuses on fun and inclusiveness, the NBA continues to make inroads into the elusive youth market. According to market research, almost half of NBA viewers are under 35, and the average age of NBA viewers is considerably younger than their NFL or MLB counterparts (Maese, 2018).

Key Point @DoctorGC ⌄

Social media can be a very negative place, especially in sports. Social media workers and audience members are both susceptible to hostility and criticism. #SocialMediaAndSports

essay to the concept of outrage taking over the lives of those on social media, noting that "over the past decade or so, outrage has become the default mode for politicians, pundits, critics and, with the rise of social media, the rest of us" (Benedikt, Kirk, & Kois, 2014). Connor Friedsdorfer of *The Atlantic* wrote that "in America's digital culture, outrage is packaged to almost every niche in the citizenry" (Friedsdorfer, 2018).

Unfortunately, sports social media is no different from the other forms of social media, and outrage is often the order of the day. The outrage cycle on social media seems to be constantly in search of a new subject, which could be something as mundane as bad officiating in a game (Risdon, 2019), the reaction to years-old tweets by momentarily popular people (Associated Press, 2019), or something as silly as an NFL player tweeting out spoilers for a popular movie (Crist, 2019). Sam Laird of *Mashable* described the process as "another episode of America's favorite modern game show, *Person Says Dumb Thing Then Gets Dragged on Twitter Then Offers Flimsy Apology*" (Laird, 2017).

Craig Newmark, the founder of online classified advertisement site Craigslist, voiced an interesting perspective regarding online outrage and social media fights, proffering the concept that those conflicts are manufactured. "Americans are much more reasonable and moderate than what you might guess when you see a little Twitter war. But I'm guessing that the purpose of many Twitter wars is to polarize people . . . we've seen that happen because you can often trace some of the fighting groups to the same location. Outrage is profitable. Most of the outrage

Theo Wargo/Getty Images for Spotify

Social media outrage has led to sports and media figures becoming lightning rods for criticism. Broadcaster and writer Jemele Hill came under fire for Twitter comments she made while at ESPN.

Sports, Media, and Online Community

Jerod Morris

Twitter: @JerodMorris

Twitter: @AssemblyCall

Instagram: www.instagram.com/assemblycall/

Facebook: www.facebook.com/assemblycall/

LinkedIn: www.linkedin.com/in/jerodmorris/

YouTube: www.youtube.com/channel/UCybLgKCtOU8L-w_1NX5MIzqQ

Courtesy of Jerod Morris

Jerod Morris has experienced a fascinating side of the social media world since he graduated from college in the mid-2000s. As a podcaster, blogger, and copywriter, he has been part of several ventures that sit at the crossroads of social media content and audiences. He has used social media to build online communities but has also seen those communities take a negative turn as networks such as Twitter have matured.

"It all began with Midwest Sports Fans, which was a sports blog. I had started working for a social media marketing company, and I started Midwest Sports Fans to learn how to use WordPress."

WordPress, the open-source blogging software, was omnipresent in the online sports community during this time, and Morris was one of many private citizens in that era who learned the platform and discovered a way to connect with audiences interested in sports. The success of the Midwest Sports Fans site led him to create a Twitter account and develop a larger online presence while also extending his professional experience into content marketing, site hosting, and how social media fit into the big picture of audiences and messages.

"By 2011, I was transitioning out of operating Midwest Sports Fans—I had grown tired of the hamster wheel of creating content for advertising revenue," said Morris.

Morris' next sports-related venture was to start a podcast centered on his main sports passion, Indiana University men's basketball. *The Assembly Call* podcast was born.

THE ASSEMBLY CALL

Launching a podcast and finding an audience in 2011 was quite a challenge. Podcasts were hardly mainstream at this time, particularly in sports, and the majority of sports fans online didn't know where to find podcasts or how they worked. For Morris, social media—and Twitter in particular—provided a vehicle for the audience to find the podcast.

"Marketing *The Assembly Call* was the first place that I had a strategy developed for using Twitter. We have this hashtag for IU basketball that gets used by media members and fans when they are talking about the team. So we would jump in on the hashtag, and I would spend two hours tweeting my commentary on the game. Then when the game ended, we would drop the link to the podcast on the hashtag and start the show."

The strategy certainly paid off for Morris and his cohosts. *The Assembly Call* rapidly grew in popularity and quickly became a fixture of Indiana basketball fandom for those who followed online. The popularity of the podcast eventually led to a weekly radio version of the show as well as a content partnership with the highest-traffic online news site covering IU basketball and a Twitter audience of over 14,000 followers as of late 2019.

THE EVOLUTION OF TWITTER

Morris has been involved in a number of other ventures, developing and hosting several podcasts that focus on entrepreneurship, content management, and the business of creating and maintaining successful podcasts. He has both observed and used Twitter during his career, and has seen both the network and its audience grow, change, and mutate over that time.

"Twitter was such a unique service when I first got onto it because it was a way to have a touch-point with media members that you had previously just seen on television or read about. Then athletes started getting on Twitter, and now it's a touchpoint with them too. It opened up this new world of communication, and it gave you a better way to follow the news and stay up-to-date."

Morris notes that the business of sports media worked in symbiosis with the way that Twitter operated.

"Soon after I opened an account, I noticed that if you're etrafficking in viral sports content, you need to keep the account open all the time," he said. "Especially for sports news commentary and conversation. It all seemed to gravitate toward Twitter. And it felt like there was a purity to the conversation in the early years. I didn't notice as much of the negativity and the 'Gotcha!' type of stuff."

But as Morris notes, there has been a gradual coarsening of the conversation on Twitter.

"Twitter was always a place for hot takes because of the character limits, but it feels even more that's what it is now. Especially over the past few years, I have to turn my mentions off during an IU basketball game because of how much negativity there is. And I'm just a guy with a podcast. I can't imagine what working media or players have to deal with."

What does he think caused the change?

"It's been a few different things. There seems to be an understanding, whether it's implicit or explicit, of how to get attention on social media. Being loud, being negative, being incendiary, posting rumors—those things cut through the noise and get attention. I notice it happening to me, where I'll see 10 tweets that agree with me but one that calls me a nasty name, and it's that one that stands out.

"It also seems like the tone of societal discourse has changed, not just on social media but overall. People feel a different sense of freedom to say mean or toxic things. That's just become more accepted in society."

THE FUTURE OF ONLINE DISCOURSE

With Twitter and other traditional online social networks often falling prey to toxicity and negativity, Morris sees changes in future online conversations in sports.

"The reason social media succeeded was that people all over the world were allowed to come together efficiently and openly to have conversations. People have a real, genuine, almost hardwired desire to use the Internet to connect with each other, but anymore, you find trolls or advertisements that get in the way and make it an unpleasant experience. So you have to take the part that people want, which is the connections to others, and give people a place to connect that provides that and keeps a gate around it."

Morris sees the emergence of more private, curated social networks as a potential future for online social discourse, a trend that is already developing in certain corners of the social media world.

"Curated and moderated social networks allow people to have connections and meaningful conversations online while walling off some of the bad stuff," he says. "Many people are fed up with free discourse on social media because of all the bad things that come with it."

I've seen in the online world—I would guess 80 percent—someone's faking it for profit" (Smith, 2019).

Some social media platforms are more susceptible to outrage culture, largely because of their infrastructure. Twitter's approach of equal importance for all accounts and messages is great for the democratization of content, but the price of that approach is that the divisive messages and responses end up being seen by far more people. Facebook's infrastructure tends to relegate the outrage to the comments section of a post, but that ends up making the comments unreadable in many cases.

The unfortunate reality of social media outrage is that provocative content tends to drive traffic. This is not a concept unique to social media, as the growth of debate shows on ESPN and other sports television programming over the past two decades indicates. But it is a concept that's arguably more important in the advertising-driven model of social media, where clicks and eyeballs equate to revenue.

Costs are associated with aligning your sports social media brand to outrage, but there are also benefits. A brand like ESPN is not likely to incur many negative costs by associating itself with online outrage because the outrage is almost always presented as the opinion of the journalist, rather than the opinion of ESPN.

For many large media organizations, this calculus has served them well. But for the journalist, aligning with outrage on social media can end up causing the audience to disregard your messages as a crass attempt to be relevant and gain audience, rather than as an expression of learned fact. The benefits come from increased exposure, and the inclination of online audiences is to gravitate toward outrage, either because they feel compelled to express an opinion (Benedikt et al., 2014) or because they find the social media exchange entertaining.

However, when it comes to using social media to provide political opinions, even sports media brands as big as ESPN can find themselves struggling to maintain their voice. After a series of political controversies involving former anchor and reporter Jemele Hill (Miller, 2018) and a number of high-profile incidents involving politics, social media, and accusations of liberal or progressive bias, ESPN president James Pitaro set ESPN's content on a path that would avoid overt political commentary or statements (Strauss, 2019). Research showed that the perception of ESPN as being politically biased toward liberal and progressive ideology had hurt its perception among those with a conservative political perspective (Clavio & Vooris, 2018). In short, conservative viewers perceived ESPN as a media outlet hostile to their interests as a result of the coverage.

Trolls and Argumentation

A related phenomenon to outrage culture on the Internet is the existence of **trolls** in most social media spaces. As with outrage, this is not a phenomenon that originated with social media. One of the first studies that I conducted on online audiences focused on college sports message boards (Clavio, 2008). The purpose of the study was to better understand why people spent time on message boards discussing college sports and what the users got from that exchange. I discovered that most people were there for two primary reasons: interacting with other people and gathering information on their teams.

However, there was a group of people using these message boards who were focused on a cluster of uses that I labeled as **argumentation**. These people were there to engage in trolling behavior: to argue with other users online and talk smack to

other people. If you spend any amount of time on social media, you've likely run into those types of accounts. They often appear to be there solely to ruin conversations, send mean-spirited messages, or engage in debate for the sake of argument instead of persuasion.

Trolls can be quite sophisticated in approach, often using the infrastructure of social media platforms to increase their effectiveness, such as using Twitter lists to identify a clustered group of targets for harassment (Feiner, 2019). Social media sites are identified as one of the main locations where the worst kinds of online trolling take place (Moreau, 2019).

 Key Point @ DoctorGC
A small number of people go on social media with the primary purpose of simply making other people mad. #SocialMediaAndSports

But not all people who are angry online are trolls. Particularly in sports, there are many instances of people being upset with some aspect of their fan or consumer experiences, so they opt to vent displeasure on social media. Trolls are a special category whose online existence is designed to disrupt the normal give-and-take of a network for their own enjoyment.

Working in sports social media is going to put you in contact with trolls who could focus on your account or on fans in your social media network. Deciding how to handle trolls is an important aspect of being a social media professional, and this is often done in consultation with your coworkers and superiors.

Todd Clarke of Hootsuite wrote nine separate suggestions for how to deal with trolls, and the first recommendation was to develop a policy for how to consistently deal with that kind of behavior (Clarke, 2019). This is an excellent starting point because the policing of behavior online should be consistent and evenly applied so that your audience knows what actions are permitted or not. The rest of Clarke's recommendations fall on a spectrum, including ignoring trolls, banning them, correcting them, and using the power of your community to deal with them for you.

 For more information about how to interact with trolls and deal with community management, consult the web resource.

That range of solutions can work well for brands, but what about a person? As a journalist or athlete who is the target of trolling behavior, you have a wide range of potential responses at your disposal. In many cases, we see the targets of trolling just ignore it, preferring to not give the troll any oxygen. In other cases, popular people will use their far larger follower bases to obliterate the troll in full public view. Sports journalist Michelle Beadle became known for her willingness to blow up trolls on Twitter (Graham, 2015; Lucia, 2014; Sussman, 2016). Her explanation for that approach, on Bill Simmons' podcast, was instructive:

> When I retweet those [trolls], my dream is not to be like "oh, hey, let me engage with you." My ultimate dream, and what I hope happens at least once before I die, is that an employer of one of these morons one time is reading these and seeing the kinds of things that their employees are tweeting publicly and then just fires them. And then, you know, a downward spiral for that particular person. I would love that. (Johnson, 2014, ¶5)

While this approach may not work for most people, it does represent a different kind of philosophy than the turn-the-other-cheek approach that many people use. In certain cases, it may be more effective than simply absorbing abuse online.

Key Point @DoctorGC

It is wise for your organization to come up with a consistent and unified approach to dealing with trolls and online troublemakers. Establishing community guidelines can make your social media experience more enjoyable for both fans and employees. #SocialMediaAndSports

The Online Disinhibition Effect

Closely related to trolling and argumentation is the broader wave of poor behavior online by many. Trolls may be online to annoy and disrupt, but social media has seen unfortunate behavior by many people, even those who are otherwise good people and good social media citizens. Much of this behavior can be attributed to a psychological tendency called the online disinhibition effect. Simply put, people will say things to other people online that would never be said in a face-to-face conversation with those same people.

Dr. John Suler identified this phenomenon before social media had become widespread (Suler, 2004). In his paper on the online disinhibition effect, he noted that there were at least six factors that contributed to the trend of people doing and saying things online that they would not do or say in the face-to-face world. The Online Disinhibition Effect sidebar highlights each of the factors and their characteristics.

These factors often exist in combination and may not be the only factors involved in people acting unpleasantly online. But the online disinhibition effect provides a useful framework for understanding why some people act the way they do on social media.

Understanding these factors and the reasons people are willing to go out of their way to be critical, spiteful, or dramatic in social media conversations helps to show how best to reduce that behavior among your own social media followers. There are ways to use the social interactivity present in this form of media to short-circuit antisocial behavior from audience members who aren't bad people, which can make it easier for you to banish people who are just there to create problems.

For instance, combatting factors like dissociative imagination and solipsistic introjection can be as easy as hosting video chats where you answer the audience's questions. Allowing the audience to put a face and a voice to the text that they see on social media helps personalize the account, thereby reducing the potential feelings that there isn't a person behind the account that can exist online.

Similarly, finding a way to give your audience a voice, whether that is through retweeting good comments they make, featuring their questions in online Q&A sessions, or running small user-generated content contests can help the audience feel like a part of the social media community that your sports or media brand is maintaining online. Those kinds of tactics don't always work, but they can have a positive effect in many cases and are worth trying if you are struggling with negative audience action or reaction.

Sports, Social Media, and Toxicity for Women

As difficult an environment as social media can sometimes be for all who work in it, the social media environment is considerably more difficult for women. Amnesty International issued a report

ONLINE DISINHIBITION EFFECT

1. *Asynchronicity:* Online communication doesn't generally happen in real time, creating a communication style that lacks the social cues of face-to-face interaction.

2. *Dissociative anonymity:* When people can separate their actions from their in-person identities and lifestyles, they feel emboldened to act out.

3. *Dissociative imagination:* Users may view others they communicate with online as characters in an imagined reality, rather than as human beings engaged in conversation.

4. *Invisibility:* Not being seen provides people with the courage to say or do things they would otherwise not do.

5. *Minimization of status and authority:* A lack of status and power symbols online relegates authority figures to the visual role of peers, rather than superiors whose rules must be obeyed.

6. *Solipsistic introjection:* Online communication can feel as if it is taking place in a person's mind, rather than as a social interaction between them and others.

titled "Toxic Twitter—A Toxic Place for Women." It described the abuse and degradation that women regularly face on that social media platform (Amnesty International, n.d.). News outlets have written stories about harassment and toxicity present in comments posted on Instagram (Lorenz, 2018).

In 2016, two female sports media figures, Sarah Spain and Julie DiCaro, were the face of a public service announcement video that was created by a group called Just Not Sports, which was posted on YouTube and went viral on Twitter. Using the hashtag #MoreThanMean, the video appeared to start as a take-off of a popular late-night TV segment, where celebrities read angry but largely harmless tweets directed at them.

However, the video quickly took a dark turn as the text of the tweets changed to reflect the harassing, sexualized, and demeaning language often directed at female sports media members by certain members of the Twitter audience (Mettler, 2016). The video would go on to win a Peabody Award for highlighting the misogyny and trolling that is often present on sports social media (Deitsch, 2017).

The negative and misogynistic comments aren't limited to sports media figures either. WNBA players, and the WNBA itself, have been regular targets of this type of negative language and behavior, largely on Twitter. Many WNBA players have taken the stance of confronting trolls and negative responses directly on Twitter, rather than sitting by and allowing people to say whatever they feel (Spector, 2018).

People of any gender can and do get trolled, harassed, and dehumanized on social media. But for women in sports and sports media, it is a consistent

and significant problem, one that makes the social media environment an unpleasant place to work. As a longtime social media observer, I am regularly appalled at the way in which female sports media members and athletes are talked to on social media, particularly on Twitter.

While some of the comments and responses to women focus on a supposed lack of sports acumen or knowledge, many comments simply focus on a woman's appearance. Look at a female sports media member's Instagram or Facebook comments, and you are likely to see several comments focusing entirely on her physical appearance, with no additional reason or context. This is not good behavior, and it makes social media in general a terrible work environment for many women.

Social media platforms have been called on to do a far more comprehensive job policing responses and comments, but there are many difficulties in trying to address the kind of toxic behavior the audience engages in. It becomes incumbent on media organizations, sport organizations, and enlightened fans to help police toxic behavior. Organizations and community members demonstrating that certain behavior is not acceptable within their online networks can go a long way toward improving the way people act. There are

 Key Point @DoctorGC
Sports social media is particularly inhospitable toward women, and online communities must go out of their way to establish acceptable behavioral guidelines for audience members. #SocialMediaAndSports

Nuccio DiNuzzo/Getty Images

Successful women in sports, both on the playing surface and on press row (such as broadcaster Erin Andrews), are unfortunately the target of much social media negativity.

rules and expectations of conduct at games and in public places. Why wouldn't those same rules and expectations apply to where people come together on social media?

Summary

Social media audiences engage with online content in fascinating ways. People migrate from social network to social network based on their perceptions and feelings toward their options, and those elements can and will change over time. Audience behavior is not always predictable, but the factors that influence that behavior are not secret.

While many audience members online are enjoyable people with a sincere desire to connect, some elements of the online audience are not nice to be around. Understanding the tendencies that lead to this kind of behavior and grasping how and why people choose to act in particular ways is important to anyone planning on working in sports social media.

Review Questions

1. What are the three primary beliefs that influence behavioral intention within the theory of planned behavior?

2. What has made NBA Twitter so unique among sports leagues and their approaches to social media?

3. What are the potential negative effects of using outrage and controversy as a communications tactic on sports social media?

4. How can a sports or media organization combat the online disinhibition effect among its audience members?

The Technology Curve

CHAPTER OBJECTIVES

Social media changes constantly at a pace that makes even veterans dizzy. How can you keep ahead of these changes? This chapter focuses on those issues by doing the following:

- Breaking down social media into its technological and content basics
- Developing strategies for how to fit your ideas to the technology
- Helping you understand how to spot change in social networks

When I first started studying social media, I used to get comments from article reviewers that would go something like this: "Why are you wasting your time studying Facebook and Twitter? Everybody knows these networks are going to disappear in a year or two anyway and be replaced by something else." That mentality used to drive me crazy for two reasons. First, the first decade of the 2000s certainly had its fair share of failed social networks, and the demographics and user bases for networks like Facebook and Twitter showed that they weren't going anywhere anytime soon.

But second, and more importantly, Facebook and Twitter's networks contained the **building blocks** for future online social communication, and even if the brand names changed, the process of people interacting with one another in an online space was worth studying. There were important clues from both practical and theoretical perspectives in the way people approached social media, and we still see many of the same trends today.

The smart social media practitioners in sports realize that the social network used is far less important than the message. The network is important for delivering the message, and as we've established, each network does different things for different people. But rather than get hung up on "How do I use Facebook?" or "How do I use Instagram?" to get your message out there, you need to think about how to use the tools within social media—and realize that the networks and their features are those tools.

Why Technology Changes

It is important to start this chapter by considering why technology has changed as rapidly as it has since the start of the 2000s, particularly in media. Innovation in both hardware and software have been a near constant, and that stands in marked contrast to the previous 50 or so years of technology. But from a historical perspective, rapid change has been the exception rather than the rule, and ultimately professionals and consumers have had to deal with some unprecedented shifts in the landscape due to the newness of Internet-based communication.

A Paradigm Shift in Media

Before the advent of Internet-based social communication, the last major advance in communication technology occurred in the 1970s and 1980s, when cable television was adopted by the masses and most of the video-based news ceased requiring a broadcast signal to reach the audience. Even that innovation fit within the existing paradigm of how people received news and information, a paradigm that had existed, relatively unchanged, since the post–World War II period of the 1940s and 1950s.

Most content was transmitted through mass media sources (e.g., newspapers, television, radio) and the content was one-way in terms of information flow. In other words, the audience's ability to respond to media or create widely available media was practically nonexistent.

The paradigm shift started in the mid-1990s as the World Wide Web standardized the Internet for users and changed the communication experience— first for a small number of people, then gradually more as Internet access became less expensive and less difficult. Instead of a small number of content producers, Internet users were able to access voices and ideas that previously were not given space or time within the mass media structure.

Additionally, Internet users were able to communicate with one another and with media content creators, both through email and on public message boards and USENET forums. These elements ended up being the building blocks of social media development in the following decade.

Key Point @DoctorGC ⌄

The shift from a mass media model of communication to the Internet has changed the way that people consume information and entertainment as well as how content is produced. #SocialMediaAndSports

Hardware, Convergence, and Portability

Before the Internet age, media were largely separated into their own categories, each distinguished by physical characteristics. In other words, print (i.e., newspapers, magazines, books) was its own category, audio (i.e., radio) was its own category, and video (i.e., television, movies) was its own category.

While there were occasional and less-than-successful attempts to find ways to combine these forms of media during the mass media era, the advent of the computer and the gradual growth in popularity of Internet access started to make these efforts more successful. Once processor speeds, display quality, and internal memory improved enough, people could suddenly consume different types of media on the same device, whether that media was written, aural, or visual.

The Portable Computer

Initially, these devices were computers—both stationary desktop computers and early laptop computers. While laptops were certainly portable versus heavy desktop computers, they were still cumbersome to transport and were at the mercy of primitive Wi-Fi and mobile data connections.

As computers started getting smaller and more portable, so did telephones, mutating from the bulky handset devices of the mid-20th century to the early mass-produced cellphones of the 1990s. Cell phones became popular among some of the population, but as of 2000, half of the adults in the United States still did not have a cellular phone, and half of the adults who didn't have one said they never planned to acquire one (Saad, 2018). But while the prospect of owning a mobile telephone that simply made phone calls didn't appeal to those consumers, **technological convergence** would end up changing many minds.

The Smartphone

The advent of the iPhone in 2007 was talked about at length in chapter 4, and it's important not to underestimate how much of a game changer that device was in terms of the technology curve. Phones were no longer just devices to place phone calls. The iPhone and its competitors were basically mobile computers, capable of doing everything from checking email to surfing the Internet to catching up on your social media (Saad, 2018).

Apple's 2010 launch of the iPad and the new generation of tablets would further cement the technological platform of the new communication paradigm, one that was centered on all-inclusive hardware devices that users could easily transport and that broke down the preexisting physical separations between types of media. No longer did consumers have to change media sources for different types of activities. As the initial press release for the iPad trumpeted in its opening paragraph, the device could be used for "browsing the web, reading and sending email, enjoying photos, watching videos, listening to music, playing games, reading e-books, and much more" (Apple, 2010).

Modern Hardware and Convergence

The hardware paradigm launched by the iPhone and its technological descendants has remained largely unchanged in the intervening years. Media delivery is now aimed primarily at "smart" devices—phones, tablets, laptops, and televisions—that are capable of handling multiple forms of media.

A few single-use forms of media still exist, including the increasingly rare printed edition of the newspaper, the physical copy of a book, and a

© Human Kinetics

Tablets are an excellent example of media hardware convergence, combining digitization with portability.

car radio. But many consumers, and most younger consumers, now digest all forms of media via smart devices, and it is that environment that social media platforms are best equipped to deliver content to audiences.

Additionally, the portability of hardware has changed the nature of the type of content being delivered. In prior media generations, creating content that required an investment of time on the part of the consumer was commonplace because the nature of the media being used lent itself to that form of storytelling, and the additional space allowed for the organic insertion of advertisements into the consumption process. Newspaper stories could and would run long across multiple pages, television programs were lengthened to run in 30- or 60-minute blocks to accommodate a 24-hour broadcasting clock and the selling of commercials, and full-color high-quality pictures were generally only available in glossy magazines that were packed with advertisements.

In the current media era, the portability of hardware and the convergence of different forms of media into the same delivery system has made content smaller, shorter, and more directly delivered. Broadcast companies like ESPN, which once focused on hour-long sports highlight television shows such as SportsCenter and Baseball Tonight, now partner with startup technology companies like Quibi to create short, five- to seven-minute shows that are aimed at mobile devices for audiences on the go to consume (Sperling, 2019). The convergence of content into one stream means that audiences can focus on more things but have less time and attention to do so (McClinton, 2019).

Key Point @DoctorGC

Portable media technology has helped to spur convergence in media consumption by incentivizing media companies to fit different forms of content onto the same devices. #SocialMediaAndSports

Software Development

As hardware has become more converged and more portable, the software used to bring media content to users has become more important. The emergence of software as an intermediate delivery device for media content is a relatively new phenomenon. For many decades, the hardware itself was the delivery system. But as smartphones, tablets, and computers have taken over the delivery process and multiple forms of media have started to occupy the same space, software has become a key part of the system. This is most apparent in the importance of apps, the programs that act as portals for access to social media platforms and networks.

Well-designed social media apps do an excellent job of seamlessly transporting the user into the network environment. The familiarity of your home content feed, the ability to quickly post your pictures or your thoughts, and notifications to tell you what you have missed are all key components of these apps because they create a sense of ease in the user and make it simple to read and create content. For many social networks, having a well-designed and functional smartphone app is a key component of gaining or maintaining mass popularity. Platforms that have yet to design an attractive or enjoyable app can struggle to have people adopt their networks as a result.

Software development isn't just for the big social media platforms. Media and sport organizations also have invested heavily in the creation and development of smartphone apps that can deliver information to users. For instance, ESPN has focused

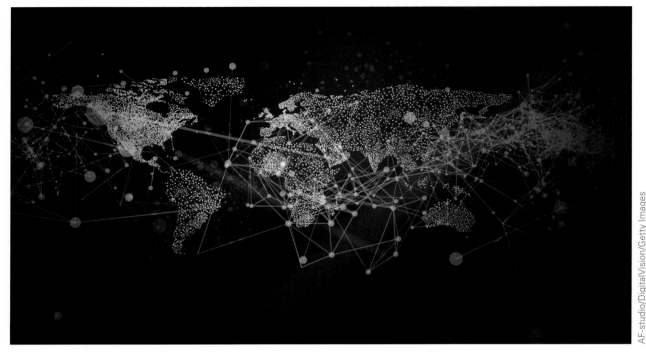

AF-studio/DigitalVision/Getty Images

Communications networks have used a balance of hardware and software innovation to connect the world.

a great deal of attention, money, and time on the development of its core ESPN app, which delivers news, video, and notifications to audiences.

ESPN has worked to streamline its app environment, creating a single smartphone app that handles its written material and delivers highlights and live games (Adler, 2019). The English Premier League's official app integrates a wide variety of features, including live updates on fixtures, statistics for the league, news and features written about all the clubs in the league, and even a built-in fantasy sports management feature.

Most teams have also worked with developers on their own apps as well, with the NBA featuring links to all 30 team apps on its website. One Pittsburgh-area tech company, YinzCam, has developed team-specific apps for a global array of organizations, including English Premier League clubs, Australian Rules Football clubs, NBA teams, and college teams in the United States (Torrance, 2019).

App development is likely to coordinate closely with hardware development over the next decade. The introduction of new hardware features will continue to expand the media creation and interactive capabilities of social media platforms, and the companies competing for audience members on social media will need to be focused on who can best

harness those new hardware capabilities within the confines of their software.

 For the latest information about social media apps and how to maximize their effectiveness, be sure to check out the web resource.

Social Media Building Blocks

The brand names and delivery systems of social media content change regularly. It is a mistake to get caught up in features and functions of social networks or technology due to the regularity of change. You should understand that social media is largely an assemblage of individual pieces of content arranged and presented in unique styles based on the characteristics of a network.

The best way to approach the creation of social media content is to first uncouple the various elements within social media content, breaking the entire exchange down to its component parts. Social media building blocks encompass all the types of content one can create within the structures of this type of communication. The categories of building blocks that you should be thinking about are the following:

- Written content
- Images
- Preproduced video
- Live video
- Audio
- Graphics
- Dynamic visuals
- Responses

By understanding how these building blocks operate both individually and in combination, you can help future-proof your thinking about social media and avoid getting bogged down in the inevitable technological changes that will come along.

Written Content

Written material is the most prevalent social media building block, largely due to its efficiency as a transmitter of information. Organizations can fill social media written content with a tremendous amount of detail, and almost every social network has written content built into its default display.

Twitter's primary display focus is on portraying written content, sometimes in concert with other building blocks. Facebook's default input is writing, and even images or dynamic content are generally accompanied by writing. While certain social networks, such as Snapchat, don't use writing in the primary display, written content is ubiquitous.

Simply linking to an article on a website that is text-based doesn't qualify as writing in the social media context. Writing as a social media building block involves creating text that displays natively within the social media visual environment. On a platform like Instagram, the writing is generally subordinate to the visual elements, while on Twitter, the writing is often the star of the show.

Deciding how much or how little writing to include in your social media content can be tricky. For instance, ESPN's company policies regarding writing as a primary content type on social media have evolved over time. Adam Schefter, the ESPN NFL reporter, noted in 2012 that writing on Twitter as a story evolved was viewed by some in the audience as him being wishy-washy, but in fact it was a public version of real-time reporting (Fry, 2012). For a time, ESPN reporters were expected to tweet links to their stories without much additional context, with the company's rationale being that directing traffic to its website made more sense than Twitter keeping all the traffic for itself. That approach may

fit your organization, particularly if you generate money from advertising revenue that relies on click-throughs and on-site advertisements.

Images

With social media becoming increasingly visual in orientation, images have become another key social media building block. Whether serving as primary content (as they do on Instagram) or as supporting content (as they often do on Facebook and Twitter), images can be the primary social media message delivered to the audience or frame written social media messages by providing insight and understanding to the intended audience. This images category includes photos as well as Photoshop or design creations.

Preproduced Video

Of all the social media building blocks, video has seen the biggest increases in both prevalence and importance over the last half of the 2010s. This is largely due to a combination of gradual increases in digital bandwidth, thereby making it easier for social media users to view video, and responses from social networks and software makers, who have made video far more central to the social user's experience in 2020 than it was a decade earlier.

Preproduced video closely mirrors the historical media platform of television by providing audiences with what is essentially broadcast content. In other words, there is no direct audience interaction with the content itself, although you may invite them to provide comments after the fact on whatever social media platform you are using. This type of video runs the spectrum from simple highlights or interview segments uploaded with no additional context to fully produced shows that involve multiple cameras, angles, and graphics.

This type of video is increasingly popular among sports media outlets due to its natural storytelling qualities and its similarity to television programming. Learning the ins and outs of video editing and sequential visual storytelling will help make you an in-demand job candidate for both media and sport organizations because both are increasingly turning to preproduced video as a key building block for reaching audiences and capturing attention.

Live Video

While prerecorded video and live video are similar in that they both involve using video, they qualify as different building blocks because their usage within social media is and should be different. Whereas prerecorded video is generally used to provide audiences with one-way broadcast content, live video provides the opportunity to interact with your audiences in real time.

Several major social media platforms now provide a distinct portal in their apps for you to send live video streams to your audience, with these portals generally allowing you to see audience interactions on screen. Leveraging those interactions effectively while providing the live video is an important part of managing this building block.

Additionally, live video can be used to provide audiences with real-time reporting in a way that is more effective and evocative than simply writing accounts of what is taking place. One of social media's greatest communication aspects is the ability to provide audiences with on-the-scene and in-the-moment reporting, and in many cases, live video is the best possible content type for that purpose.

The primary caveat with this building block at sporting events is to make sure you are not violating any contractual rules on video content. For instance, the team or media personnel working live sporting events that are televised will aggressively shut down attempts to livestream video from the event itself. Rights fees and exclusivity clauses on live video at sporting events are among the most carefully guarded of media deals.

I have seen journalists threatened with expulsion from sporting events for livestreaming even a few seconds of the crowd at games. However, generally that prohibition does not apply to livestreaming your own face as you provide an on-site report. Be aware of what rules might affect your use of live video and social media.

Audio

Audio may be the least prevalent of any of these building blocks as a standalone item. Many social networks assume that the user wishes to view content with audio turned off—for instance, Instagram set the default audio setting to "off" for autoplay videos on users' streams. However, audio remains a powerful form of content, and sports social media content has found many uses for audio, both in concert with video and as standalone embedded content.

For instance, short snippets of podcasts are used by media companies such as The Ringer and ESPN to provide audiences with a sneak preview of what the full podcast sounds like or to provide access to an interesting portion of the conversation. Apps such as Anchor have allowed audiences to create podcasts and post them online, sharing links to the audio across social media channels. Additionally, many radio stations stream their audio on social media.

Graphics

There is a distinction between standalone text (as one finds in Twitter, Facebook, and on Instagram posts) and text that is graphically embedded into video (as one finds in Instagram story posts, Snapchat posts, and other video). In the former context, the text operates in either a primary or subordinate position to other content, whereas in the latter context it becomes part of a converged video format.

Although **graphics** can include this type of embedded writing, they also involve other forms of written communication. This category includes emojis, stickers, and undynamic filter effects that can be used to alter the visual representation of a post. Graphics can also include combinations of visual imagery alongside textual and graphical information.

Dynamic Visuals

While writing, audio, images, and video all existed as standalone media content categories before the social media age, **dynamic visuals** are unique to the converged media environment that social networks provide. This building block consists primarily of animated GIFs and animated filters. This category provides more dynamic material than still images but lacks the length or compositional consistency to qualify as videos.

Dynamic visuals can be used in various situations on different networks. Animated GIFs on Twitter are often used humorously, relying on pop culture references that audiences will recognize and appreciate. Animated filters can provide everything from unique visual effects to augmented reality (AR) and can be used in both image-based and video-based settings.

Dynamic media is often used as a support element in social media content, providing additional context to a different kind of social media building block. But dynamic media can also stand alone as social media content, and this type of content is often the most memetic by nature. Effectively using dynamic visuals requires a good understanding of the current cultural environment in the area in which the content is being posted.

Leagues such as the NBA see plays from their games turned into animated GIF files on a regular

Courtesy of Indiana University Athletic Department

Sports teams use a combination of visual elements and links to produce work that falls under the graphics building block.

basis (Giphy, n.d). Smart social media departments in both the NBA and the media who cover the league should use those GIF files as both primary and secondary content on Twitter and Facebook, due to the positive response they get from fans and the ability to include dynamic media in what they are publishing.

Responses

You may not think of **responses** and comments as a social media building block, but they are. When content is posted on most social media platforms, the content acts like flypaper, attracting audience interactions and responses that stick to the content visually and become viewable parts of it. Instagram comments, Facebook comments, and, to a lesser degree, Twitter replies have varying levels of visibility but exist as part of the content once they are created. Similarly, responses from the content creator to those comments become a viewable part of the content.

Many content creators respond to the responses either passively (e.g., liking a response) or actively (e.g., replying to the response). Some social networks

(particularly Instagram and Facebook) allow the original content creator to delete or disable comments, which further reinforces their status as a social media building block.

When used and moderated properly, responses can be a powerful tool for sport organizations and sports media companies in this field. The public nature of quality responses to social media posts can lead to higher rates of engagement as audience members see the responses and feel more inclined to add their own perspectives. This strategy requires that you or your company assign someone to monitor responses and to enforce a set of community guidelines, but it can pay dividends.

What About Stories?

Snapchat, Instagram, and Facebook have all integrated stories into their app infrastructures, and while it is tempting to think of the story itself as a building block, it does not qualify because it is a delivery system for building blocks.

Stories can be used to provide a montage of still images, video, and embedded text to showcase an event or to simply capture slices of life that wouldn't

Key Point @DoctorGC ⌄

Social media stories are a key part of the social media structure for most platforms, and content creators should think of them as ways to provide consumers with multipart narratives or multifaceted ideas. #SocialMediaAndSports

otherwise fit easily into standalone pictures or videos. Stories are a bit like social media versions of traditional television broadcast packages. They bring together multiple types or instances of content, collecting them into an easily deliverable package and using notifications to essentially deliver them to users. Stories also include the ability to alter the length of time that content is displayed, and social media creators should be conscious of how timing and presentation order can affect the ways audiences process content.

Building Block Evolution

Thinking about social media through the concept of building blocks allows you to deal with technological evolution more easily. Rather than getting wrapped up in worrying about new features being offered through hardware or software updates, focus instead on how your organization's messaging intersects with the building blocks.

As new social media platform development has slowed down, we have seen a gradual reduction of new content avenues being added. This allows the apps to refine how various building blocks are presented to the audience and allows content creators to refine how they use the building blocks.

Some building blocks are unlikely to evolve much beyond their current states. Writing, images, and prerecorded video don't have a great deal of obvious growth or change opportunities. It is possible that the way social media apps display these building blocks or allow audiences to interact with them will change, but the core elements of the content are unlikely to shift much.

By contrast, I would expect further evolution in areas such as live video, dynamic visuals, graphics, responses, and audio. These building blocks have a lot of room for growth because most of them are still in the early stages of adoption and integration within the social media communication environment.

For instance, AR features are likely to increase over the next several years as camera and processing power improve in hardware. AR technologies are still somewhat speculative; however, social media companies such as Snapchat and Facebook have continued to invest in AR extensions to their applications (Mastorakis, 2018). New AR-like filters for Instagram emerged in 2020, including a Disney-themed filter that assigns a randomly chosen character (Garrison, 2020).

The popularity of AR features comes down to their inherent power for increasing interaction between the user and the social media platform. It is likely that continued development in AR could end up fully transforming the dynamic visuals building block from a largely predetermined set of visuals to an in-the-moment set of computer-generated content additions.

Your job as a social media professional is to keep abreast of these developments and consider how best to apply them to your work environment.

Which Building Blocks Are Best for Your Content?

Before you start creating social media content, you should think about which building blocks are most effective for what you are trying to do. If this sounds similar to the message earlier in the book about carefully choosing which social media platform(s) your content will be most effective on, good! That's exactly how you need to think about it, and the choices of platform(s) and building block(s) should lie at the heart of all your social media decisions.

The social media network you choose for your content should affect your decision-making process on the building blocks you are using. Facebook may work best with a focus on preproduced video and images, while Twitter may work best with a focus on live video, written content, and dynamic visuals. Effectively leveraging a platform like Instagram is certainly going to require effective use of images but will also likely require you to think about dynamic visuals and graphics.

Some building blocks are easy to use, provided you have experience in creating types of content. For instance, dynamic visuals are generally not building blocks you have to create yourself; you just have to know where to find them on your social media app and how to effectively use them. However, some building blocks require greater technical skills to craft something that your audience will enjoy and appreciate. Both prerecorded video and live video are excellent examples of this. Good video requires much planning in terms of goals and storylines (Gallegos, 2019) and requires a working understanding of the various technical tools related to video

PROFESSIONAL INSIGHTS

The Evolution of Social Media in Sport

Dr. Ann Pegoraro

Twitter: @SportMgmtProf

LinkedIn: www.linkedin.com/in/annpegoraro/

Academia.edu: https://laurentian.academia.edu/AnnPegoraro

Courtesy of Ann Pegoraro

Dr. Ann Pegoraro has been among the leaders in researching sports-focused social media over the past decade. Currently serving as a full professor and the director of the Institute for Sport Marketing at Laurentian University, Dr. Pegoraro's research has focused specifically on how social media is used within sport, including examining social media networks, framing messages, and using social media strategically to position sport organizations and athletes in the broader public consciousness. She spoke with me about her perceptions of social media evolution and where she thinks it might be headed.

Q: What's your perception of where social media is at as we enter the 2020s?

AP: Well, I think from where it started, it's certainly changed. I think back a decade ago when organizations first started using social media, most of them used it as a traditional media platform. It was broadcast only, pushing messages out, and not understanding that it was a dialogue platform, a two-way communication platform. Most organizations just weren't ready for that.

When you look at sport organizations now, you see they've shifted the tone and voice of what they use. They engage on these platforms, understand the value of engaging with fans, and understand that fans are a tremendous source of value creation for them.

It also seems that sports teams are taking themselves a little less seriously on social media than they did a decade ago. It's not so much a corporate communication focus. They seem to realize that's not what fans want.

The rise of visual platforms certainly has shifted the way communication happens, and the behind-the-scenes approach has shifted into the format of stories—the ability to focus on telling a story through digital means. Now we see organizations understanding the value of telling the story of their athletes and their teams.

Q: Has the development of the various social networks gone the way you expected it to when you first started researching social media?

AP: Everything outside of Instagram has turned into a media platform in a traditional sense. For instance, we can now stream sports live through Twitter or through Facebook. As much as Mark Zuckerberg claims otherwise, Facebook is a media company. It's not a social network anymore. The social network side of Facebook is what it can provide to advertisers, but it has shifted into a news agency and a media broadcast platform. People are using it very differently than they were a decade ago.

Twitter is also very much a broadcast platform. A few people still use it as a social network, but they are no longer in the majority. These platforms are focusing less on building connections between people and more on reaching people in some way and getting them to consume content.

Q: Does that evolution hurt the concept of social media in terms of how it is researched?

AP: The sports world on social media is unique because sports fans still like to talk to each other. The sports bar has moved online—we will still debate our favorite players and teams on social media, so there's still a network connectivity there. That is valuable to sport organizations who are creating content—they can share the content and that network effect is there. Sports fans have stayed connected more than other groups online.

(continued)

Professional Insights *(continued)*

The network ties are weaker now than they used to be. Now, weak ties are important because they allow new communities to move in, but people aren't as tightly connected because social network use has moved beyond family and friends and into connecting with strangers.

Q: How do you feel about the gradual coarsening of discourse on sports social media?

AP: It parallels a lot of what's going on in society. The rise of disrespect and hate speech has found its way into social networks. It happens and it grows because the platforms won't do anything about it. They need to be able to say they have a billion active users, for business purposes.

Twitter very rarely deals with hate speech, particularly when you think about death threats against athletes who miss field goals and things like that. The fact that you can say terrible things online without having to say it to someone's face, that was the first step. Now it just keeps escalating, partially because social networks won't deal with it but largely because it's also escalating in society.

Q: What is the proper way to preemptively combat a toxic atmosphere?

AP: The teams that have limited hate speech successfully have done two things. First, they have a highly identified fan base who helps to police it for them. We've seen some amazing takedowns from fans who go after and shut down bad comments. That has been a benefit for teams.

Second, the teams themselves have done some takedowns of people who have come out with awful things about athletes.

The shift to visual media makes things easier as well: More pictures and video means there's less text for people to react to. Visual stories and video clips are helpful in that they are not giving users something to get angry about.

Q: Where is it going in the next five years? Do you see a new social network on the horizon, or will we see the current group of networks maintaining their market shares?

AP: I'm in the camp that says we won't see a new social network.

First, the predominance of the ones already there is hard to overcome. A new social network would have to offer something different and would have to take away users from one or more of those other platforms. People only have so much time to dedicate to interacting with others on social media. While they may have two or three accounts, they're not super active on all of them—they tend to have one that they primarily focus on.

Plus, the current lineup of social networks keeps evolving. Facebook, Twitter, and Instagram are constantly studying their users. They keep taking away certain network aspects and adding new aspects based on their users' behaviors. The barrier for entry is getting high for a new social network to enter the picture.

Q: What do you think is worth keeping an eye on in terms of hardware and other consumer access portals to social media?

AP: Augmented reality interfacing is worth keeping an eye on. That could shift the way people use social media. Emojis and face recognition tools and other things of that type are starting to appear in team apps. The first social media platform adaptations to that shift could end up being game-changing.

Another key element is the shift in the actual abilities of smartphones. For instance, the new iPhone is going to make it easy for some amazing content to be created. Suddenly you've got user-generated content that will rival the quality of what sports teams are putting out.

In terms of how people interact with the social networks, most of the consumption of social media is now mobile and happening through apps. Everything that the major social networks decide to do will be about keeping eyes on the apps.

Key Point @DoctorGC
Understanding how your social media platform choices interact with your message approach will help you choose the right building blocks for your content. #SocialMediaAndSports

creation, many of which were discussed in chapter 2 of this book.

In some cases, the unique functionality of a social media app leads users to turn one content building block into another. For instance, younger social media users who primarily use Instagram have started creating images of text or text-and-image composites using material from Twitter and elsewhere, screenshotting it, and then posting it on Instagram (Farokhmanesh, 2018).

This transformation of content from one building block to the next can appear confusing to people who haven't used the social media platforms regularly for content creation. But in that case, content users are taking written content from another user and repurposing it in an environment where the original writing isn't intended to be directly interacted with; rather, the content is now being displayed as an image (or series of images) where the primary focus is comments and responses about the implied or real message of the original text.

 The web resource discusses how each of the social media building blocks integrate with major social media platforms. Be sure to check there for the latest updates in how to effectively leverage content on those platforms.

Cross-Posting

Many social media platforms have built-in functions that allow for the automatic **cross-posting** of your messages to more than one social network. These functions are often attractive to social media users because they provide a seemingly easy, time-saving approach to reaching your audience across multiple platforms.

However, be cautious cross-posting on social media and understand the limitations of it. Cross-posting functionality changes regularly, and the audience norms on social media networks can change over time. Be conscious of what each platform allows you to do and how it handles cross-posted content.

Summary

Social media networks are the thriving offspring of technological change and evolution. Advances in hardware and software will constantly alter the social media environment, causing audiences to change their consumption habits and patterns and leading to further change and evolution.

Understanding the history of technological change in social media communication is an important aspect of anticipating future changes. Breaking down content creation into the social media building blocks allows you to evaluate content choices effectively and make the right moves to facilitate your or your organization's communication needs.

Review Questions

1. What did the media content paradigm shift in the 1990s change about how media was transmitted and consumed?

2. What kind of impact has modern media convergence had on sports media consumption?

3. Which content building block is the most prevalent on social media?

4. How does social media platform choice affect decisions about what social media building blocks to use in content creation?

7

Framing Your Presence

Effective social media usage in sport is heavily reliant on successfully framing messages. In this chapter, you can expect to do the following:

- Understand how agenda setting operates in sports and social media
- Learn the basics of framing theory and how your decisions about framing can affect your social strategy
- Identify the positives and negatives of certain types of brand positioning on social networks

The impact that social media messaging can have on the public perception of you or your brand is hard to fathom for people outside of media and public relations. But it's definitely there, and it's something that a sports media professional must always keep in mind.

NFL quarterback Sam Darnold discovered that impact during his playing days at the University of Southern California, as he related to *Sports Illustrated*'s Jacob Feldman (2019):

I didn't have Twitter. All I had was Instagram. Someone created a fake Twitter account about me, and it was the most ridiculous stuff that you could ever think about. I was just like, "What, dude? Come on." And people thought it was me, though, people who didn't know me.

People would search Sam Darnold. This account popped up, and they were like, "Oh, must be him" because they didn't see any other account. So, the negative part of social media . . . My great friend now, one of my best friends, is Cam Smith, a linebacker at USC. He didn't know me. He thought that was me, and so he didn't talk to me, like at all, our whole first semester of freshman year.

Then, as the year went on, we kind of found ourselves with the same group of friends because we had very similar personalities and he was just like, "Man, I got to ask you, you're a lot different

in person than you are on Twitter." And I was like, "On Twitter?" He pulled it up, and I was like, "Dude, that's not me. That's a fake account." So, I ended up getting it deleted.

I thought that was just super funny. But, just the whole, like, reputation versus who the actual person is, it's a huge, huge deal in sports, even for me. (¶13)

While Darnold was able to reach out to teammates who were under a mistaken impression of his personality and address those items directly, there were still many people who followed college football who might have formed a false or incomplete picture of him based on the fake Twitter account. And although the ultimate damage to Darnold's reputation was likely minimized due to his not yet having become that popular, this incident still provides a good example of how it doesn't take much in the way of bad social media messaging to negatively affect what people think of you and your brand.

The unfortunate thing about bad social media messaging is that people and brands generate it without ever having to deal with a malicious or fake account. Instead, the people and organizations manage to create bad messaging all by themselves.

Social media can help you control the way your organization is perceived. This chapter explores a couple of important academic theories, agenda setting theory and framing theory, and explains why a smart social media manager should have a firm grasp of what those theories represent and how he can shape a social media content strategy.

Agenda Setting

When we hear the word "agenda," we are almost preconditioned to assume that it's a negative thing. But when you are running a social media account and your job depends on getting the ideas and information that you think is important out in front of an audience, you absolutely want to be the one setting an agenda.

People who research and teach communications for a living are very familiar with the theory of agenda setting. It is one of the most important audience consumption theories in communications, and understanding its basic ideas and tenets can help you with your approach to social media. This section looks at the background of agenda setting from a research perspective, then focuses on the applied lessons from the theory and how you can use them in your approach to social media messaging.

Agenda Setting Theory

In the early days of communications and media research, scholars were not certain how people processed information that they came across in newspapers, television, or radio. Some early scholars were convinced that media messages had a direct impact on the human mind and that people immediately believed any messages they saw. This process was known as the hypodermic needle theory or the magic bullet theory—the idea that information was injected straight into a person and became what they believed.

Subsequent research disproved that theoretical approach to communication and found that media did not have that type of direct power or impact on people. What emerged instead was a series of theoretical approaches that emphasized the importance of the flow of communication, the interpretation of information, and the establishment by media organizations of what is (or is not) news.

Agenda setting theory focuses on the way the media affects the perception of news in the eyes of audiences. The theory, first put forth by Max McCombs and Donald Shaw (1972), argued that media do not tell people what to think but do tell people what to think about. Media publish articles and commentaries that focus on certain stories, people, and issues, and those become the things that are discussed, both in media conversation and by the public.

Agenda setting theory helps to explain why certain things are newsworthy in sports media and others are not. Think about the way that ESPN approaches coverage of major sports leagues. There are 30 teams in Major League Baseball, yet most of the discussion surrounding MLB seems to focus on just a few teams: the Boston Red Sox, the New York Yankees, and the Los Angeles Dodgers. While all three teams have had success, a disproportionate number of stories and segments focus on those franchises. By featuring those teams, ESPN engages in agenda setting, and audiences react accordingly. If the audience consistently sees the same teams featured in the news, many will believe that those teams are the most important and newsworthy.

A study by *Deadspin* that looked at ESPN's flagship program *SportsCenter* throughout 2012 found that the financial value of a sports team had a stronger correlation with coverage by the show than did winning percentage. Furthermore, *Deadspin* found that if you "add coverage of golf, NASCAR, club and international soccer, the Olympics, and tennis to what the NHL got, you *still* don't reach half the time spent on the NFL. Football and basketball . . . took up well over half of *SportsCenter*'s time between them" (Burns, 2013).

A similar phenomenon happens with the coverage of individual athletes. Sports media outlets engaged in a tremendous amount of coverage of former Florida Gators quarterback Tim Tebow in the early 2010s. That level of coverage turned Tebow, an excellent college quarterback whose professional football prospects were subpar at best, into perhaps the most talked-about athlete in the sport for a few years.

Some of the coverage reached embarrassing proportions, with ESPN getting chided by the *Columbia Journalism Review* for its breathless coverage of all things Tebow (Weintraub, 2012). Even in the late 2010s, after Tebow's NFL career had petered out, ESPN and other major outlets were still covering his progress through Major League Baseball's minor league system as a prospect, something that almost never happens for traditional baseball prospects. Tebow entering the agenda of the media made him newsworthy and kept him newsworthy long after the original reason for his inclusion in the news had expired.

Kyodo News via Getty Images

Consistently featuring the same teams in national sports coverage is a product of agenda setting.

Media organizations make decisions about newsworthiness through various considerations and factors.

- Perceptions of how compelling or interesting a team or person appears to be
- The perceived levels of popularity of teams
- The perceived importance of what is being covered within the context of society at large

This can often lead to entire leagues and groups of people feeling left out of coverage. For instance, researchers have highlighted the lack of coverage of women's sports across many different aspects of sports media (Springer, 2019), despite the emergence of the WNBA and the sustained success of the United States Women's National Team in soccer. Soccer has struggled to garner media attention despite the worldwide popularity of the sport and the emergence of professional teams that regularly sell out stadiums.

Agenda setting theory can extend beyond media outlets telling people what to think about and can also extend to how audiences think about those items. Denham (2014) researched a series of articles in the *New York Times* regarding doping and fatalities in horse racing and found that initial reports by the newspaper seemed to shape how subsequent news stories about the issue were written by other news organizations.

Another study by Denham (2004) highlighted an even more interesting aspect of the media's ability to affect policy in sports. The magazine *Sports Illustrated*, which was arguably the leading voice in sports journalism during the late 1990s and early 2000s, wrote an exposé regarding former MLB player Ken Caminiti and his use of performance enhancing drugs (PED). Denham's study highlighted how *Sports Illustrated's* piece had used **agenda building** (Lang & Lang, 1983) by not just making people think about PED usage in baseball but also causing a reformist reaction and outcome from authorities, which manifested itself in MLB promising steps would be taken to mitigate the problem of PEDs in baseball.

 Key Point @DoctorGC
Media can be used to raise or lower the perceived importance of a subject or topic by choosing which subjects get covered and what stories are shared with the public. #SocialMediaAndSports

Social Media's Impact on Agenda Setting

Agenda setting theory was conceived of and tested in an era of mass media that featured a very small number of media channels sending the same messages to many people. While some major media companies still command a broad audience, social media channels now allow far more messages to enter the public sphere. We still do not know exactly how that will affect agenda setting theory, but we do know that agenda setting is no longer limited to a few large media outlets.

Included in the social media agenda setting mix are accounts whose messages are not predicated on objectivity, as traditional mass media messages claimed to be, but rather on the individual agendas of organizations, fans, and other entities with vested interests. Team accounts, league accounts, fan accounts with large followings, and athlete accounts all have viewpoints to share and items they wish to advance as important in the overall discussion of sports. For the average consumer, it can be difficult to distinguish between objective and unobjective viewpoints.

Your work in social media should always keep the concept of agenda setting in mind. Whether you are a journalist using social media to disseminate news and inform the public or a social media worker operating a corporate brand with millions of followers, the core components of agenda setting still apply. Your followers pay attention to your messages, and the content of those messages leads them to consider things as important or not important.

The messages that you create and publish are, by their very existence, going to be perceived as more newsworthy and important than the items that you choose not to create messages about. The messages that others create in your area of the social media mix are also going to affect the viewpoints of your followers, so it is important to monitor the conversation, see what is being said, and adjust your posting approach accordingly.

Framing

If agenda setting helps media to tell people what to think about, framing focuses more on how media shapes the interpretation of news through the way they report it (Sanderson, 2013a). This section gives you a closer look at the concept of framing, how it affects the perception of people and events, and some examples from research.

Framing Theory

When communications scholars talk about framing, they are referring to a theory of how people process information. Framing as a theoretical concept was originally proposed by a scholar named Erving Goffman (1974), whose book, *Frame Analysis*, theorized that people evaluate the world around them via specific frameworks rather than by some universally held truth. Further investigation of the concept of framing has led communication science to the idea of the media-imposed frame, a concept captured in framing theory.

Framing in media occurs when coverage of an event, a group, or a person is placed within a certain context. In traditional media coverage, issues are often framed in positive or negative terms; for instance, a politician may be covered within a frame of their legislative successes as opposed to their legislative failures. Framing occurs constantly throughout sports media coverage, as journalists provide fields of context and meaning to place events and people in a larger narrative.

One example in sports media is the way that NBA superstar LeBron James is covered. You might think that a consensus perspective would exist about a player like James, who won multiple titles and was clearly the dominant player in the league for several years running. However, the way James was framed in the media during the prime of his career in the 2010s varied quite a bit.

Positive framing

- LeBron James is the greatest player of all time.
- LeBron James is a global icon of sport and entertainment.
- LeBron James has carried most of his teams with his amazing talent.

Neutral or negative framing

- LeBron James hasn't accomplished nearly as much as Michael Jordan.
- LeBron James is more concerned with branding than with winning.
- LeBron James is a poor teammate whose roster micromanagement has kept him from winning more titles.

The interesting thing about framing is that a media commentator or a fan could find examples and context to portray James within any of the frames listed above. In many cases, framing isn't about truth or

Stacy Revere/Getty Images

Even the best players in the world, such as the NBA's LeBron James, can see their public perception affected by how they are framed in media.

falsehood but rather about how the person doing the framing wants to portray the athlete. Audience members who are constantly exposed to the framing of James as the greatest player ever are going to be more likely to take for granted the idea that James is the greatest player ever.

 Key Point @DoctorGC ⌄

The way that people or topics are discussed in media has a major impact on how they are perceived by the public. The framing of a story influences how people think about the people or things involved. #SocialMediaAndSports

Sports Media Framing Research

This section highlights a few examples of sports media framing research and how the concept of framing can extend to coverage of sports. As with the description of agenda research above, it is not a comprehensive review of sports media framing research.

Examinations of framing in sports media often focus on traditional media outlets like television and the implications of those outlets' approaches to covering major sports and events. An article by Mirer and Mederson (2017) looked at how the

NBC television network had framed the National Football League's (NFL) concussion crisis during its broadcasts of the popular Sunday night show, *Football Night in America*. The study concluded that while NBC did talk about head injuries on an ad hoc basis, it tended to ignore the larger themes of player safety or a broader crisis with brain injuries in the league. Rule changes to help minimize concussions were portrayed as having a potentially negative effect on the quality of the game because of the uncertainty around how defensive players were supposed to tackle.

Athlete self-framing on social media has become a hot topic for researchers because it is so unique to the social media era. In previous eras, all but the most powerful athletes were at the mercy of media companies in terms of how they were framed to the public. However, social media allows athletes to enjoy a measure of control over their communication with audiences while allowing them to combat framing from media that could be considered negative (Sanderson, 2008).

Frederick et al. (2014) looked at the way athletes used Twitter and found that athletes on Twitter were largely using it to either respond directly to fans or to interact with other athletes. Sanderson (2013b) looked at Twitter usage among rookie athletes in sports, including the four major professional sports in the United States (i.e., the top professional levels of baseball, basketball, football, and hockey), and found that athletes were going beyond tweeting solely about their sports and including references to pop culture and information about their day-to-day activities.

Lebel and Danylchuk (2012) looked at male and female professional tennis players and how they presented themselves on Twitter. They found that these athletes used a combination of backstage and frontstage personas on social media. The backstage approaches athletes take on social media included focus on behind-the-scenes information, discussion of non-tennis activities, and interactions with fellow athletes and celebrities.

Meanwhile, the frontstage approaches that the study uncovered focused on expressing gratitude toward fans and using Twitter for promotional purposes. In simpler terms, the backstage approach athletes used appeared to "break the fourth wall" and let audience members behind the curtain, whereas the frontstage approach was in the vein of more traditional media presentation.

A study by Frederick and Clavio (2015) on high-profile high school football recruits and their usage of Twitter found an even more informal backstage approach was being taken. When you consider that high school players had almost no ability to talk directly to large numbers of fans even a decade ago, the fact that they are now actively framing the way that fans think about them is remarkable and demonstrates the unique powers that social media networks have to affect audiences.

Social Media Framing Concepts

How does framing affect your efforts on social media? It requires your usage to follow a logical pattern of presentation to provide the audience with a framework to view your brand and assign meaning to it. When you're applying framing theory to your social media usage, you're not just giving your audience things to think about. You're also giving them the context of how to think about those things. Providing that context is critical.

It is important not to get too caught up in what kinds of messages to craft on social media before first figuring out what overarching narrative you intend to use for your brand. Sports industry social media tends to be a copycat field, where message types across platforms that find success are quickly copied and used by other people and organizations hoping to cash in on the popularity of the original message. However, establishing your brand's narrative and voice is going to generate far greater returns on social media than reposting the latest meme.

Figure 7.1 highlights a simple but effective process that social media managers should use when considering message framing. This process always requires a deep understanding of the core elements of your brand. Unless you are beginning from nothing, these elements are likely already part of your organization's understanding of itself. Think of the core elements as what makes your organization special and distinct from other organizations.

Equally important to the core brand framing process is understanding the nature of your social

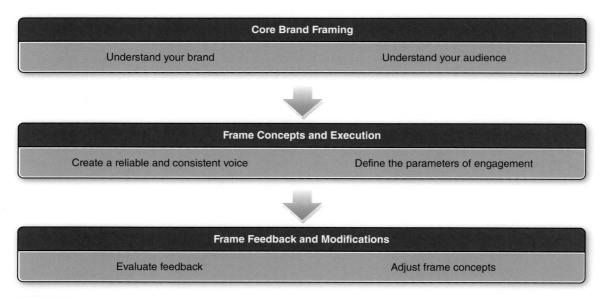

FIGURE 7.1 Social media framing process.

LEVERAGING SOCIAL MEDIA FOR FRAMING PURPOSES

Coleen Rooney (left) and Rebekah Vardy (right) became embroiled in a social media spat that captured the sports world's attention in 2019.

The way social media is used to establish frames and narratives continues to change as the way media organizations and fans interact with social media change. Elements of media coverage that once took place only in newspapers now can get significantly more attention on social media. An excellent example of this occurred in October 2019, where a strange mix of social media, sports culture, tabloid journalism, and celebrity gossip all collided.

Former England international soccer player Wayne Rooney's wife, Coleen, posted a tweet detailing a supposed violation of social media trust, where someone who followed her personal Instagram account had been leaking details of her posts and stories to a British tabloid (Rooney, 2019). After using a sophisticated disinformation campaign intended to discover the person doing the spying, she revealed that her investigation showed that the culprit was Rebekah Vardy, the wife of one of her husband's former England teammates (Jennings, 2019).

The way Rooney's initial tweet framed the situation was nearly perfect, with a list of fake stories and a seemingly logical process of elimination pointing the finger at a person who already had a less-than-stellar reputation among soccer fans in Great Britain and elsewhere (Jennings, 2019). The tweet garnered a tremendous amount of attention, receiving over 300,000 likes and over 56,000 retweets within the span of a few days.

Although Vardy would try to engage both traditional and social media in responses afterward to recover her reputation (Waterson, 2019), the damage had been done and in a way that underlined interesting media ramifications, including the power of social media for framing purposes, the declining importance of traditional tabloid newspapers in the framing of athletes, and how supposedly authentic social media posts are often anything but that.

Had Rooney gone to a tabloid newspaper to air her grievances with Vardy, the story might have been little more than momentary front-page news in Great Britain. However, by releasing it on Twitter, Rooney tapped into the breadth of the platform's network of journalists and sports fans and turned it into a far bigger story than it would have been otherwise.

media audience and how they interact with the brand. As noted earlier in the book, it is important to remember that your social media audience is likely different from your overall audience, generally skewing younger and with different priorities and interests than the general population. However, it is also important not to radically alter your core brand priorities simply to attract a social media audience. Pretending your brand is something that it is not won't yield long-term success.

 For more information on using specific social media platforms for framing, check out the web resource.

Differences in demographics and engagement patterns across different social media platforms will make it important to alter certain aspects of the core brand framing to maximize your effectiveness. As Blake Zimmerman pointed out in chapter 2, you will likely want to alter the way your brand frames messages depending on which social media platform you are using.

After you have figured out your core brand elements and understand your audience, the next step involves conceptualizing the nature of the frame(s) you plan to use. These elements form your **brand narrative**, something discussed in more depth later in this chapter.

A major aspect of that process relies on developing a consistent, reliable **voice** on social media. The goal here is for audience members to immediately identify your posts as belonging to your account because the way they are composed is so recognizable. This can apply to written posts, images, or any other form of media. The compositional style, aesthetic approach, and tone of your posts should have a familiarity to them for the audience.

Equally important to your frame concept and execution process is deciding what the parameters of your social media engagement will be. For instance, interacting with fans is generally a good thing that can help your organization, but there are things to consider when it comes to those types of interactions.

- Do you plan to interact with every fan or be selective?
- Are you going to ignore the trolls who will inevitably leave nasty comments under your Instagram posts?

 Key Point @DoctorGC
Establishing a consistent social media voice is important because it provides your brand with an identity that audiences can easily recognize. #SocialMediaAndSports

- Do you plan on turning the brand's Twitter feed into a quasi-living being, sending out tweets that are filled with emotion and being reactive to things happening in your area of the sports world?
- Or are you going to keep it straightforward and use the Twitter feed as primarily a one-way channel of information that broadcasts news and events to your audience?

What you choose to do is up to you and your bosses, but you need to actively think about and plan your approach.

The final two steps of the social media framing process are evaluating feedback and making adjustments. While the total of feedback you receive is valuable to consider in any media venture, it is important to not overreact to individual pieces of feedback, particularly in social media settings where reactions can be overly emotional and negative. The audience is too vast and too anonymous to warrant taking each item of feedback to heart. However, it is important to note trends in audience response, and both active feedback (i.e., direct comments) and passive feedback (i.e., the presence or absence of interaction with the content).

It's important to keep in mind that while "framing process" and "brand voice" sound very PR-heavy and bland, your actual social media content should be vibrant and full of personality. Use these guidelines to make your overall presentation more coherent and consistent, but make sure your content is something that the audience wants to see over and over again.

Branding Narratives and Framing

The concept of a social media brand needing a narrative probably sounds a bit phony, like you are being asked to create a fake story when all you want to do is communicate with audience members. However, there's nothing fake about a brand narrative, and a well-conceived one can provide your audience with something to grasp mentally and emotionally.

What is your brand and how do you or your company want audiences to view it? For an aspir-

PROFESSIONAL INSIGHTS

Framing in Social Media

Dr. Evan Frederick

Twitter: @evanfrederick83

Courtesy of Evan Frederick

The University of Louisville had a rough few years in the late 2010s. Major scandals rocked the school's men's basketball team, with one causing it to be stripped of its 2013 NCAA title and another causing the university to fire both its athletics director and head men's basketball coach.

Dr. Evan Frederick, a sports media professor at the University of Louisville, has had a front-row seat to these and other controversies in college athletics. As an expert in framing and sports communication, Frederick talks about how public relations and crisis communication can affect the perceptions people have regarding not just a sports team but an entire university.

"Framing on social media allows you to bypass traditional media and therefore control the narrative," says Frederick. "It shouldn't be a snap decision to frame on social media. You need to think of ways to frame messages to keep fans on your side, keep them informed, keep people identified with your organization, and stem the tide of negative media you may be getting. Aim for being honest, supportive, and transparent in the way you structure your messages."

While media bypass can make social media appear to be an attractive option, Frederick notes that hazards are associated with that approach.

"An organization could lose control of the narrative very quickly on social media as other influencers jump in and try to affect the conversation.

"Social media messaging and framing is definitely an imperfect system because it's only been around for about 15 years or so. Before that, this environment didn't exist," says Frederick. "For better or worse, everybody has a voice on social media, but many times it's 'for worse.'"

Frederick's advice to social media communicators trying to frame crisis situations is to keep in mind the organization's long-term goals, not just the short-term implications of messaging.

"It's all about the inclusion or exclusion of information on a topic," he says. "If you're engaging in traditional public relations or crisis communication, you're always putting a positive spin on everything. But if it's image repair, you can't put a positive spin on egregious transgressions. Your greatest fear as an organization is that bad news will make fans defect. So you have to choose a path that encourages fans to ride out a storm and stick with your team."

Frederick notes that many traditional public relations approaches don't work on social media because of the expectation of immediate communication and response.

"If you remain quiet for too long, people view that as complacency or think that you are hiding something," he says. "But if you're too up front with defending people and it comes back to bite you, your organization ends up having to do a lot of cleanup as a result. The natural reaction is to jump on social media and defend people without knowing all the facts, and that can be very dangerous."

He notes that certain interesting aspects of social media make it a very useful tool for public relations and framing, despite its drawbacks.

"There's still this perception of authenticity on social media—even though you're hiding behind a screen, the idea is that what comes out on a team's social media accounts is being communicated directly to the masses, not filtered through someone or coming through a press release," says Frederick. "If an organization communicates a message through social media, it resonates with people more than if the same message came via a formal press conference. The perception is that the team is apologizing to the fans' faces, even though that's not what's happening."

ing sports journalist, brand narrative may be constructed as a talented, hardworking young professional who takes their job seriously but also has a fun or interesting personality. Many sports media members incorporate aspects of their personal lives into their feeds alongside their tweets about recently published stories or Instagram posts about games they are attending. These bits and pieces of life outside of work help humanize the journalist in the eyes of the audience and may make the audience react more favorably to reporting or other content that the journalist posts as part of the job.

Narratives are important to sport organizations using social media messaging. A college athletic department's brand narrative may be constructed as a serious organization committed to promoting student-athletes and excellence in athletic accomplishment. An NBA team may decide to focus its brand narrative on being a young, hip organization that is committed to multiculturalism and youth culture.

If you're working on your own social media, crafting your brand's narrative will be up to you. Try to think about the way in which you are likely

Key Point @DoctorGC

Brand narratives are important to establish because they help dictate how social media audiences feel about you or your organization. #SocialMediaAndSports

to be perceived, both in the core messages of your content and the way that content is delivered, and consider how that audience perception compares to the other content creators in the space.

YouTube star Emma Chamberlain is an example of this process. Chamberlain has used a low-key appearance and editing approach that stands in stark contrast to the glitzy, slick production that many of her rivals use (Lorenz, 2019). This style appears to be more relatable to viewers than the overproduced approach that had become common. By making a conscious decision about the way her work is constructed and presented, Chamberlain provided her brand with a different type of visual framing and an overall different narrative and found tremendous success with both.

Kevin Abele/Icon Sportswire via Getty Images

Former NFL receiver Antonio Brown became a well-known example of using social media for public leverage in 2019.

On the other hand, doing social media on behalf of another entity, be it an athlete, media company, or sport organization, will probably entail working within a brand narrative that others have developed over time, something that may not necessarily interface well with social media messaging. In some cases, you may be able to work some social media magic through making a team's brand appear youth-oriented or sympathetic.

The 2019 saga of professional football player Antonio Brown is an informative example in this context. Brown, who had been recognized as one of the best wide receivers in the NFL during the first few years of his career, grew dissatisfied with his team and successfully lobbied for a trade to the Oakland Raiders in March 2019 (Rosenthal, 2019). However, a series of increasingly bizarre clashes with Raiders front office personnel led Brown to force the team to release him (Tasch, 2019).

In the week leading up to his departure from the Raiders, Brown reportedly sought advice from social media consultants on how he could accelerate his release from the Raiders (NFL on ESPN, 2019) through strategically releasing documents and professionally produced videos on social media. This may not have been the first instance of a player purposefully using social media to force a change in teams, but it was certainly the most high-profile and orchestrated example.

Your brand's narrative helps to provide a framework to the social media content producer within which content can be crafted. It is important to remember that the messages you are creating on social media need to contribute to that framework, and not detract from it.

Social Media Voice and Framing

We've already talked about creating and maintaining a consistent voice on social media, but it's also important to consider how the tone of that voice affects the way that your organization is perceived. A college athletic department will want its messaging to have a different tone than an NBA team, just as a sports journalist is likely looking for a different social media tone than what would be preferred by an athlete.

An effective voice can even build reputation and audience where none is present. A useful example of this happened during the 2018 NCAA Men's Basketball Tournament, during and after the famous upset of first-seeded Virginia by underdog 16-seed University of Maryland, Baltimore County. The 74-54 victory by UMBC over Virginia was the first such upset in tournament history, and it was accompanied by the unexpected emergence of the @UMBCAthletics Twitter feed as a social media phenomenon.

The person behind the account during the game, Zach Seidel, used a playful but feisty tone that gained a significant amount of attention. In fact, it generated so much attention that the account had gained over 35,000 followers and had been retweeted over 48,000 times from the start of the game to its conclusion (Andrews, 2018).

The NBA's Atlanta Hawks received positive media coverage for its social media presence in the mid-2010s (Atkinson, 2016; Brooke, 2015; Prada, 2014), yet the social media coordinator at the time, Jaryd Wilson, noted in an interview how establishing the voice that he and his team used on Twitter involved pushing boundaries that others in the Hawks organization were not always comfortable with (Prada, 2014). For popular and tradition-rich sports brands such as Manchester United and for media organizations such as the *Washington Post*, the voices their social media accounts use are generally going to have more restrictions imposed by management than organizations with less national or international cachet.

In chapter 3, we discussed evaluating large numbers of social media accounts and considering what created the differences between successful and unsuccessful accounts. Social media voice plays a huge role in the differences between accounts, and your own efforts at crafting a social media voice that is both appropriate and memorable will likely be assisted by extensively studying accounts. That process, combined with your own abilities and characteristics as a communicator, contribute to developing a strong, memorable social media voice.

Summary

Social media messages have a powerful effect on how audiences perceive athletes, teams, media members, and leagues in sports, and there are academically valid theories as to why and how that process happens. Media engage in a process called agenda setting, which helps to direct people toward thinking that certain things are newsworthy, and then audiences tend to focus on those items as being important.

Meanwhile, both traditional media and individual accounts on social media engage in a process of framing, which affects how audiences think about people, places, and things. Social media framing can be affected by several factors, including audience perception of an organization's brand, the way an organization uses social media, and the way that messages are voiced.

Review Questions

1. What are some factors that media organizations consider when deciding what stories to cover?
2. How does framing work in media messages?
3. What are the two primary areas of core brand framing?
4. How does a person's social media branding voice differ from that of an organization's?

Editorial Content

This chapter addresses how people working in the editorial field effectively use social media, with a focus on the following:

- Understanding what editorial content is and how it differs from industry content
- Evaluating the strengths and weaknesses of editorial content and how those strengths and weaknesses play out within social media spaces
- Developing strategies for using social media as a sports journalist or media member

Historically, when people have thought about sports media, their frame of reference has been independent editorial content as produced by journalists, entertainers, and cultural observers. As we learned in chapter 1, the mass media era featured a small number of content producers and an even smaller number of venues from which to consume that content. There were a limited number of newspapers, radio stations, and television stations, and ownership of those outlets was often regulated by the government. Athletes, teams, and leagues had to work with media outlets to reach large audiences because most of them could not directly communicate with audiences before the dawn of social media.

But as access to digital communication methods has expanded and as social media platforms have grown, these sport organizations and entities have developed their own parallel content streams that audiences can access. In many cases with sports media, the traditional editorial content producers are in direct competition with sport organizations for fan attention.

We will talk in depth about the content that sports industry produces in chapter 9. This chapter focuses on editorial content in the social media age, what it has inherited from past generations of editorial content, the challenges that editorial content faces, and the opportunities that exist for journalists and others working in this space.

Defining Editorial Content

For the purposes of this book, editorial content is content produced by people or entities that are independent from the control of athletes, sports teams, and sports leagues. This definition includes many of the traditional forms of media and content ownership that audiences are used to, including newspapers, radio stations, and most television stations as well as digital multimedia platforms such as ESPN and independent digital-only content producers.

In the current media environment, it is easy to confuse editorial content with industry content because the forms of content are often the same. For instance, a cable package might contain ESPN, which qualifies as editorial content, right next to the NHL Network, which ultimately is owned by the National Hockey League and therefore should be classified as industry content. While both are cable channels, the nature of ownership and the relative levels of independence from the sports industry are key factors in determining which form content is taking.

Another example involves written content that is promoted on social media. An article from *Sports*

Illustrated, a blog post on *Awful Announcing*, an athlete-authored piece on *The Players' Tribune*, and an insider access story written by an employee of the communications staff for the Buffalo Bills all look very similar on Facebook or Twitter, but the first two would qualify as editorial content while the last two would be classified as industry content.

Expectations of Editorial Content

The distinction between editorial content and industry content is important for young social media creators to understand. As we have learned so far in this book, so much of effective social media content creation relies on the effective and appropriate usage of voice, personality, and perspective. In an environment where different types and forms of media share the same spaces, it can be a struggle to understand what is appropriate or inappropriate for editorial content on social media.

In the United States, editorial content on social media is generally expected to follow the same guidelines for objectivity that traditional editorial content has historically followed. In other words, if you are creating social media content for a news website or broadcast station, you should not be openly rooting for teams or players in your messages. Furthermore, your primary job is to promote your organization's content, not the interests of a team or athlete.

The role of an independent sports news organization on social media is to provide an objective perspective unafraid to offer critical commentary on the actions or inactions of sport organizations and their members. This approach does not mean that editorial content on social media has to be negative, but it does mean that it can (and possibly should) be negative when the moment calls for it. Social media content can also be positive if the situation calls for it. Objectivity does not have to equate to "digging up dirt" or publishing negative stories; it simply means that editorial organizations are using proper journalism to report and comment on stories.

You will likely receive negative interactions and responses from people on social media when you are objective in social media posts that discuss sports teams. Fans may accuse you of bias or dislike toward their teams. These types of responses do not mean that you are doing anything wrong. In fact, these types of responses probably mean that you're doing your job correctly. Some fans simply want media that reinforces the good feelings or attitudes they have toward their teams, and anything they

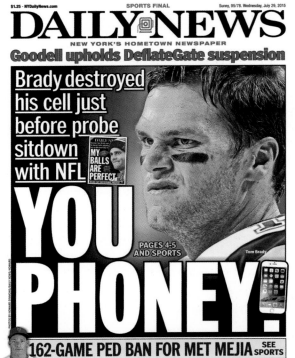

Editorial sports media content features news reporting, commentary, and analysis from independent reporters.

see that runs counter to that is going to lead to a negative reaction.

This era of sports media has seen some changes in the way that sports journalists approach their jobs. As sports media audiences have adapted to the digital era of media, sports journalists have seen the industry's stance on objectivity altered. Their employers now often encourage these journalists to play up their ties to the game or the teams that they cover. As *Sports Illustrated*'s Tim Layden noted, "The voice of sports media has changed as well. Increasingly, sports journalists have abandoned neutrality in favor of writing (or broadcasting, or podcasting) in the voice of the fan" (Layden, 2017).

This shift does not mean that reporters are abandoning objectivity in the way they report on sports.

 Key Point @DoctorGC ⌄

Within United States media, approaching coverage of sports objectively is considered a cornerstone principle of journalism. #SocialMediaAndSports

Instead, it means that reporters are expected to walk a line where journalistic principles and sports fandom intersect to better connect with audiences and encourage them to consume content.

Many journalists, particularly older ones trained in prior eras, are uncomfortable with this trend. For younger journalists, it is important to remember that your authority and credibility with the audience rests on them trusting you as someone who will tell a straight story. This applies to social media content as much as it does to written stories or broadcast news.

It is worth noting that for visual social media content, you can and should use your access to provide compelling content that taps into audience emotions and excitement. For instance, it is perfectly acceptable for an independent multimedia outlet to shoot and edit video of a sporting event where the final product focuses exclusively on the team that the outlet is there to cover and to have that content focus on the positive plays and emotional reactions from the players and coaches on the team. It would be impractical to capture every single visual aspect of a game in a two-minute video, and the nature of visual content online requires you to pick a perspective and communicate through it.

Advantages of Editorial Content

The biggest advantage that editorial content has in the current sports media marketplace is the industry infrastructure that has built up over the past several decades. For audiences, the idea of consuming news still generally equates with getting information from an independent media source that has demonstrated its expertise or relevance in that area. Sports audiences still turn to ESPN for the latest news, and sport organizations still broadly rely on independent media to broadcast games, write stories about games and athletes, and report on important information relating to the sport.

The brand names and forms of media may change over the years. For instance, *Sports Illustrated* and *The Sporting News* aren't nearly as popular as they were in the 1980s, while *SB Nation* and *The Athletic* have become key players in certain areas of sports. But the idea of audiences turning to independent media to find out what's going on with their favorite teams continues to be commonplace across the world.

Sports media coverage has long been a significant driver of audience traffic to both the media

Reporters use access to sports figures to produce quality sports journalism.

Charles Trainor Jr./Miami Herald/Tribune News Service via Getty Images

organizations that provide the coverage and the sport organizations that are the subjects of it. In the United States, that relationship has guaranteed access for journalists covering teams, even if the nature of that access has changed over time. It is still important for most sport organizations to have independent editorial content produced about their games because the audience reach of traditional media is still much greater than what sport organizations can reach on their own.

Within the confines of social media, the editorial content has allowed reporters and commentators from both local and national media organizations to act as opinion leaders within the online conversation surrounding sports teams. Sports journalists are often among the most-followed accounts in any sports team's social media network, and content from those journalists is among the most shared or retweeted content relating to the team. Even when a sports journalist leaves a beat and is replaced by a new sports journalist, the replacement rapidly gains followers and attention within the network due to the reputation and importance of the outlet for whom they work.

Social media audiences are very portable as well. For instance, during the late 2010s, the rapid growth of *The Athletic* saw journalists from other media organizations moving to the new publication. In many cases, these journalists brought huge social media followings with them in the form of established Facebook and Twitter audiences. This led to content from *The Athletic* having far greater reach than it would have managed if it were starting with no accrued social media following.

These examples highlight the continued importance of the independent media voice within the sport social media environment. While it may seem sports fans only want to hear positive news about their teams, many fans are intelligent enough to want truthful reporting, analysis, and commentary. Most fans do not want to see cheerleading from the media; they want to see insightful coverage from interesting people who care about the sport as much as they do. Your platform as a social media creator

Key Point @DoctorGC

Fans still look to reporters and journalists for information and framing that helps to establish opinions about what goes in on sports. #SocialMediaAndSports

for editorial content can provide a wide audience for your reporting and analysis as long as you can fulfill those expectations.

Disadvantages of Editorial Content

While editorial content still has plenty of advantages, the disadvantages in the eyes of sport organizations and fans have steadily grown in the social media age. Because sport organizations can reach audiences more easily than in the age before social media, many organizations have started to limit the access that journalists and other editorial content creators have enjoyed in the past.

ESPN commentator J.A. Adande complained about this trend in the United States in 2015, saying, "The one thing that has gotten worse for sports media is access. We hardly get to see, talk to, and most of all get to know the players and coaches anymore. What limited interaction there is takes place primarily in the teams' workplaces. Who feels like opening up while at work?" (Deitsch, 2015). Veteran Fox Sports commentator Joe Buck shared a similar complaint, noting, "Specifically to baseball, I would make players more accessible. There is no way networks can be able to talk to NASCAR drivers before they stuff themselves into the driver's seat of a race car to go over 200 miles per hour while we are all forbidden to talk to the starting pitcher of that night's game" (Deitsch, 2015).

 Key Point @DoctorGC

Journalists and other editorial content providers are often limited in the level of access they get to athletes, coaches, and team personnel. #SocialMediaAndSports

The limited access has increasingly been paired with athletes communicating to fans and audience members in different ways. Many choose to use Twitter or other social media outlets to speak directly to fans. Additionally, many athletes communicate to fans through team-based media, taking questions and giving answers to people who are presented to the public as reporters but who lack editorial independence from the teams or leagues that employ them. NBC Sports NFL reporter Mike Florio commented about the trend of sport organizations hiring their own media personnel and the problems that creates for traditional reporters:

I'd prohibit sports leagues and teams from hiring reporters. The phenomenon, which has become more and more prevalent over the last decade, creates an inherent conflict of interest for those covering the leagues and/or teams that employ them . . . it makes it harder for truly independent reporters to compete with those who embrace the status of employee-journalist, making them more likely to get that "exclusive" interview *that is in reality a meeting between coworkers* [emphasis added]. (Deitsch, 2015, ¶9)

These problems are new in the United States but have manifested for years in other sports media markets. For instance, Premier League teams in Great Britain are not nearly as willing as professional sports teams in the United States and Canada to work with media organizations to give them access to players and managers for quotes and stories. Media outlets in Great Britain agree to **embargo** sports news publishing in both traditional and social media venues until certain times, largely because the organization gives media outlets such little source material to work with (Curtis, 2019). As described in that piece, within the Premier League:

Players don't make their way to a podium after a match. There's no requirement that they talk to the media after a game at all. There's no equivalent of a midweek NFL practice where you can track down every member of the squad. "What the clubs and the associations don't want is daily access between journalists and the athletes," said [*Sunday Times* soccer correspondent Jonathan] Northcroft. After a match, reporters must wait in a mixed zone, an area players pass by on the way to the team bus, in hopes they'll stop for a quick word. Because reporters never know when they'll talk to a player again, they're tempted to pelt him with questions to float weeks' worth of stories. (Curtis, 2019, ¶29)

That level of rationing of access is commonplace in many countries around the world, and it makes the job of the editorial content producer that much more difficult.

Access has shown signs of decreasing in North America. As early as 2011, NBA owner Mark Cuban went on the record on his blog stating that he didn't see a need for **beat writers** from any websites, including high-traffic sites like ESPN and Yahoo, to ever need to be in the Dallas Mavericks locker room before or after a game. Cuban's rationale was that while newspaper and television reporters needed to be in the room to reach the demographics that do not use the Internet for news, reporters working for Internet sites are geared toward generating pageviews and use approaches that run contrary to the team's best interests (Cuban, 2011).

Cuban would later go on to revoke **media credentials** to Mavericks games for two ESPN reporters, possibly because he was unhappy with the way ESPN was using the reporters to cover the team (Reigstad, 2016). During the heyday of the Kevin Durant and Russell Westbrook teams that the NBA's Oklahoma City Thunder featured in the mid-2010s, the team and its two stars were infamous among local media for making no effort to allow any sort of working relationship to form with the reporters whose job it was to cover the organization (Curtis, 2015).

Moritz (2011) points out an issue that independent media have to confront when it comes to issues relating to editorial content, access, and how audiences evaluate what media to consume. In relation to a point that Cuban makes about sports teams being capable of communicating all the facts to consumers about the organization and its personnel just as effectively as independent media can, Moritz writes:

This is one of the great unspoken fears in the sports media world. Teams, through their own websites, are able to communicate directly with fans. As a Buffalo Bills fan, I don't need *The Buffalo News*. I can get the stats, the raw interviews and other information right from the team's website . . . Now, I like that *The News* provides me with news and analysis that may not align with the team's best interest. But I would not be surprised if, at some point in the future, a team cuts off press access, citing this very reason. And would there be a big fan uproar over this? (Moritz, 2011, ¶5)

What we have seen in the intervening years since these questions were first asked is informative for the future. Fans generally prefer favorable coverage of their teams, but there has not been any regular pattern of teams taking steps to ban reporters in favor of their own coverage. The two exist side-by-side in the social media environment, with independent media having gravitated toward more opinion-based content and teams providing more insider content.

However, the increasingly visual aspects of social media make this issue more concerning for editorial content producers. Sports fans have shown a preference for video and images of athletes and sports figures, and the potential lack of access to these figures for independent media makes it difficult to regularly produce that content. Adding to the concern is that the primary competition for independent media on social media is the sport organizations who have that access and use it to produce their own social media content.

The Blurring of Content Lines

As one might expect in an environment where media forms are merged and content types can be difficult for audiences to recognize, there are blurred lines in the divide between editorial and industry content. Some media organizations have opted to work directly with organizations and athletes to produce media messages that are likely to generate much traffic but also don't fit the traditional paradigm of how stories are produced and delivered to audiences.

In the summer of 2019, ESPN allowed NBA players Tobias Harris (Harris, 2019) and Khris Middleton (Middleton, 2019) to write first-person pieces on its platform explaining their free agency decisions. While insightful and interesting to NBA fans curious about why two free agents made the decisions that they did, ESPN's choice to publish their words directly, rather than allowing a journalist to interview them and put the moves into context, represented the continuation of a gradual shift by some traditional independent media entities to breach the editorial wall in an effort to make inroads with an audience that increasingly values direct insights just as much as objective reporting.

Even *Sports Illustrated*'s scoop of LeBron James' announcement that he was returning to the Cleveland Cavaliers in free agency during the summer of 2014 was accomplished in an unusual way. The story (James, 2014) was written by veteran reporter Lee Jenkins but was told in a first-person format, as if James was speaking directly to the audience. While Jenkins' reporting chops and trustworthiness with sources allowed *Sports Illustrated* to get the story in the first place (Valade, 2014), the format of the piece

served as a template for media ventures such as *The Player's Tribune* that provides first-person accounts from athletes. Would Jenkins still have gotten the exclusive if the story was not written in first person from the perspective of James?

Best Practices in Social Media Editorial Content

For those working in sports social media editorial content, it is important to remember that your work is rooted in journalism and its associated media theories. You are engaging in the expression, marketing, and advertising of news and opinion. This approach is not tremendously different from what's been done within traditional media in the past. However, it is being done in a modern marketplace where all content, editorial and industry, is on an equal footing in the eyes of the audience. You're trying to win a popularity contest among various types of content, including the industry content that often contains the type of access that audiences crave.

So how do you win that battle against leagues, sport organizations, and athletes and their popularity? How do you simultaneously work with those entities to maintain a good level of content and interaction? You're also likely competing against other independent media for audience numbers. How do you use social media in that environment?

There are two areas of social media effectiveness that you'll need to master in sports media:

1. Managing your own social media branding and presence

2. Managing your organization's branding and presence

For the sports journalist, this distinction is important. Your brand must always play a primary role in your social media presence because ultimately you are the only one who is going to take responsibility for that brand. The media organization you work for will almost certainly promote you and your work, right up until you don't work there anymore. Changing jobs, whether it involves moving up, moving sideways, or getting fired, is a reality of the sports media business. You cannot and should not rely on any organization managing your social media presence. As mentioned earlier, social media audiences are portable from position to position, and the more effort you put into cultivating and main-

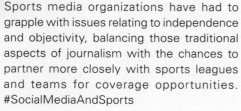

Key Point @DoctorGC

Sports media organizations have had to grapple with issues relating to independence and objectivity, balancing those traditional aspects of journalism with the chances to partner more closely with sports leagues and teams for coverage opportunities. #SocialMediaAndSports

PROFESSIONAL INSIGHTS

Sports and Social Media in Europe

Patrick Berger

Twitter: @berger_pj

Instagram: www.instagram.com/p_mountainer/

Courtesy of Patrick Berger

Patrick Berger is a print media specialist who works for *Berliner Zeitung* and uses social media regularly in the course of his job as a reporter. I spoke with him about the role that social media plays in sports within European countries, and how various social networks are viewed by fans, athletes, and media.

Q: What role does social media play in your day-to-day role as a sports reporter? Is it considered an important part of your job?

PB: Social media can be seen as a major aspect of my daily work. I'm using various platforms, each one for a different purpose. Twitter and Instagram especially are a fixed component of my job.

I use Twitter to inform myself about the latest news: the different clubs' official tweets, tweets from players, other journalists' assessments, and—more generally—match reports, transfers, rumors. Whatever I might miss (matches, press conferences, etc.), Twitter helps me to get the highlights at a glance and directly read important athletes, agents, or managers' reactions on this.

Instagram helps me to get private insights into the players' lives: What are they doing in their free time? Who are they friends with? In addition, it's the best option to get in touch with them or agents I haven't been in contact with yet.

Another effect of social media is the information I get about my readers and my audience. Many stories I write are based on and emerge from comments or posts helping me to get an idea of what they might be interested in. Sometimes, I also integrate comments into my stories to show different reactions of fans to a certain transfer.

To present myself as a sports reporter, I like to use social media to share my latest articles and stories. Other parts of my own social media content include insights into the mixed zone and my trips to different events and matches.

Q: How do sports fans in Germany use social media? What kind of content do they expect from reporters?

PB: I think that sports fans in Germany use social media as a source of information. They want to be informed about sport. They do this by following media companies (newspapers, websites, channels) and club channels, but also journalists. Also, I have the impression that they like to see video footage—short videos with good content.

The fans expect us sports reporters mainly to be up-to-date: Who does my club want to sign? Is a player transfer about to be completed? Why did the transfer break down at the last second? I think that this is even more important to the fans than just providing insights and giving behind-the-scenes impressions. It's all about assessments and above all about opinions! The fans expect clear thoughts and opinions from us reporters. Interacting with the fans is especially important.

Q: What is the online community like for sports-focused social media in Germany? Is it an enjoyable place to interact with others?

PB: I think it can be a meaningful place for exchange. Especially on Twitter, the conversations are often very fruitful. Unfortunately, there are many problems with that here as well. Fans who only see things from their club's perspective become angry whenever the journalist publishes a negative message.

(continued)

Professional Insights *(continued)*

Q: In the United States, social media has become a key channel for sports teams and athletes to communicate directly with fans. Does that happen in German sport?

PB: Germany is currently moving in this direction but is still far away from being as advanced as the USA. This is because German athletes are still very cautious, probably out of fear or respect of the club's own media representatives. There are clear briefings before the season and recommendations from the club representatives in certain training sessions: What may the players post on social media? What should they not post?

Of course, German athletes like (football/soccer stars) Mesut Özil, Jerome Boateng, Manuel Neuer, or Mats Hummels also have an incredibly large number of followers. But they rarely, if ever, use direct communication. Unfortunately, many accounts are also "clinically" managed by service agencies. This often doesn't seem very authentic. However, Mats Hummels is a positive example: He often reacts to Twitter and Instagram fan comments, answers questions, and sometimes writes back. This is very well appreciated by the fans. But that's the exception.

Q&As are made now and then, but they are often led by the clubs and last about 20 to 30 minutes. Since the clubs monitor these, the players can't answer without any restrictions.

During the 2019 FIFA Women's World Cup, I made a comparison between German players and those from other countries. It's noticeable that the Germans don't stand out. The best-known German player, Dzsenifer Marozsan, has just 75,000 Instagram followers. Melanie Leupolz has 153,000 followers, and Giulia Gwinn has the most followers with 167,000 (as of October 2019). The 2.4 million followers of the Brazilian Marta (Viera da Silva) or the 9.2 million followers of Alex Morgan are a huge number by comparison.

The Germans still have a different attitude toward social media than Americans do.

Q: Twitter is very popular among sports journalists in the United States. What would you say are the most used and most popular social networks in Germany? Do you see any imminent changes in the future as far as what networks are used?

PB: Twitter and Instagram, quite clearly. On Twitter, however, the exchange is more stimulating and meaningful. The intellectual level seems to be higher there. On Instagram, people are very superficial, looking for beautiful photos, etc.

The acceptance of fans and readers for the work of sports journalists is, I think, much higher in the United States or in other countries than it is in Germany. With Marc Behrenbeck from Sky or Christian Falk from BILD, a few sports reporters have 30,000 to 40,000 followers on Twitter (as of October 2019). In the United States, on the other hand, well-known reporters who are close and inform about current topics every day very quickly reach 500,000 to 1 million followers.

Raphael Honigstein works for many newspapers as a correspondent in England and has, for example, 490,000 followers on Twitter (as of October 2019). That would hardly be possible for him in Germany.

Q: Do you feel like social media has changed the role and job expectations of sports reporters in Germany?

PB: I don't think social media has changed expectations much. But it's an incredibly important element in day-to-day work. Many stories can be discovered via social media. If you use it wisely, you can make yourself more popular, strengthen your position, and become a better-known brand.

taining an audience of social media followers who are interested in what you do, the more audience you can deliver to your next employer.

Key Point @DoctorGC ⌄

Take care of your own social media identity and presence, regardless of what organization you are working for. #SocialMediaAndSports

Managing Your Branding and Presence

Due to the positioning of independent sports media within the social media networks of sports teams and fans, your social media presence as an independent sports media member provides you with opportunities for personal branding. Within these opportunities are questions you need to ask yourself about framing and public perception.

Your identity online should be consistent over the years, with minimal changes. Try to avoid integrating your employer's name into your Twitter or Instagram handles or Facebook page unless you are required to do it, and even then I would suggest pushing back and attempting to keep it independent. Listing your employer in the About Me section is fine and including links to your employer's social media handles and site make sense. But remember that you are cultivating an online brand that will need to survive multiple employers over multiple years.

Additionally, try to be consistent with your branding across platforms if you intend the public to consume them. Your Twitter handle should be the same or similar to your Instagram handle and YouTube channel. You don't necessarily need to use your full name on these sites, but try to use something that is easy to remember and easy for audiences to connect to you. Your Facebook page in most cases should be your full name, with links to your other social media somewhere on the page.

Social Media Platform Choices

The first consideration is which social media outlets you plan to be active in and why. For most North American sports journalists, the first outlet to focus on is Twitter, due largely to the popularity of Twitter among media members and the importance of making connections within your industry. Twitter provides sports journalists with a venue to publish links to their work, interact with some fans and audience members, and engage in public conversation about sports in real time with both fans and other media.

As a sports media member, you may also wish to become active on one or multiple other platforms, depending on your goals for audience development and the types of content you are publishing. Facebook may be the best choice for connecting with older social media users, while something like YouTube would be useful for media members that publish a large amount of visual content. You need

Indiana Daily Student - idsnews
March 12 at 5:42 PM · 🌐 ···

The announcement ends the IU sports calendar in the 2019-20 academic year.

IDSNEWS.COM
NCAA cancels March Madness, Big Ten cancels all spring sports

Grace Ybarra and 24 others   1 Comment 7 Shares

Courtesy of Indiana Daily Student

Media organizations can use various social media platforms to report on game results and other important sports news.

to make these decisions based at least in part on where the audience that you are trying to reach is located, and that answer may change from sport organization to sport organization.

 The web resource discusses the appropriateness of each major social media platform and its use for sports media members, so be sure to check that out for the latest information.

Reporting on News and Games

A major element of your social media presence is going to involve reporting on news and games. The methodology by which you do that is going to differ from platform to platform, but ultimately many social media followers are going to follow you because you are considered an expert source of information.

On sites like Twitter, this reporting will likely be real-time updates on factual events taking place in games you are watching as a working member of the media. In this reporting, you should emphasize your on-the-scene presence and expertise in observing both the sport and the specific team you cover to burnish your information's appeal to both existing and new audiences.

For sites other than Twitter, such as Facebook or Instagram, you will likely be posting a single piece of content, perhaps a link that leads audiences back to your organization's website. Always be conscious of not overpopulating your audience's newsfeeds unless that approach fits with the social media platform you are using.

Commenting on News and Games

If all you did was report facts and information, social media audiences would have very little reason to follow you. Analysis and commentary on what is going on within sports is a major aspect of social media presence. As a sports journalist, you possess expertise and knowledge to make learned and informed commentary and analysis on what is going on in a game or with a news story. Use that ability and provide audiences with that perspective. For example, the Twitter feed of *The Athletic*'s Brendan

Reprinted by permission from Brendan Quinn

Live-tweeting games and providing analysis and commentary is an important part of being an active media member on social platforms.

Quinn provided real-time commentary during a Michigan State basketball game.

Providing Personal Context

Many sports media professionals choose to provide certain details about their personal lives to the audience. Of my friends in media, I've seen several examples of this, including the following:

- A sports talk radio host who mentions on occasion about how he is terrified of birds
- A basketball and football writer who regularly tweets about his favorite soccer club
- An NBA writer who likes to discuss cooking and restaurants in various cities
- A sports broadcaster who weighs in on political questions that her audience asks

In all these cases, the sports media member is engaging in a calculated display of personal context. You may alienate some members of the audience who don't care about your interests or who expect you to simply "stick to sports." But you can also more fully engage audience members by providing some personal context. It helps to humanize you in an otherwise antiseptic digital space, and that can be helpful when it comes time for audience members to interact with you.

I recommend finding an aspect of your personal or sporting interests that doesn't directly conflict with your role as a sports journalist and using social media to occasionally talk about it. Don't provide all the details of your personal life, but give your audience a sense of who you are and that you have interests and a life outside of just reporting on sports. Successful examples of this include CBS Sports' Matt Norlander, a college basketball reporter and commentator who regularly talks about his pursuits as a musician, and *Sports Illustrated*'s Pat Forde, who tweets regularly about his children's pursuits.

Interacting With Audiences

Social media is largely built on interaction, and sports media's positioning within social media as a kind of real-time sports bar lends itself to journalists interacting regularly with audiences. Your choice of how to interact, and how often to interact, can set the tone for your social media presence.

Generally speaking, audiences enjoy interacting with sports media organizations and figures. If you are regularly reporting on news and games, providing analysis, and throwing in some personal context, it is likely that audiences will want to interact with you, ask you questions, and become more curious about your opinions on things. Even basic prompts, such as the one used by *The Ringer*, can generate a good amount of interaction. See Tips for Interacting With Audiences on ways you can improve your back-and-forth with social media audiences.

Social media interaction is generally a positive thing, although there can be situations where those interactions are negative. Always protect yourself in social media interactions and do not feel compelled to interact with anyone who is behaving in a threatening or disturbing manner.

Managing Your Organization's Branding and Presence

Sports media members on social media will normally receive some level of instruction from their employers about what is expected of them in terms of social media content and interaction. Your employer will likely want you to interact and engage

The Ringer
21 hrs · 🌐

All right. Give us your Super Bowl matchup prediction. Which two teams are going to make it, and who is going to win?

👍 15   104 Comments 1 Share

Use your presence on Facebook, Instagram, and other social platforms to invite contributions from the audience.

TIPS FOR INTERACTING WITH AUDIENCES

- *Be where the conversation is happening.* Use hashtags where appropriate to ensure your comments are seen. Interact with other sports media professionals covering your space to broaden the network of people who see you commenting.
- *Invite audience interaction.* As a sports media member, you likely have a network of followers. Use a social media message to invite that group of followers to respond to a question or comment about the team or sport that you cover. Audience members enjoy being engaged in this way, and this can generate goodwill between you and the audience.
- *Incentivize good behavior.* Once you start interacting with sports audience members, you will have many responses, some of them good and some of them bad. Don't give the bad responders any satisfaction. Choose to respond to the best questions and comments and leave the other ones unaddressed.
- *Highlight and feature audience members.* When you are interacting with the audience, use the tools at your disposal to make them feel important. On Twitter, use the "quote tweet" function to retweet your answer within your response. If you're using social media responses in another format such as a video or podcast, be sure to mention the audience member by her social media name.

with audience members while also promoting content that is being produced by other media members within the organization.

Creating Dynamic Content

Many sports media entities will possess or have access to advanced media equipment that can be used to produce dynamic and interactive social media events featuring you and other members of your organization. These may be live video chats, podcasts, or text-based web chats where your participation as a media member is advertised to a large audience and those audience members are invited to ask questions and interact with you. This kind of content can be mutually beneficial for both you and your organization.

If your organization is not already doing these things, suggest that it start. Most social media platforms now include easy-to-use interactive social media interfaces. Facebook, Twitter, and YouTube all allow video chats with comment sections.

Promoting Organization Content

Sports media members promote the content other members of that organization produce. On Twitter, this is often retweeted links to content, with a note from the retweeting media member about why the audience would be interested in the piece.

In the eyes of the sports media organization, having all journalists engage in this cross-promotional behavior on social media will expose work to audiences that might not otherwise see it. You probably will not be asked to do this too often, but

learning how to do it will help you maintain audience credibility. If possible, promote content you genuinely enjoy from coworkers, and be sure to view or read the content first so that you can promote it more organically.

 Key Point @DoctorGC

Learn your company's social media guidelines, both in terms of how you should approach posting your own content and how you should handle promoting your coworkers' content. #SocialMediaAndSports

Directing Traffic

In the early 2010s, ESPN famously forbade its reporters from breaking news on Twitter, with sourced or proprietary news having to go through the ESPN editorial desks and be released first on ESPN's family of media outlets (ESPN, 2011). The rationale for this was to make sure that ESPN was getting the benefit of the clicks and eyeballs for breaking news stories rather than surrendering them to Twitter.

When you use social media to promote editorial content, remember that in many cases, you want to use the various social media platforms as **conduits** to where the story exists, rather than using the platforms for the story or the interaction that accompanies the story. Writing a compelling tweet or Facebook post should be the first step in getting the audience to click through to your organization's

PROFESSIONAL INSIGHTS

Sports Journalism and Social Media

Dr. Brian Moritz

Twitter: @bpmoritz

Twitter: @TheOther51Pod

Website: www.sportsmediaguy.com/

LinkedIn: www.linkedin.com/in/dr-brian-moritz-ph-d-9b7308/

Courtesy of Brian Moritz

Dr. Brian Moritz has experience as both a practitioner of sports media and a researcher who studies the business of sports media. After a decade covering college basketball as a beat reporter, Moritz made the move to academia and has focused his attention and time on research into the nature of sports journalism in the 21st century.

Social media has played a big role in the changing definition of the sports journalist, but Moritz is quick to point out that much of that change is focused more on the types of things that are published.

"One of the things the research has shown is that social media has both dramatically changed the job of sports journalism, and also not changed it at all," he says.

I talked with Moritz about the effects of social media on the profession of sports journalism and how it has changed the roles and responsibilities of those who work in the field.

Q: Has social media both changed and not changed sports journalism? I'd love to hear you explain that more fully.

BM: Social media has changed a lot of the publication practices of sports journalism. The day-to-day content, the nuts-and-bolts news and information stories, all work well on Twitter. But what's interesting is that on the bigger, more conceptual level, social media hasn't changed sports journalism.

Sourcing is still the same as it always has been. News judgment hasn't changed. News coverage has grown a bit to include women's sports, but on the whole, many practices and attitudes of sports journalism are the same as they ever were.

What the research continues to show is journalists have brought many traditional practices, attitudes, and norms to social media platforms. As a result, Twitter and other social media platforms become an extension of "traditional" journalism, rather than a different approach to journalism. Journalism on Twitter is very much the same journalism as it's always been, just sped up.

When I was coming up in print media in the age before social media, there were these clearly delineated roles and silos within sports journalism. And now everything has gotten messy and unclear in the social media age. For 50 years, there was a routine in the profession of sports journalism. It got changed very quickly, within a few years, and during a time (2008-2012) when there was a great deal of economic uncertainty. That shifted the ground under sports journalism and the profession is still trying to find its legs.

Q: Thanks to social media, audiences have a lot more direct access to athletes and teams than they ever did before. What kind of an impact has that had on sports journalism?

BM: It has accelerated the process of sports journalism. Social media has made it so that the nuts-and-bolts information on any story is out there immediately. People know who won the game already, they know the score, and they know where Kawhi Leonard signed in free agency. So that opens the door for more analysis pieces. The "day one" story isn't "Kawhi Leonard joined the LA Clippers for X dollars" because that story is already on Twitter. So news judgment now takes you to a new "day one" story that focuses on what it all means.

Your lead story isn't the what; it's more of the why.

(continued)

Professional Insights *(continued)*

Q: In 2019 NBA free agency, superstar Kevin Durant famously announced his choice on Instagram, bypassing the process of making an announcement through traditional media. When players and teams can produce and publish their own profile pieces through social media, does that have a negative impact on sports journalism?

BM: It has definitely had an impact, but I'm not sure if it's negative or positive. For many years, those types of stories—the free agency signings, the profiles of new coaches—were the bread-and-butter stories that sports journalists did during training camp. But now, as a reporter, you're not going to do those stories because they've already been done by the team and with a level of access to sources that you're not going to be able to achieve.

Because teams and players are starting to do those types of stories themselves, you have to find different stories to write about. That has been a challenge for traditional sports media outlets. You're no longer going to write "Kevin Durant signed with the Nets" because he already announced it on Instagram. The pieces after that become more of an instant commentary, a "what does this mean?" sort of piece.

Q: Does that create a problem for objectivity in sports journalism? There used to be a cast of reporters that was there to report the news and then a separate group that analyzed it.

BM: The hardest-hit figure in the traditional newsroom hasn't been the beat writer; it's been the general columnist, particularly in midsized markets like Buffalo or Indianapolis. Social media, especially Twitter, has made everyone a columnist, so to speak.

Social media has certainly blurred the traditional lines on the beat writer position. In the era before social media, it was very comforting as a beat writer not to have to express an opinion, to be able to play things down the middle. You didn't have to put something out there and be wrong; you didn't have to endanger your access to sources.

But it's important to remember that beat writers always have had opinions and views, and many times those opinions were more informed than the columnist's because the beat writer was there every day, talking to people, and paying attention. Beat writers have taken to this new role well because the job allows them to. And after a while the question became, So why do we need a columnist, exactly?

An analysis piece doesn't mean it's not an objective piece. It's a game story with opinion, but it's an informed opinion based on reporting.

website or podcast. Ideally, the audience will engage with the content in your organization's web space as well.

Summary

Editorial content remains a key aspect of sports journalism, with social media being an important space for journalists and media members to operate. You can use social media to connect directly with audiences, promote your work, and develop and expand your own brand. Understanding the difference between editorial content and industry content is important, both for the purposes of marketing your work to the audience and for understanding what types of messaging to avoid.

Review Questions

1. What makes editorial content different from industry content?
2. What is objectivity in sports content?
3. Why do media members struggle sometimes with issues of access to athletes and coaches?
4. Why is providing personal context on social media important for media members?

Industry Content

Industry content has been the greatest growth area of sports media messaging in the social media era. This chapter focuses on several important aspects of industry content within social media, including the following:

- Marketing sports team and sports league through social network content
- Marketing content for athletes and other sports professionals via social media
- Dealing with mistakes, public perception, controversy, and other elements of social media, and understanding how these items can be used to your advantage in certain circumstances

Chapter 8 presented how social media content fits into the broader picture of modern sports media practices. The other half of the picture is in this chapter, and it focuses on the rise of sports entities—athletes, teams, and leagues—creating their own content, disseminating that content directly to audiences, and short-circuiting the traditional workflow of sports media.

Sports entities entering the competitive media marketplace has marked a significant change in how sports media careers play out. Students in 2000 who wished for a career in sports media had to focus almost entirely on traditional media and roles; in other words, careers in sports media meant journalism jobs in print, television, or radio. The few sports media jobs within the sports industry were almost entirely in public relations or as team-employed play-by-play broadcasters.

Students entering the field in the 2020s are presented with a far more diverse set of potential jobs and career paths, although with that diversity can come confusion. Industry content allows sports entities to employ writers, broadcasters, social media professionals, artists, production staff—the types of jobs that have existed, and continue to exist, in traditional editorial content positions.

What makes things even more confusing is that many students entering sports media and sports social media will likely find themselves working in both editorial content and industry content positions at various points in their career. Because the skill sets for media are so similar, expertise in media creation can lead to opportunities to jump in between editorial and industry content seamlessly.

Defining Industry Content

Industry content is media produced by sports entities, be they athletes, teams, or leagues. This includes the entire spectrum of media—website stories, social media posts, branded audio and video, images and photography, and more. It includes athlete-authored pieces on websites like *The Player's Tribune*, Twitter feeds for NBA teams like the Atlanta Hawks, Instagram feeds for college athletic

 Key Point @DoctorGC
Industry content comes from athletes, teams, and leagues using social media for communication, persuasion, and media bypass. #SocialMediaAndSports

PROFESSIONAL INSIGHTS

Team Social Media Strategy

Eileen O'Malley

Twitter: @eileenmomalley

LinkedIn: www.linkedin.com/in/eileenmomalley/

Courtesy of Eileen O'Malley

Eileen O'Malley is the manager of marketing and social media with the Boston Celtics. A graduate of Clemson University, she is in her third year of operating the social media channels for the franchise. I had a chance to engage with her in a Q&A session about her educational background, what it's like working for a hallowed franchise like the Celtics and the interesting opportunities and challenges for a social media content creator, and what sorts of things aspiring students should focus on if they want to work in professional sports and social media.

Q: How did you get started in social media?

EO: While I was in college, I was involved in marketing with Clemson athletics. I learned how to market to people and how to create buzz around an event. Ultimately, that is what translates to social. You're trying to create that buzz for fans, that interest level, and have them want to feel the attachment to your brand. I was able to use the lessons that I'd learned in creating interest in some small sporting events on campus.

My college experience in the classroom helped as well. My professors at Clemson had us focus on Twitter and how brands are interacting with each other and with fans and how trends in that space are constantly evolving.

I paid such close attention to what the industry was doing digitally for a couple of years, so even though I wasn't necessarily doing it, I was looking at what they were doing and focusing on why they were doing it. Was this Twitter campaign a strategic move to help them with any business objectives? Are they just trying to paint a story? It helped me understand why teams were posting things, which I don't think many people think about when they look at social.

Q: The Boston Celtics are a unique franchise in the NBA, with the most championships in league history and a proud and traditional brand. How do you translate that to social media, which tends to be very young, edgy, and untraditional?

EO: It's something that has become one of the biggest challenges of my job—making sure that we're translating the Celtics' traditional championship-caliber brand that the world has known for decades into this digital space. What's harder now is that we're that championship brand living in a "what have you done for me lately?" society. When you harp too much on that traditional championship brand, it doesn't always resonate with the online audience.

Finding a way to balance that tradition with the NBA culture and be a little more outside-of-the-box in the digital space is something that we're constantly evaluating. We have to stay true to our brand first and foremost, but you have to push the boundaries at some point. It's figuring out strategically which points are the ones worth pushing for. It's a challenge.

We spend a good amount of time making sure that all our departments are in lock step over what we want to be communicating to the fan base. We have a list of brand pillars and guidelines for who we are in a very general sense. Those are the guiding principles for what we are constantly doing. Our brand is very traditional, championship-caliber, and community-focused.

We are definitely more traditional on Facebook, email, and our website. We take the most liberties on other platforms. We take many liberties on Twitter because of the nature of that platform and how big NBA Twitter is. Snapchat and Instagram are our most informal to give a behind-the-scenes feel on those platforms.

Q: Have you noticed a change on NBA Twitter since you first started doing this job?

EO: Twitter has definitely evolved. It seemed like there were a few teams sticking their necks out brand-wise a couple of years ago, and now it's more commonplace. Now I feel that some brands who used to be way out there and very outlandish are teetering back a bit. But it also could just be that other brands are doing more. It feels like there are fewer extremists at this point.

Q: How do you and the rest of the Boston Celtics social media team define success in what you do?

EO: We are very revenue- and data-driven at the Celtics. We look at engagement and video view numbers. We created an internal algorithm to see how our various pieces of content stack up, to help benchmark our pieces against each other. We use that to determine success as a concept.

Ultimately revenue is big. If we can tie revenue to it, it's a success for us. If we can get it to be a branded content piece, that's big. If we can do something that's engaging the audience well and shows that people are interested and care about it, and also attach a partner and make money from it, that's a very big win for us.

Q: Do you go into everything with the idea that it will become branded content?

EO: We have a few different strategies. In-game social messages are more reactionary and in the moment. So with those, we don't necessarily go in thinking, "How can we repeat this piece of content?" Instead, it's more of a focus on how we can react and build off the excitement of a play or amp up the excitement for the game.

Much of what we're coming up with, we're thinking maybe we test it like this as a proof-of-concept piece, where we can at some point build this out to be a five-part series. Or we can post this throughout the season with a certain amount of frequency. Our group will consider how we can package content and messages in some way, but it's not always the driving decision for why we may or may not post something.

Q: What advice would you give a student who is interested in doing your job some day?

EO: If you have some sort of design background, even if that's just understanding the basics of Photoshop, Illustrator, and InDesign, or if you're able to do something with video and motion graphics, that gives you a leg up.

I do much of the copywriting. Being able to convey messages in a brief format is huge. Understanding how to adapt your writing style to be the voice of a brand, and the ability to be consistent with that, is important.

Being able to stay organized and manage your time is important, as is being able to juggle multiple tasks simultaneously.

When we hire at the Celtics, we always look for the people who have the most transferrable skills and a good attitude fit. If you can understand the brand and immerse yourself in that, then it becomes a lot easier to be in situations where you have to post something quickly. Since you already know the brand, you can convey the situation to the fans through the lens of the brand.

Q: What do you think is the best way for an interviewee to convey that he understands the brand of the team he is interviewing with?

EO: My best advice is to do your research beforehand. Be able to pinpoint more than just recent content campaigns from the brand, ones that you can tell have been landmark campaigns for them internally. If you've spent enough time studying social media channels, you can see the different levels of support being put behind messages and campaigns.

departments, and any other media instance where a sports entity controls and disseminates its own media to the digital audience.

As we mentioned in chapter 8, there is some crossover between industry content and editorial content that can make the lines appear a bit blurry at times, such as active NBA guard J.J. Redick hosting a podcast on *The Ringer* or Milwaukee Bucks player Khris Middleton penning a first-person perspective for ESPN about his free agency decision during the summer of 2019. But even in those cases, the delineation we are using would classify that content as editorial, rather than industry content.

Advantages of Industry Content

Purveyors of industry content in social media have some innate advantages over those trying to market editorial content. The primary advantage in the present media landscape is the access that industry content has to material the sports audience seems to covet. We heard from sports media experts in chapter 8 bemoaning the lack of access that journalists have to athletes in the present day. That's just in the United States—in many countries across Europe, access to athletes and coaches is practically nonexistent, with media members forced to ration quotes and embargo information to squeeze stories out of what meager items they are given.

Insider Access

For industry content, the access is far greater because sports entities have finally woken up to the idea that they can leverage insider access to their personnel for both public relations and monetary purposes. Sport organizations can bring the team or player directly to the audience and do so in a way that showcases personality, insight, and narrative-affirming aspects of the person.

The traditional era of media required teams to partner with reporters to tell the stories of their athletes, while the new era of social media allows the teams to tell those stories themselves, and for athletes to bypass both traditional and team media if they so desire. Organizations can also bring audiences into areas that traditional media may not care to go. For instance, German football club Bayern Munich produces a series called *Inside FC Bayern* that takes fans behind the scenes of their favorite clubs and features episodes that focus on aspects of being a footballer, including everything from how contracts are signed to what happens at a team medical examination (FC Bayern Munich, 2019).

Sports Popularity and Social Media

Industry content has also shown a capacity for unbelievable levels of popularity, especially when compared with traditional editorial media outlets and their employees. While even large media entities like ESPN or the BBC might struggle to exceed 10 million social media followers, the Twitter accounts of worldwide phenoms like Cristiano Ronaldo and Lionel Messi exceed 100 million, and the social followings of global sporting brands like Real Madrid can stretch across multiple regions and dozens of countries. This popularity can lead to incredible earnings potential. A 2019 report indicated that Cristiano Ronaldo earned US$48 million in income from his Instagram feed while only earning US$34 million in salary from Juventus, his club soccer team in Italy's Serie A (Lane, 2019).

Another advantage is the built-in friendliness of the social media audience for the sports entity. While traditional media outlets are supposed to be bound by the rules of objectivity, industry content has no such barrier. A sports team's social media feeds are almost always going to focus exclusively on positive news, spin negative news into something palatable for the audience, ignore negative news entirely, and present the team's actions and personnel in as rosy a perspective as possible.

Changing the Rules

The lack of journalistic restrictions on media content from the sports industry has led to a great deal of innovation and creativity in the way that content is created and distributed. In her book, *Social Media for Strategic Communication*, Freberg (2018) notes how both sport organizations and athletes have consistently pushed the boundaries of what can be done with social media, using it for fan-focused marketing and promotion, public-minded charity, and sports operations-minded items like recruiting.

At its best, sports industry content on social media leverages sport's existing relationship with the audience. Athletes can use social media to talk directly with fans, sell products, or make political statements that are important to them. Sports teams and leagues can position themselves culturally or socially in ways that make them more attractive to certain segments of the population, such as we saw earlier in the book with our discussion of the NBA and the way its teams use Twitter. The sports industry can also use social media content to connect fans with other fans, allowing people with a vested interest in the team and its successes to share a greater sense of community.

 Be sure to check out the web resource for ideas on how to use various social media platforms to successfully publish industry content.

THE NBA, SOCIAL MEDIA, AND HONG KONG

Ivan Cheung/SOPA Images/LightRocket via Getty Images

Protesters in Hong Kong used signs to express thanks to Houston Rockets general manager Daryl Morey and to criticize LeBron James' Twitter response to the controversy.

The National Basketball Association (NBA) spent years developing a grassroots business approach to cultivating interest in the NBA in China. Friendship tours, the success of Chinese star Yao Ming in North America, and the popularity of American-based players in China had by 2019 turned the NBA into a sport that was embraced by both the Chinese people and the censorious Chinese government (Mozur & Qin, 2019).

But one tweet sent in late 2019 by an NBA team executive led to a chain of events that threatened to undo years of work, simultaneously creating a firestorm among Western audiences and media about freedom of speech, democracy, and the business practices of sport.

Houston Rockets general manager Daryl Morey sent a tweet that appeared relatively innocuous, supporting pro-democracy efforts in Hong Kong (Gonzalez, 2019), a special administrative region of China that had seen protests throughout the preceding summer (BBC, 2019). The tweet was very poorly received by Chinese officials, who would eventually and unsuccessfully demand the firing of Morey, according to NBA commissioner Adam Silver (Deb, 2019). Chinese fans would go on to protest the NBA, and league games that had been a fixture on Chinese television in the past were not shown during the opening weeks of the 2019-20 NBA season (Deb, 2019).

Meanwhile, NBA team personnel struggled to deal with the situation in ways that one might have anticipated. LeBron James, the league's top star, withheld comment on the situation at first, then made a seemingly out-of-character statement accusing Morey of being misinformed about the situation. What made the statement appear out of step with James' normal approach to such statements was his prior support for a wide variety of social justice issues (Yeung & Levenson, 2019).

The entire situation served to highlight an important point about sports entities trying to leverage social media for business purposes. When teams or athletes can focus social media messaging on positive game results and entertaining aspects of sports culture, the stakes are low and the possibility of building meaningful audience engagement is high. But when confronted with weighty real-world issues, sports entities are often faced with the reality that involvement in social media content is ill-suited for effective commentary and can backfire in several ways.

Some sports entities want to build brands around controversial topics and are unafraid to post messages and engage in conversation about those topics. For them, such an approach is part of their identities. For a huge organization like the NBA, or a worldwide star like LeBron James, the risks often outweigh the financial rewards, and the financial rewards are the reason they operate in the social media space in the first place.

Athletes as Influencers

Athletes are historically very popular people among the masses, which makes it no surprise that they wield considerable influence in a networked environment like social media. It is surprising that athletes are increasingly becoming more powerful within social media than the influencers who came to prominence on Instagram and other platforms in the last half of the 2010s.

Increasingly, athletes are using social media influence in concert with brands and corporate partners. Rather than the simple advertising as one might have seen in television commercials, social media influencer partnerships between companies and athletes focus on important elements of messaging and audience engagement, including the following elements:

- The alignment between the athlete's story and the brand's market positioning
- The promotion of the athlete's origin or success story by the brand
- The ability of both athlete and brand to give the audience memorable and entertaining content (Lucken, 2019)

Social media analysis of NBA players like Russell Westbrook, Giannis Antetokounmpo, and Luka Doncic demonstrates the ability to provide media value in the hundreds of thousands of dollars per post (Nielsen, 2019).

This phenomenon extends across the globe within sports. Formula One driver Lewis Hamilton, who had over 12 million Instagram followers as of 2019, was estimated to be earning nearly US$50,000 per Instagram post (Tan, 2019). Even younger and lesser-known international athletes can affect influencers on social media. As Somalia-born boxer Ramla Ali explained, "Being a millennial athlete means you have to manage your own image correctly, appeal to fans, respond to requests, and stay current through fashion, music, or sports, all while still training at an elite level and competing around the world" (Pitcher, 2019). Ali had over 39,000 Instagram followers as of 2019.

 Key Point @DoctorGC
Athletes now can leverage their global popularity within social media, earning money for endorsing products on a worldwide scale. #SocialMediaAndSports

Social media content can even be effective for sports personnel who you wouldn't immediately expect would be able to take advantage of it. Research has shown that elite high school football athletes in the United States maintained follower counts on Twitter that numbered into the thousands, and that the athletes used Twitter for self-promotion and interaction with the audience, among other uses (Frederick & Clavio, 2015). College football stars had follower counts and engagement numbers that dwarfed many professional athletes and celebrities, with Alabama quarterback Tua Tagovailoa's social media feeds eclipsing 579,000 followers (in October 2019) and featuring a **user engagement rate** of nearly 12 percent (Heim, 2019). User engagement rates are important across all kinds of content because they represent the percentage of the audience that interacts with the content through liking, commenting, or sharing the content with others.

Disadvantages of Industry Content

With the types of advantages listed above, one would think that industry content would reign supreme over the social media landscape. But there are some disadvantages of industry content, some of which are self-inflicted.

First, despite sports entities having the same capacity to produce media as traditional media entities, not all of them are interested in doing so. For every Atlanta Hawks, Oregon Ducks, or Manchester United, dozens of sports entities don't appear willing to invest in their media approach. There are still sports entities who regard social media as unnecessary and distracting, college athletic departments that lag in using video and images to portray sports and athletes, and football clubs that lag in using social media to disseminate messaging.

In many cases, sport organizations do not value social media positions, with other employees within the organization considering the jobs unimportant and the positions paying very little (de la Cretaz, 2018). Much of this can be attributed to the newness of sport organizations needing to create and distribute their own media. In an industry long conditioned to considering media as the enemy, the cultural shift required to support and care about social media creation is still likely many years away.

Problems With Storytelling

Even sports entities who have a vested interest in producing media content can struggle due to a lack of understanding of what makes a story interesting

Key Point @DoctorGC

Industry content often lags professional media content because sport organizations are focused on selling tickets and sponsorships, with media content still viewed as a secondary function. #SocialMediaAndSports

or appealing. Unlike editorial content, there is no long-standing tradition of compelling media content being produced by sports teams or leagues. While there have certainly been strides made in the past two decades, such as the NFL Network's *A Football Life* series or some of the best material from *The Players' Tribune*, the sports industry still lags traditional media in terms of the depth, breadth, and compelling aspects of **storytelling**.

Part of the reason for this is that industry content often suffers from being too close to the subject matter. Because industry content is almost uniformly positive in nature, it leaves its creators in a box where they often cannot honestly approach the portrayal of a subject or person. For instance, a team-produced interview with a coach or player will tend to be either too lighthearted or too technical, and that can lead to audience members becoming disinterested in the interview. While audience members like to hear positive things about their teams, they also like drama and controversy, and those items are sometimes difficult for creators of industry content to portray.

Audience members who are not already fans of the sports entity producing the content will often have a hard time finding the content in the first place. For established teams and leagues this is generally not a problem since their built-in audiences are already large. But for up-and-coming sports entities, teams, and younger athletes that do not have a history of success, this can present a major hurdle. Casual fans will tune in to ESPN or Sky Sports and be exposed to whatever newsworthy items are happening in sports. If a sports entity is outside of that spectrum of news, it can be difficult for them to attract new fans and unlikely that those fans are going to randomly decide to check out the media that the sports entity has posted on social media without some other kind of news cue.

Lack of Authenticity

Industry content still risks being deemed as more advertising or public relations than news. Sport organizations have to be careful in how they approach social media content.

Sports organizations can fund sports media production facilities that rival professional media companies.

Courtesy of Indiana University

The successful Premier League club Manchester City ran afoul of this in 2019 after hiring a public relations firm to hype up the public about attending games in UEFA's Champions League competition against lesser-known competition. The decision to hire the firm turned into a fiasco after the firm placed an advertisement seeking social media influencers who would use social media accounts to tell the story of what it was like to attend one of the games (Hickman, 2019). The club was widely ridiculed for the advertisement, and the public relations firm was fired.

This came on the heels of additional unfortunate social media news for Manchester City, when it was shown that the majority of followers on social media channels were fake accounts. They were hardly alone in this regard because popular apparel and merchandising firms Nike and Foot Locker also had large percentages of fake fans (Hickman, 2019), but for a club like Manchester City that has struggled with questions of authenticity in the tradition-rich Premier League, such controversies with social media accounts do not help.

Authenticity matters to sports fans when it comes to their favorite teams and athletes. Modern fans want to be let in on the authentic passions of the athletes that they follow, and social media allows them a small window into those passions if the athlete is willing to show them (Caporoso, 2016). Sports teams have the capacity to provide audiences with authentic and emotionally appealing content via social media by promoting when things are going well, but it is important for teams to be sensitive to fan attitudes and emotions when things aren't going well. Many communications strategies in sports approach social media as if it is straight up advertising, and that approach can turn audiences off (Patterson, 2015).

 Key Point @DoctorGC

Sport organizations must be careful about keeping social media messages authentic to their brands. #SocialMediaAndSports

Mistakes and Controversies

The popularity of sports on social media ensures a wide audience for the successes that sports entities enjoy, but it also creates a wide audience for mistakes and unfortunate occurrences. Organizations and athletes alike are susceptible to mistakes on social

media, and the results of those mistakes range from harmless gaffes to career-ending crises.

One of the most common types of controversy involving athletes and social media involves the dreaded deep dive into an athlete's popularity before social media. Numerous athletes who have gained sudden fame have later been subject to intense scrutiny and criticism of their Twitter archives, including such varied examples as current NBA player and former college basketball star Donte DiVincenzo (Temming, 2018), MLB stars Trea Turner and Sean Newcomb (Brunt, 2018), and NFL quarterback Josh Allen (Eisenberg, 2018). For sport organizations and athletes, investigations into social media histories can lead to negative media repercussions.

But are they fair? In many cases, athletes are held accountable for tweets they made years earlier, often as minors. As Fieldhouse Media's Kevin DeShazo argued, "Should we be held accountable for things we've said in the past? Absolutely, if those things were said as an adult. But here were talking about teenagers. To hold a 14- or 15-year-old to the same standards as adults, that seems unfair to me" (Eisenberg, 2018). But ESPN baseball broadcaster Jessica Mendoza disagrees, saying, "Regardless of who you are now, and what you meant then, I don't think the messaging can be that it's okay because you were young or you didn't know" (Bird, 2018).

Sports media outlets have made a cottage industry out of focusing on social media gaffes and mistakes, whether they were committed by teams or by athletes. Writers and video content producers regularly construct year-in-review content pieces reviewing the top sports social media gaffes (Olojede, 2017; Temming, 2018), a trend that exists both in the United States and in other markets, such as England (talkSPORT, 2017). In some cases, even relatively low-impact mistakes such as a player wearing an erroneously worded T-shirt have taken on a life of their own, thanks largely to the amplifying impact that social media platforms can have on news (Farmer, 2019).

Athletes and others can do things to fix past mistakes on social media, including using web services to delete old Twitter posts or paging back through archives to manually eliminate questionable content. However, these methods are tedious and imperfect. Many people forget to do them until a crisis hits, and by that point there's a good chance that a media member or other interested party has located and archived the offending posts.

Voice and Control

Not all social media issues in industry content deal with old tweets. Some of them focus on present-day tweets. One revealing episode was discussed at length in a *Sports Illustrated* article, detailing how teams told an NFL draft prospect to curtail his usage of Twitter. His agent revealed the reason, stating "When Twitter started taking over, teams didn't understand it. They didn't like the players having another way of sharing their voice. They don't want any of them having non-football thoughts or focuses, so teams were freaking out" (Kahler, 2019).

Many colleges in the United States that maintain major collegiate athletics programs have struggled with how to handle social media usage among their athletes and staff. Athletes can enjoy broad support from fans on social media, but they also can experience significant criticism and negativity. Coaches often dislike what they feel are distracting elements of social media when it comes to athletes and their mental approach to the game (Hale, 2018).

Meanwhile, schools must balance the free speech rights of their athletes with the potential for negative public relations from what these popular students say on social media. Most college athletic departments have social media policies that athletes must sign to participate, such as the example shown in figure 9.1 from the University of Southern California. This document advised athletes about the types of social media content that the university considers inappropriate and offensive and laid out a series of penalties for lack of compliance with the guidelines (University of Southern California, 2012).

Best Practices in Social Media Industry Content

Theoretically, it is important to remember that at its core, social media industry content is a public relations function for the organizations and people who produce it. Ultimately the purpose of industry content is to serve a sports entity's audience directly while providing an idealized, but still authentic, image of the entity.

Managing Your Branding and Presence

For the social media specialist in the sports industry, your most important initial investment of time and resources will be devoted to understanding the core tenets of the brand you are creating for, and then using those tenets to guide your voice in your created content. There's no such thing as a one-size-fits-all approach when it comes to social media, and even if your bosses give you a great deal of latitude in your content creation, you still need to understand what makes a sports entity important to its fans.

You are likely working as part of a larger social media content team in your sport organization. Understand your role within that ecosystem and focus on producing content that meshes well with the other content the team is producing. Meet regularly with management and team members until you feel confident in your abilities to create content that fits the parameters of the organization without having to think too much about the process.

Most young people are hired into social media roles because they have demonstrated the ability to create social media content effectively. Use the skills you demonstrated before you got hired and adapt them to the sports team's content needs. Remember, your trained eye and creative capacity were likely why you got the job. The best social media teams adapt their approaches somewhat based on the strengths of the people who work on the team, just as the team members adapt their approaches somewhat based on the brand of the organization for whom they work.

 Key Point @DoctorGC
You get hired to do social media for a sport organization based on your abilities. Smart organizations will find a way to work your specializations into what they do. #SocialMediaAndSports

Social Media Choices

Much as with editorial content, industry content needs to make decisions about resource allocation, types of media created, and time spent on media creation based on which audiences the organization wants to reach, and why. You will likely be working in the same social media spaces as editorial content creators, but working from within the sports industry allows you to approach things a bit differently.

Sport organizations should make full use of media platforms that allow **serial content**. Unlike independent media organizations that may not be able to rely on doing the same thing every week, sport organizations can use their access to players, coaches, and facilities to provide content on a regular basis to audiences, with each piece of content telling a connected aspect of the story.

UNIVERSITY OF SOUTHERN CALIFORNIA ATHLETIC DEPARTMENT SOCIAL MEDIA POLICY AND GUIDELINES FOR STUDENT ATHLETES

Playing and competing for the University of Southern California is a privilege. Student-athletes at USC are held in the highest regard and are seen as role models in the community. As leaders you have the responsibility to portray your team, your university, and yourselves in a positive manner at all times. Sometimes this means doing things that are an inconvenience to you, but benefit the whole team.

Facebook, Twitter, and other social media sites have increased in popularity globally and are used by the majority of student-athletes here at USC in one form or another.

Student-athletes should be aware that third parties—including the media, faculty, future employers, and NCAA officials—could easily access your profiles and view all personal information. This includes all pictures, videos, comments, and posters. Inappropriate material found by third parties affects the perception of the student-athlete, the athletic department, and the university. This can also be detrimental to a student-athlete's future employment options, whether in professional sport or in other industries.

Examples of inappropriate and offensive behaviors concerning participation in online communities may include depictions or presentations of the following:

- Photos, videos, comments, or posters showing the personal use of alcohol, drugs, and tobacco (e.g., no holding cups, cans, shot glasses, etc.).

- Photos, videos, and comments that are of a sexual nature. This includes links to websites of a pornographic nature and other inappropriate material.

- Pictures, videos, comments, or posters that condone drug-related activity. This includes but is not limited to images that portray the personal use of marijuana and drug paraphernalia.

- Content online that is unsportsmanlike, derogatory, demeaning, or threatening toward any other individual or entity (examples: derogatory comments regarding another institution; taunting comments aimed at a student-athlete, coach, or team at another institution; and derogatory comments against race and/or gender). No posts should depict or encourage unacceptable, violent, or illegal activities (examples: hazing, sexual harassment/assault, gambling, discrimination, fighting, vandalism, academic dishonesty, underage drinking, illegal drug use).

- Content online that would constitute a violation of Pac-12 or NCAA rules (examples: commenting publicly about a prospective student-athlete, providing information related to sports wagering activities, soliciting impermissible extra benefits).

- Information that is sensitive or personal in nature or is proprietary to the USC Athletic Department or the university, which is not public information (examples: tentative or future team schedules, student-athlete injuries and eligibility status, travel plans/itineraries or information).

If a student-athlete's profile and its contents are found to be inappropriate in accordance with the above behaviors, he/she will be subject to the following penalties:

1. Written warning
2. A meeting with Director of Athletics and Head Coach
3. Penalties as determined by the athletic department, including but not limited to possible suspension from his/her athletic team

For your own safety, please keep the following recommendations in mind as you participate in social media websites:

- Set your security settings so that only your friends can view your profile.

- You should not post your email, home address, local address, telephone number(s), or other personal information as it could lead to unwanted attention, stalking, identity theft, etc.

- Be aware of who you add as a friend to your site—many people are looking to take advantage of student-athletes or to seek connection with student-athletes.

- Consider how the above behaviors can be reflected in all Facebook applications.

If you are ever in doubt of the appropriateness of your online public material, consider whether it upholds and positively reflects your own values and ethics as well as the USC Athletic Department's and the university's. Remember, always present a positive image and don't do anything to embarrass yourself, the team, your family, or the university.

By signing below, you affirm that you understand the USC Athletic Department Social Media Policy and Guidelines for Student-Athletes and the requirements that you must adhere to as a USC student-athlete. Also, you affirm that failure to adhere to this policy and guidelines may result in consequences that include suspension from your athletic team, and you may be subject to additional penalties imposed by the NCAA, Pac-12, or USC.

Printed name _____

Signature _____ Date _____

FIGURE 9.1   The University of Southern California's athletic department social media policy for collegiate athletes.

Reprinted by permission from University of Southern California

For instance, your organization can use a video platform such as YouTube or Vimeo to curate playlists of videos. Indiana University athletics, a member of a major college athletics conference, use YouTube for this purpose, curating playlists about their major sports programs and featuring coaches and athletes in behind-the-scenes interviews and profiles. Providing fans with serial content allows them to settle into patterns of consumption where they are anticipating new content and going back to watch previously produced content.

Remember to use various social media platforms for their strengths. Twitter is excellent for interactions with other organizations and media as well as interactions with select fans and influencers, while Snapchat is best for attempting to communicate with young audiences. Keep an eye on what your league competitors are doing on their various social media platforms, and don't be afraid to adapt someone else's good idea into something that works for your organization.

Go Where Only You Can

Insider access and behind-the-scenes content remain the sport organization's biggest advantage in the social media world, and you should be doing everything within your power to leverage that access in your content. Fans are genuinely curious about what makes their favorite teams work. They want to see pregame routines from players, what the coaches' offices look like, and what a typical off-day involves for the members of the organization.

Behind-the-scenes content can take many forms, including images, sound, short video, and longer video. Work with your sports operations department and observe the various aspects of the team's environment. Take notes on what items are interesting and which players or coaches might be willing to take part in this type of content.

Be conscious of the reality that coaches and athletes may not initially want to be a part of the content, and do not approach those groups with a sense of entitlement. Explain your ideas and why they would be effective and useful for the organization and perhaps also for the people you want involved. Work with your management to bring ideas to the table and create mock-ups or example footage of what your ideas might look like when they come to fruition.

Also keep in mind that some of your best insider access comes outside of the normal team environment. Look at facilities and the people working there to see if there are interesting stories that you can tell through social media content. Learn about your fans, particularly the die-hard fans of your organization, and try to incorporate those fans and their stories into your content. Keep a notebook or Word document of all the ideas and possible creative output that you can think of, and be sure to revisit those notes over time as you learn more about the organization and its audience.

 Key Point @DoctorGC
Take time to learn the acceptable social media boundaries within your organization and among your team's athletes and coaches. #SocialMediaAndSports

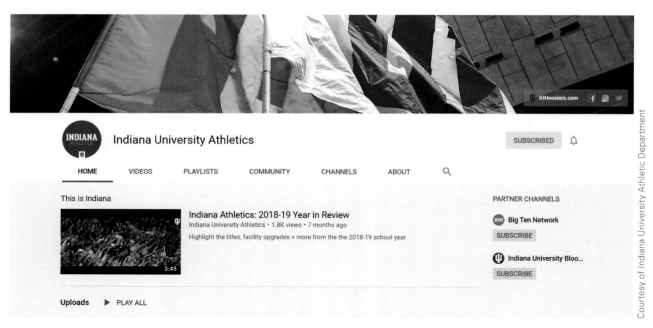

Many teams have their own YouTube channel that contains a curated list of professionally produced videos, highlights, interviews with team personnel, and behind-the-scenes materials.

Leveraging Organization Members

Smart organizational social media strategy is about more than just entertainment or marketing. Ideally, you and your social media team are working with other members of the organization to present a unified experience to fans, consumers, and potential customers. Your coworkers in other parts of the organization may not initially be comfortable with using social media, but as an expert, you can help them understand the best ways to respond to customers and create content.

While the default approach to social media messaging can often be focusing on emotion and fan engagement, your organization's social media presence can be far more expansive than that. Here are some key areas of the organization to consider for social media interaction purposes.

Marketing

Many social media departments in sports are wholly or partly run by the marketing department. If that is the case for your organization, you still need to make sure that social media isn't just seen as a means to an end for marketing ideas but rather as a holistic process through which marketing ideas are conceived and executed. A fully integrated social media approach to your organization's marketing department will allow you to effectively use the understanding of online communities that you acquired in chapter 5 and the various social media building blocks that you learned about in chapter 6.

If you are a social media manager outside of the marketing department, you should be having regular meetings with the marketing staff to keep up-to-date on what initiatives the organization is crafting while also providing the marketing department with ideas about how to best use the social media toolkit to deliver messages and engage with fans.

Public and Community Relations

If social media isn't its own department and isn't being run out of the marketing department, chances are it is being run by the public relations staff. This makes sense in a way because of the very public nature of communication that takes place on social media.

Many organizations have envisioned social media channels as an extended form of public relations, historically using platforms to issue official statements and press releases and provide basic information about games being played. While using social media solely for those purposes is essentially missing out on the communicative potential of social media, the core concepts of communicating important organizational information to audiences are sound.

PROFESSIONAL INSIGHTS

Fans, Social Media, and Crisis Response

Dr. Natalie Brown Devlin

Twitter: @NatalieBDevlin

LinkedIn: www.linkedin.com/in/natalie-brown-devlin-79118121/

Courtesy of Natalie Brown Devlin

"What's unique about social media is that it gets to the heart of what you want out of public relations—that two-way communication between organization and fan. Sometimes that works out well for sport organizations, and sometimes it doesn't."

Dr. Natalie Brown Devlin, an assistant professor in the Stan Richards School of Advertising & Public Relations at the University of Texas at Austin, focuses her research on crisis communication and digital media in sport. She has done a great deal of research on how both fans and sport organizations conduct themselves during crises, and much of that research has focused on social media's impact within that continuum.

"Social media has given fans a unique kind of power that they didn't have before," Devlin says. "They can publicly comment on crises themselves. I started my research with a question: Do fans engage in traditional crisis communication techniques? And the answer is that yes, they do."

Devlin's research has led her to examine social media fan reaction, particularly with collegiate athletics. Examining football fan reactions to crises, she found some consistent trends across both.

"In both cases, fans feel this intrinsic need to rally during times of crisis, to show that 'Even though our fandom feels threatened right now, we are still together through this,'" says Devlin. "They also aren't afraid to attack either the person making the accusations or a third party."

Devlin notes that the reactions of fans online to crises that involve their teams have a lot to do with the way fans psychologically process fandom and relationship with the team.

"You can't separate crisis communication from fan identification," she says. "As a fan, your team is now completely psychologically relevant to you, so the crisis is going to be perceived as a threat to that."

Within social media networks, Twitter seems to have an outsized effect on fan reactions to crisis communications, largely because people's comments on crises are reactionary, public, and very much in the moment as news and information break.

"Twitter encourages more of a 'social TV'-type phenomenon, where you're consuming media simultaneously on multiple devices. The comments that you're sharing on social media are reactionary to the other content you're consuming. Certainly, you have fan comments on Facebook groups and team pages, but Twitter has more of a reactionary component to it."

Devlin says that social media managers for organizations and athletes often find themselves in a tricky spot when it comes to dealing with fan communications surrounding crises. While fans can certainly help with public defense, social media managers have to be careful about how they appear to be interacting with those communications.

"If it looks like the organization is trying to intentionally drive fan reaction to a crisis, it can backfire," says Devlin.

She also notes that social media appears to be influencing tried-and-true crisis communication approaches and methodologies.

"There have been times recently where an apology theoretically should have worked, but it did not. It was almost seen as an admission of guilt. And a denial was more effective. So it seems in some cases, this approach that we see on social media, the need to 'hit back' instead of apologize, indicates that certain things may be changing and need to be examined again theoretically."

The main concerns with public relations in sports are in the bland nature of their communications efforts, which tend to not play well in a social media space and among fans. Effective coordination with public relations involves working with the department on information and timing but then modifying the presentation of the content into something more entertaining and interesting for the audience, apportioned to the most appropriate social media platform.

Team Operations

Athletes, coaches, and administrators in sports are notoriously insular with information, tending to view all media as intrusions and distractions. However, as we discussed throughout the book, insider access and behind-the-scenes content are what audiences want.

Making inroads with the team operations staff and gaining their trust is an important part of being a sports social media manager. Ask for a meeting during the off-season where you can clearly explain your tactics, describe how communicating materials could positively alter the public perception of players and coaches, and discuss parameters within which social media content can be created. Bring visual examples of the type of content you want to create and show coaches and general managers what the value of that content could be to the organization and to their own brands. Ask those same people for input on what insider content might be interesting to the audience.

Ticketing, Game, and Facility Operations

Some fans may just be on social media because they are looking for parking information, ticket purchasing options, crowd control help, or merchandise (Patterson, 2015). Have a system set up with your organization's game or event operations staff where they have a representative on the proper social media channels, and work with them on interaction approaches and information distribution. At the very least, make sure that information and assistance requests that come through to your social media channels are getting routed to the proper place.

Additionally, remember that athletes and coaches on social media are members of your organization as well! In many cases, their content is going to be of interest to large segments of fans, and you should be constantly monitoring their feeds, or as we saw in an earlier chapter with the Texas Tech University example, working with them directly to coordinate the promotion of their messages. Sharing or engaging with content from athletes and coaches through the organization's social media channels can increase their exposure while generating reactions and engagements from your organization's followers.

Interacting With Other Organizations

In sports social media, you will often have the chance to interact publicly with the accounts of other teams in your league or association. While each league is different in how it prefers to handle those types of interactions, fans and observers generally enjoy watching two teams jab at each other playfully online. This kind of interaction works best on platforms such as Twitter, which allow for relatively rapid responses that are publicly viewable.

After working in the business for a period of time, you will likely meet the operators of the other teams' social media accounts and develop professional relationships with them. That can help with managing team-to-team interactions and ensuring that the banter is playful and entertaining without turning mean. Fans of rival teams may consider each other to be mortal enemies, but teams are generally part of the same business and competitive organization. Give the fans a good show but remember that your social media office and the other team's social media office are ultimately on the same side.

Crisis Communication

Social media's public reach makes it a natural environment for crisis communication to take place. Platforms like Twitter allow organizations to make rapid statements in the face of an impending crisis, while platforms like Facebook allow audiences to interact with the organization in response to crises that are occurring.

Crisis communication on sports social media can be tricky due to the variety of moving parts that occur during a sports crisis. For instance, in November 2019, the Cleveland Browns of the NFL had to deal with the fallout from a nationally televised moment of rage on the football field involving Myles Garrett, who ripped off the helmet of an opposing player and used it as a weapon against that player.

The Browns would tweet out an apology from Garrett and then would wait until the NFL ruled on Garrett's indefinite suspension before making their own statement on Twitter. Garrett himself would maintain silence on social media until January 1, 2020, when he tweeted out a video thanking Cleveland fans and making vaguely inspirational statements (Vadaj, 2020).

The Browns organization had to deal with the immediate fallout of the event, their own organizational stance toward the incident, the NFL's stance toward the incident, their fans' stance toward the incident, and the player's stance toward the incident, with all of those entities being able to weigh in on their own social media platforms.

For sport organizations, crisis communication is the most thankless aspect of social media. Crises often bring harsh criticisms from what seems like all corners of the Internet, leaving social media teams buried in an onslaught of negativity and anger. It is important for organizations to have a plan for how social media will be used during a crisis. What platforms to use, what types of statements will be made, and what will or will not be responded to are all important social media crisis communication elements that need to be discussed before any crisis takes place.

Summary

Industry content in sports social media continues to grow in popularity and importance within the sports media scene. Almost every sports entity has at least one social media platform, and jobs in this area continue to expand as the demand for quality content creation increases. Sports entities have significant advantages in content creation in terms of access to behind-the-scenes materials and favorable audiences, but many still struggle to tell effective stories or effectively manage their advantages in a competitive media environment.

Review Questions

1. What are some advantages that industry content has in the marketplace over editorial content?
2. Why are issues of voice and control problematic for sports media industry content?
3. What are some areas of a team's behind-the-scenes content that you could focus on?

Holistic Social Media

Working in social media can be challenging from both professional and personal perspectives. This chapter focuses on the following:

- Developing an understanding of the personal challenges within the sports social media environment
- Establishing good working practices to keep your career progress strong and positive
- Learning how to maintain balance and avoid burnout

Social media use has become a requirement for almost everyone working in sports media content. Although platforms, audiences, and methods of communication continue to change over time, the core elements of personal interaction and marketing of content remain.

Working in the social media world will provide you with a huge number of both high and low points. Few media moments are more affirming and positive than when content you created goes viral due to everyone loving it or when complete strangers go out of their way to thank you for something that you wrote. On the other hand, few media moments are more negative and soul-sucking than when complete strangers make nasty and degrading comments about you on social media or when your work is aggressively criticized and ratioed. This chapter focuses on the personal, moral, and ethical elements of social media usage among practitioners.

Personal Care and Challenges

We have talked a lot in this book about technical skills, creative skills, intellectual skills, and knowledge development. All those things are certainly important to becoming a top-notch social media content creator. But the biggest and most important asset that you have in this business is yourself. Your physical, mental, and emotional **well-being** are the most important things that you need to focus on if you want to have a long and fruitful career in this field.

Social media work presents a unique and difficult set of challenges for the people who choose it as a profession. Your work is constantly being judged by others, from the consumers and fans who digest your content to the managers and administrators who employ you. The content you create is always being criticized, questioned, and compared to things that others have created. That can be a very difficult thing to deal with mentally and emotionally, particularly at early stages in your career when you don't have much experience and are probably lacking in confidence about the quality of your content.

If you think you want a career in sports social media, get experience in high school and college working in that environment first, before committing to the field. You never know until you've done it whether you will like the pressure and judgment that is inherent in the social media creation process. Getting experience doing social media work before you go pro will at least provide you with an understanding of what you are getting yourself into.

As you network with social media professionals throughout your college years, ask them specific questions about how they deal with the pressures of the job.

- Did they ever struggle with criticism of their content?
- Do they feel uncertain about what they produce, and how do they handle that?
- What kind of support system do they use to keep themselves balanced?

These types of questions can give you a better sense of what you need to think about as you enter this field.

Balance

Becoming successful at creating social media can often mean an unhealthy level of immersion into the process. Consider the highly successful YouTube star Emma Chamberlain, who had nearly 16 million social media followers as of 2019. According to a *New York Times* profile, she spends 20 to 30 hours editing each video that she makes, which has led to her experiencing physical pain and deteriorating eyesight as a result of her normal work practices (Bromwich, 2019).

Tyler Blevins, better known as the famous esports star Ninja, is an even more extreme example. Blevins earned more than US$500,000 a month as of 2018, mostly through Twitch and YouTube interactions that required him to be online constantly, streaming his games of *Fortnite* and interacting with audiences while only getting five or six hours of sleep a night and rarely taking a day off (Draper & Bromwich, 2018).

Balance is a key issue with creating social media content because of how important time online or time creating content is to the overall product. I know from my own experiences in media that it's very easy to lose track of time, not engage in regular physical activity, and neglect social obligations because I am too locked into what I'm trying to get done.

The issue with balance is that you're often going to be competing against other people who are purposefully unbalanced to gain an edge. Rob Perez, the creative genius behind the well-known World Wide Wob account popular on NBA Twitter, essentially recommended that aspiring content creators build around their content creation:

My recommendation is, whether it's fair or not, is I don't think you're going to succeed in this industry unless you make it your lifestyle. You have to be 24/7 about it because there's gonna be people like myself that don't leave the apartment for five days . . . You have to be willing to invest

Stress and demotivation are regular features of every job, and social media is no different.

in yourself. You have to be willing to not take a paycheck and commit to getting your voice and your content out there as much as possible. (Front Office Sports, 2018, ¶12)

I am torn by this kind of advice. On the one hand, Mr. Perez is correct in that people can succeed in this business because they make it a lifestyle, throwing everything into content creation and online presence and outworking everyone else in the process. I have seen many success stories in different forms of media where the people involved did exactly that.

However, I have also seen a lot of people not succeed by following this path. Sometimes it's due to bad luck, sometimes it's due to poor work-life balance, and sometimes it's due to a lack of innate talent. Making sports social media your lifestyle could eventually turn you into a breakout star, but there are no guarantees. You have to be conscious of the professional and personal risks in taking such a step.

There are ways to keep a good balance in your approach without turning your whole life into one long grind for content. Developing skills during college and continuing to add to those skills will save you a lot of time and effort. Focusing on an area that

Galen Clavio

Working in sports social media can be taxing, so it's important to keep your enjoyment of both the work and the subject matter.

you are passionate about and building your content in that space helps establish credibility, which is a key part of making it in this field.

Keeping it fun and fresh for yourself is also important. You will hit a point where the newness of creating social media goes away, just as you will hit a point where the novelty of working for a media organization or sports team will go away. Once that happens, can you find things to keep your job interesting? Are there challenges you can set for yourself? New skills to learn? Emerging social media forms to master? New ways of creating engagement with viewers and fans? If these things excite you, then there's a good chance you will be able to maintain a healthy balance in your life between your social media presence and your personal existence. If not, then you probably need to ask yourself why you want to do this in the first place.

 Learning how to effectively use each social network helps to reduce the time you spend on social media, and that can assist with balance and burnout issues. Check out the web resource for more information on each social network's best practices in sports.

Burnout

A lot of people think working in social media is both fun and easy. After all, how hard can it be, right? You take a few pictures, you write a few tweets, a bunch of people like your stuff, and then you do it all over again.

Except . . . that's definitely *not* how it works, and if you've learned anything from this book so far, you have hopefully come to realize exactly how much work goes in to being successful at social media. The profession requires hours and hours of developing skills, evaluating feedback, and keeping up with technological and cultural trends, and that doesn't even count the constant media creation cycle that you enter once you start doing social media on a professional basis.

 Key Point @DoctorGC
Even the best sports social media content creators suffer from burnout and emotional fatigue. Grant yourself the ability to walk away from things and reset your mind. #SocialMediaAndSports

Everyone processes the experience of creating and performing on social media differently. For most, there comes a point where something causes us to want to stop creating social media. Perhaps your latest social campaign flopped and your bosses criticized your work. Perhaps some audience members tweeted awful things about you and accused you of not knowing what you were doing. Wanting to walk away may be temporary or permanent, but the likelihood is that you are going to experience that feeling of **burnout** more than once in your career.

Hootsuite's Emma Brown highlighted four potential symptoms that are associated with social media burnout:

1. Compulsive desires to check your phone
2. A lack of interests outside of social media
3. Anxiety or tension at work
4. Poor sleeping patterns (Brown, 2019)

Those symptoms are by no means unique to social media, but they do exist in the profession and it is important to keep an eye on yourself to make sure those symptoms have not taken hold.

How do you deal with social media burnout? Even better, how do you keep from getting to the point where you feel burned out in the first place? Here are some important tips for protecting yourself.

- *Keep your social life alive*: Social contact with other human beings outside of work is important in any job. In social media, it may be even more important because so much of your communication with others is via electronic means. Go out with people, interact personally rather than via text, and continue to provide yourself with new and interesting social experiences.

- *Leave work behind*: There will always be a temptation to take your work home with you, and that temptation doubles when you are doing all or most of your work on your phone. There's always one more tweet to reply to or one more Instagram post to make. However, working outside of business hours is likely to increase your chances of burnout. Even if you are the sole voice of a team on social media and have to be on call, take advantage of the times when you aren't on call and force yourself to avoid work-related social media.

- *Avoid screens when you can*: Your professional life is going to require your constant attention on a screen of some sort, whether that's a phone screen or a laptop display. There aren't many things you can do about that, but you can and should separate yourself from screens when you aren't working. Excessive screen time has all kinds of negative repercussions, from muscle pain to eye strain to brain scramble. Give your eyes, neck, and mind a break for at least a few hours a day.

- *Don't take it personally*: Social media is an unforgiving place. You will make mistakes, and people will criticize you for those mistakes. You will encounter jerks online, and they will say mean things. Don't let it bring you down. Have other interests outside of work and take the time to enjoy those things.

A key element of maintaining a healthy mental and emotional approach to your work is ensuring that you're not inadvertently increasing your level of anxiety. Chances are that if you're working in social media, you're probably consuming a lot of material online, both via native social media content and through the online news outlets that promote their work on social media. But what kind of content are you consuming? Is it content that generally matches your area of work and existing viewpoints?

Research has found that **diversifying** the types of news sources that you are consuming online can have a positive effect on your feelings of anxiety (Owen, 2019). In other words, you are well served by seeking out and following social media accounts that feature opinions and perspectives that are different from your own. This can be difficult for many people to do because humans tend to follow media that reinforce their own viewpoints, not run counter to it.

A study found that people who sought diverse content on their social media timelines tended to have lower levels of anxiety than others that they surveyed (Auxier & Vitak, 2019). Given the highly political nature of so many news items related to sports in the current environment, purposefully broadening the spectrum of news, opinion, and information that you follow on social media is a good idea.

 Key Point @DoctorGC
Maintain interests and activities outside of sports and social media. Have a diverse set of things that keep you happy and engaged. #SocialMediaAndSports

Professional Tips

Thriving in the sports social media world involves more than just knowing how to create content. You have to consider emotional and ethical issues and address them as your journey through this industry unfolds, and the likelihood is that your path will be different from the path that someone else takes through the same industry.

Much of how your career in sports social media goes depends on the kind of person, people, or organization you work for. Some sports social media positions put you in proximity with tremendous people who care about you as a person, work with you to improve your skills, and provide you with feelings of support and well-being. Other positions and environments are unfortunately not so nurturing, and in a lot of cases you will have no idea what the environment is like before you start working there.

In addition to the personal aspects of the social media work environment listed above, other items and considerations are worth thinking about.

The Content Cycle

Social media is always on. There aren't periods of the day where Twitter or WhatsApp just stop sending messages. The great and terrible thing about social media is that it literally never stops, meaning that when you are charged with creating social media, you have to consider the always-on nature of the space.

For a lot of sports social media jobs, a built-in content cycle gives some definition to your work and content flow. The content cycle is the parameters of the work you produce and publish on social media, and during a sports season it can end up creating periods of very heavy work, followed by periods of less work.

The content cycle can be intense for both editorial and industry content creators during the sports season. Fans and consumers are generally dialed in and interested in content relating to their team before, during, and immediately after games as well as during off-days in season.

Working in sports social media is very similar to working in other forms of sports and sports media, where your work days and times often align with periods where the rest of the world is taking a break. Content cycles in sports social media involve a lot of work on weekends as well as weekday evenings because that is when games happen and that is when fans and audience members are free from their own work obligations and able to fully consume the content you are creating.

For sport organizations with a small number of people maintaining their team accounts, this content cycle can be a challenge. Over a long season such as Major League Baseball's 162 games or the NBA's 82 games, social media team members will often have to trade off responsibilities for maintaining the social media accounts during those games. Additionally, if news breaks in the middle of the night, someone on the social media content team is going to have to get up and post something about it.

Dealing With Trolling and Harassment

Dealing with online trolls is unfortunately a major part of the reality of working in social media, and sports is no exception. As we've touched on earlier in the book, trolling and troll-like behavior is common across most major social networks, and the networks themselves seem unable to significantly curtail this type of harassment.

Many experts have advised that people should simply not engage with online trolls at all, using the logic that engaging trolls enables them to reach a wider audience. European organizations such as the Center for Countering Digital Hate suggest that trolls should be blocked, ignored, and reported whenever encountered (Proctor, 2019).

As we discussed in chapter 5 about users and online communities, much of the harassment and trolling behavior comes from users' lack of consideration that there is an actual person on the receiving end of the negative messages they are firing off on social media. For journalists and media members, this can lead to some mean things being tweeted or commented at them, and that can take a psychological toll on the person. The same thing applies to athletes, and a person who takes those kinds of comments to heart can find themselves dealing with a lot of negative psychological stress.

 Key Point @DoctorGC
Trolling, harassment, and other forms of bad behavior among audience members are unfortunately a recurring feature of social media usage. Don't take it personally. #SocialMediaAndSports

Fans can be hard on players and coaches in the arena, and they can be even harder on journalists and team personnel on social media.

I am friends with a prominent sports journalist who told me that he has had to simply turn off his mentions and stop reading the things that most people say to him on Twitter due to the relentless negativity that fans of the teams he covers bring to the table. NBA player Stanley Johnson says that he minimizes his time using social media because the comments he receives are often negative and toxic, noting, "If you dig through garbage, expect to find trash. Instagram is perception, perception, perception. It's not real" (Haberstroh, 2018).

Sport organization accounts also get this kind of negative treatment, although it is often directed at the team itself as opposed to the person who is operating the account. A former social media worker for the Memphis Grizzlies noted in an interview that she eventually had to realize that "when people are tweeting horrible things at the team account, they're not tweeting them at me" (de la Cretaz, 2018).

Sports media has experienced tremendous problems with misogyny and harassment, and unfortunately social media in sports provide no exception. As we noted earlier in the book, female sports reporters and writers often face unduly negative comments on social media primarily due to their gender. For some females, the balance of working in the largely anonymous world of industry content provides them some degree of anonymity, and that shields them from some of the worst vitriol (de la Cretaz, 2018).

Ethics

Ethical considerations should always be in your mind when creating social media content. Unfortunately, as of the writing of this book, there isn't much of a road map for **ethics** on social media. That is partially due to how new the social media space is, but it is also due to how many types of social media approaches there are, how many different types of organizations are creating social media content, and how little thought many organizations put into the practice of ethics in communication.

Ideally your organization will have a formal code of ethics in place for social media usage. Well-formed codes of ethics for social media normally include some commonsense items like *don't lie* and

Key Point @DoctorGC

Social media ethics are important to maintain, whether you are working on behalf of yourself or for an organization. How you conduct yourself online has a big impact on how people perceive you as a person and as a professional. #SocialMediaAndSports

don't post hurtful things. As the person doing the social media creation, you should always keep in mind the ethics of the content you are making, with the following areas given specific consideration:

- *Do I have the right to post this?* Do you or the organization you work for have the necessary ownership of the content and its component parts to post it on social media? If you are using creative material from people who haven't given you permission to do so, that is an ethical violation.

- *Will this content affect someone in an unreasonably negative way?* All content creators, be they in editorial or industry content, should keep in mind the sometimes terrifying power of social media to ruin people's lives. Always think about the possible ramifications of content before you post.

- *Is the content truthful?* There are no ethical reasons you should post something that you know to be untrue. That is a rule you should follow whether you are a journalist or a sports team content creator. This is often a greater problem for people working in industry content because sport organizations, like all businesses, do not necessarily feel an obligation to tell customers the truth. Even if you work for a sport organization, your integrity as a professional communicator rests on your ability to remain dedicated to communicating the truth. If you are in a position where you are being ordered to lie on social media, then you should consider looking for work elsewhere.

Work Conditions

Social media workers across all parts of the content spectrum are increasingly **overworked**. A 2018 survey found that social media professionals were concerned about the volume of work that their bosses demanded and the speed at which that work was required to be produced (Labarre, 2018). Many online-only sports publications demand ridiculous volumes of daily content from their writers, with the idea being that constantly publishing and promoting content will lead to higher levels of advertising revenue. Sports teams, from colleges and the minor leagues up through the major leagues, are known for overworking employees in various departments, something that I found to be the case 15 years ago when I worked in the industry. In terms of social media jobs, many organizations view content creation in purely numerical terms, both in terms of posts created and in raw visitor numbers received.

This book has explained why quality of content is more important than quantity, with a focus on specific audiences being more important than simply dragging the bottom of the social media ocean, hoping to catch something in your net. Sports social media works at its best when it is natural and fits within the confines of what is going on with a team or community.

If you find yourself overworked in an environment where your employers are demanding more than you feel like you can provide, you should first think about your own work patterns and whether they are keeping up with others in the industry. If you take an honest look at your peers and competitors and discover that your work output is not up to par, you should consider how you are approaching the job and whether you need to make changes. This is certainly a possibility, especially if you are a younger social media worker who doesn't yet have a lot of experience in the field. Reach out to other people who work in your field and talk with them about your employer's expectations. They should be able to give you a sense of whether those expectations are reasonable or not.

If the expectations are not reasonable, have a conversation with your employers. Detail what you are doing, when you are doing it, and how much or little time you have to create the content they are asking for. In many cases, employers are not aware of how time-consuming social media creation can be, particularly when it comes to things like video editing. You may be able to come to an understanding about how much social media creation can reasonably be done by one person or group.

If the expectations remain unreasonable, be realistic about your situation. Sports social media is a lot of work, but it shouldn't be so much work

Out in the field or inside of an office, social media content creation can be frustrating and time-consuming.

that it forces you to cede all other aspects of your life to get the job done. There are other sports social media jobs out there that won't make you work to that degree. It might require you changing jobs, but that is preferable to getting worked into the ground.

Job Instability

The reality of working in social media is that you're likely not going to stay in the same job for very long. Your first job might find you overqualified for what you're being asked to do and lead you to a new opportunity with a bigger organization. Your next job might end up with you being fired. The sports media environment has a lot of change and turnover in positions, and social media is no different.

The constant reality of job change should be a reminder that you have to keep your personal and professional mindsets separate when doing your job. Make sure that you understand that sports social media is a business first. I have worked with many students who got a dream job early in their careers doing social media work for a sports or media organization that they love or respect, only to watch them grow bitter and disappointed at

how the organization actually does its business or feel heartbroken when the organization eventually decides to part ways with them.

Keeping a professional mindset when it comes to working social media for a sports team can be difficult because much of your social media work requires a high level of energy and enthusiasm in the content you are creating. It is important to learn how to manufacture that level of energy for your work without being emotionally invested in the process. This is a key element of professionalism in social media work that in some ways resembles the profession of acting. You play your role to the hilt, give it everything you have, and then learn to leave it behind when you go home that night.

 Key Point @DoctorGC

You aren't going to work at the same job in social media your whole life. Changing jobs is a natural part of the employment cycle within this industry. #SocialMediaAndSports

PROFESSIONAL INSIGHTS

Professional Media, Personal Challenges

Courtney Cronin

Twitter: https://twitter.com/CourtneyRCronin

Instagram: www.instagram.com/courtneyrcronin/

LinkedIn: www.linkedin.com/in/courtneycronin/

Courtney Cronin, ESPN.com

Courtney Cronin's role as ESPN beat reporter for the Minnesota Vikings has kept her in the public spotlight since she got the job. As the lead reporter covering a perennial playoff contender, Courtney's work appears regularly across many traditional and social media platforms. SportsCenter television hits, ESPN radio appearances, ESPN.com web stories, and the ever-presence of Twitter mean that she is never very far from her audience. And that connection has both positive and negative effects.

"The first thing about social media is that we're all connected, even when we don't realize it," Cronin says. "I have my phone with me 24/7. I have an Apple Watch that alerts me to every text and every tweet. Even if I wanted to 'unplug' and not check my social media, it's so hard not to. So ultimately people always have access to you, even if you say to yourself that you're not going to focus on it."

Cronin says the always-on nature of social media, combined with the nature of her job as a beat reporter, means that social media is a built-in part of her day-to-day life.

"They have so much access to you now. Even if I want to get away from it, I can't. During the season, I don't have the luxury of saying, 'I'm going to delete the Twitter app from my phone for a few days.' We're not paid to tweet, but that's where I break my news. It's a part of my job. So that means that the interaction part falls under that same umbrella."

She says that social media interactions with audience members aren't all negative or all positive but tend to change from situation to situation.

"It's a mixed bag," says Cronin. "I wrote a feature story recently that was well received—people loved it, they commented on it, and they shared it. So of course that feels good as a writer, people sharing your work and giving it a bigger platform by retweeting it.

"But then you'll have situations that are bad. I've written stories about how the team is going to rest their starters for a game, and people have gotten really angry. They weren't necessarily angry with me, but they were replying angrily to that piece of news.

"And then there have been times where people have come at me and made nasty personal comments directly to me before. That really hurts. You can mute people or block them, but it doesn't change the fact that it was said."

She also says that the nature of social media in sports makes things complicated, especially when trying to balance how to use the different social media platforms available.

"I try to show personality on Twitter. I'm not a robot. It's silly for people to say, 'Oh, I'm a beat writer; I can't tweet anything about myself.'

"My Instagram is a public account. I've gone back and forth and debated whether or not I should have it public or private. But it's a catch-22. I promote my work through Instagram. If I'm on SportsCenter, I'm going to post it on my Instagram story. But what if I want to post a picture of me and my family at Christmas? But that's the life I signed myself up for, being a public figure. Everybody can see what goes on in my life.

"I've run into some creepy situations before, where people I don't know meet me in real life and will reference social media posts, reference things that you said or did, and act like they know you as a result of that. That can be terrifying."

Summary

This chapter focused on the mental, emotional, and other strains that can exist in sports social media work. Being conscious of the pitfalls that social media workers may face in the business is important. By bringing ideas and plans for how to cope with those stressors, aspiring sports social media workers may be able to avoid some of the more negative aspects of the business and set themselves up for a happier and healthier career.

Review Questions

1. Why is maintaining work-life balance so important with social media jobs in sports?

2. What are two signs of potential social media burnout?

3. When does the sports social media content cycle generally require the greatest amount of work during the season?

4. How should you approach a situation where you feel like you are being overworked in the sports social media field?

Afterword

As I mentioned in chapter 1, the social media world is the most dynamic media environment the world has ever experienced. The strange recipe of evolving audiences, technology, and changing methods of adaptation by businesses has created a world that will never stay the same for long and will consistently be bent and shaped by forces both within and without.

Sports social media is particularly dynamic, largely because of the unique nature of sports audiences and how sports entities, athletes, culture, technology, and audiences interact with one another in this environment. The last 20 years of sports media have seen the social media effect on sports media grow from practically nonexistent to arguably the most important element. During that time, the addition of sport organizations, athletes, influencers, and fans to the media mix has changed the expectations of what sports media is, how it is created, how it is delivered, what is valued, and who is trusted.

The social media world mutates far too often for any one book to definitively tell you how to best use social media, but my hope is that you now have a clearer understanding of the influences affecting social media in sports and how to leverage your skills and abilities to take advantage of those influences.

My final message to you is simple: Arm yourself with skills and knowledge that are useful in social media, and then work diligently to become comfortable producing social media content. Don't worry about learning "the right way" to do something because there is no singular right way. Your own special mix of culture, knowledge, and technical ability may hold the key to a new and exciting way of producing social media content that nobody has yet tried.

I'm looking forward to seeing what you can do.

Glossary

access—Reporters having the ability to interact with players or other team personnel.

active consumer of content—A process of social media consumption where you focus less on the sport being described and more on the method by which the message is being communicated.

agenda building—A second level of agenda setting, where media messages can influence how people think about certain items in the news.

agenda setting theory—A theory that states that media do not tell audiences what to think but do tell them what to think about.

API—Abbreviation for "application programming interface," this is the portal through which market research companies can extract information for social media analysis.

app—A shorthand term for "application," apps are programs on smartphones and tablets that allow users to access specific services and information. Social networks like Facebook and Twitter can be accessed through apps.

AP Stylebook—The *Associated Press Stylebook* is a regularly published guide for media professionals who work in the creation and editing of content.

argumentation—A factor in online behavior where certain audience members feel compelled to argue with others for entertainment purposes.

attitudes—The set of beliefs that your social media audience brings to their online experience.

audience access—The kind of reach a social media network allows you to have in connecting with people who are members of that network.

audiences—The collection of users who populate social media networks.

audio—A social media content building block that includes standalone audio clips, podcasts, and the audio signal present in social media video.

audio editing—The process of altering an audio file from its original format to one that matches a creative need or vision. Audio editing can be used to clip highlights from podcasts or other audio sources for use on social media.

augmented reality (AR)—The use of special software or hardware to superimpose a computer-generated image over a real-life image.

backstage—A type of self-presentation strategy used on social media that emphasizes a personal connection between the audience and the person using the account. Used largely by athletes in giving fans a behind-the-scenes look at their sports or daily lives.

balance—Finding an equilibrium between hard work at your job and a well-adjusted life outside of it.

beat writer—A media member whose primary job is to report on the news, games, and happenings of a team.

behavioral intentions—How a social media audience member plans to act online.

brand narrative—The overarching story that your organization's social media messages combine to tell about who your organization is and what you want it to mean to your audience.

broadcast channel—A social media platform that focuses on sending a message out with the intent of many users seeing it.

b-roll—Video that is used to capture the general atmosphere of an event or activity. Often used as background video for narration in video packages.

building blocks—The core content functions of social media on which all content is built.

burnout—A phenomenon where someone is overworked or demotivated to the point of no longer wanting to do a task or job.

conduit—A process by which social media links are used to take audience members from the platform and put them on a media organization's website for the purposes of consuming content or engaging in conversation.

content cycle—The pattern by which social media content is published and consumed.

control beliefs—What your social media audience thinks they can or cannot do.

coolness factor—How a product or service is perceived, particularly by young audiences. As of 2020, Facebook's coolness factor is low due to so many older people using the service, while Snapchat and Instagram have high coolness factors due to young people using them for communication.

core technical skills—Building blocks of social media content creation and usage; this group of skills includes functional knowledge of how to edit audio, images, and video as well the basics of graphic design.

cross-posting—A functionality present in some social media apps that allows for the same content to be shared simultaneously across more than one social media network.

cultural knowledge—An understanding of what is going on outside the world of sport.

daily active user (DAU)—Someone who uses a social media network or website every day.

design—The graphical architecture of a social media platform.

digital audio workstation—A software program used to edit audio files.

digitization—The process that most media have gone through over the past 25 years, where previously analog media such as film, paper, and sound waves have been transformed into a digital environment. This has had the effect of flattening the media environment, since all these media types can now be transmitted in the same channel.

diversifying—Spreading out your content consumption to include multiple types of content and points of view.

dynamic visuals—A social media content building block that includes animated GIF files, dynamic filters, and augmented reality features.

editorial content—Media content produced by independent media organizations.

embargo—A process by which information is mutually decided to be left unpublished until a specified time.

esports—A global collection of online sport matches where the competition is a video game. Most esports are streamed via social networks.

ethics—A code of conduct and behavior that involves doing the right thing.

Facebook—The dominant social network during the 2010s, Facebook's combination of social connectivity and sharing led to it becoming a worldwide phenomenon.

fair use—A legal doctrine in United States copyright law that allows for the expressive use of copyrighted materials.

fake news—A disturbing trend noticed on Facebook and other platforms in the aftermath of the United States' 2016 presidential election, where demonstrably false information was being published by rogue actors and consumed as if it were legitimate news by unsuspecting users.

feedback—Opinions about the quality of your content.

forums—Online discussion places that allow websites to subdivide discussion into multiple topical areas. The concept of subreddits descended from the original idea of forums.

framing theory—A process by which media provide fields of context and meaning to place, events, and people in a larger narrative.

frontstage—A type of self-presentation strategy used on social media where the account is acting the part of a public figure with an impersonal interactive approach to dealing with the audience.

gaming—A social media feature used by Snapchat and others that allows for users to play games within the platform's infrastructure.

General Data Protection Regulation (GDPR)—A 2018 European Union code that regulates user data collection practices of social media websites.

GIF—A looping animated image that can be published on social media. GIF stands for "graphical interchange format," and GIFs differ from traditional images in that they possess the movement qualities of video. Thousands of GIFs are available for use on Twitter.

graphic design—The process by which images, graphics, text, colors, and other elements are assembled into a combined media form.

graphics—A social media content building block that includes embedded graphical text, artifacts, and images as well as graphical characters such as emojis.

hypodermic needle theory—One of several early disproven theories of media consumption that hypothesized that media had a direct influence over how people thought about events.

image editing—The process of changing the visual aspects or components of an image; this can include applying filters, cropping or resizing of an image, and adding external graphics, symbols, or text.

images—A social media content building block that includes still images, collections of images, and software-designed images.

industry content—Media content produced by sport organizations, including athletes, teams, and leagues.

industry literacy—An understanding of the events and actions taking place within the broader fields of sports and sports media, rather than simply being focused on the individual team or league that you know.

influencer—A social media personality whose popularity can be leveraged to influence consumers in their purchasing practices.

informational interview—An interview with an industry professional that is not intended for reproduction and distribution to a wider audience. Informational interviews are ways for you to network with key personnel and gain insights into the profession.

infrastructure—The programming and design of a social media platform.

insider—A perspective that can only be provided by someone within an organization.

Instagram—The most popular and successful photo-sharing app, Instagram allows users to connect visually by sending images and videos both publicly and privately to other users.

intermediate delivery—The existence of software as an additional step between creating media and its consumption, rather than relying solely on hardware to deliver media to the consumer.

live video—A social media content building block that includes livestreaming video delivered through a social media app, often involving direct and live interaction with a social media audience while the live video is being produced.

media credentials—Permission from a sport organization to access athletes, team personnel, and team facilities; only media members who hold this credential, which the organization decides to issue, have this access.

meme—A shared cultural communication artifact that is virally transmitted.

messaging—Social media functionality that allows a user to communicate directly and privately with one or more other users.

moderators—Used primarily on sites with publicly visible comments, moderators are users who are given special administrative powers to modify or delete posts and suspend or ban users for impermissible behavior.

Myspace—An early social network that allowed people to connect with other users online, Myspace was initially very successful but gradually lost momentum due to a lack of innovation.

native functionality—Functions or features that are available within an app, rather than relying on third-party software or hardware.

NBA Twitter—The collection of fans, media, teams, and athletes that use Twitter to interact with each other about the NBA.

network environment—The visual space that users experience when interacting with a social media network through an app.

objectivity—A bedrock principle of journalism that calls for unbiased and fair reporting of news.

online disinhibition effect—The collective name given to a group of psychological impulses that have been known to affect the behavior of people online, often causing online interpersonal communication to differ significantly from its face-to-face equivalent. People are often more likely to say negative things to others due to the lack of physical proximity and interaction.

opinion leader—A person in a communication setting, particularly in a large network such as is seen in social media, whose opinions are viewed as more important and influential than most others.

overworked—The process by which an employer places too many demands on an employee.

personal connections—The social media network connections that people share directly with one another.

personal context—Aspects of a sports journalist's life the journalist chooses to make public on social media to humanize the journalist and positively influence how the audience views the journalist.

pin—A type of post on the social media platform Pinterest.

pop culture—The collection of people, places, and things that constitute a shared mass culture. Pop culture is almost always youth-oriented.

popularity—The level of success one has with attracting and retaining an audience.

portability of hardware—The ease with which a person can carry computers, tablets, and phones.

posting schedule—A method of creating a consistent presence on social media by planning out an intent to post on social media at certain times on certain days throughout the week.

preproduced video—A social media content building block that includes video published after it is taken, including simple quotes and footage as well as more complex edited projects.

privacy controls—Settings controlled by users on social media sites that can restrict access to a user's data or content.

profile—The building block of many social networks, the profile is the online representation of self. Users create profiles and fill them with pictures and information about themselves, then connect their profiles with those created by others.

promoted tweets—A type of paid native advertisement on Twitter that causes an account's message to appear in the newsfeed of targeted users, whether or not they follow the originating account.

reflective notes—A series of notes on your social media posting history that allow you to recall the circumstances that led to certain posts being successful.

responses—A social media content building block that includes audience responses and comments to social media posts that become part of the visual representation of the content.

serial content—Content that revolves around the same or similar themes and is curated in the same media space over time.

Snapchat—A social network popular with young adults in the late 2010s, Snapchat's innovations included the ability to send pictures that disappear after viewing.

social capital—A group of factors that exist within a functioning social group that can include identity, understanding, shared norms and values, and relationships.

social media dashboard—Browser or app-based software that allows users to manage multiple aspects of social media content and in some cases a platform that provides analytics and engagement numbers to the user.

social media experience—The aesthetic or emotional environment that a social media platform and network provide a user.

social norms—A group of behaviors and standards of interaction that are generally agreed to by a social group.

software suite—A collection of software titles designed to work seamlessly across multiple phases or stages of media content design.

stories—Originally a feature of Snapchat, stories are a series of connected media images and augmentations that can be strung together and published within social media platforms.

storytelling—The process of effectively communicating interesting or compelling facts to an audience in a media format.

subreddits—Areas of topical interest on Reddit that allow users to congregate in separate spaces from each other.

suggested accounts—An algorithmically determined process that exists on multiple social media sites, suggested accounts are regularly shown to users so that they might potentially increase their network of personal connections or connections to brands.

technological convergence—A process of technological evolution where two or more types of media reception or creation merged into the same device.

theory of planned behavior—A behavioral theory that attempts to explain the factors that motivate people to choose certain actions.

third-party apps—Programs created for smartphones, tablets, and computers and made by companies or programmers other than the one who created the original piece of hardware.

training videos—Online video explanations of software and hardware functionality, often available to users for free.

trolls—Individuals in online environments whose sole purpose is to argue, criticize, and interact negatively with others.

Twitch—A social network focused on the streaming of video games and other content, Twitch allows users from across the globe to interact with one another, primarily through chats and video streaming.

Twitter—A social network that allows users to share information in 280-character bursts, Twitter is best used for breaking news and quickly sharing information.

upvoting/downvoting—A system that allows users to vote positively or negatively about a piece of content on Reddit, with the votes affecting how Reddit's algorithm evaluates the content.

user communities—Online communities that feature users of software titles and hardware devices. Members of user communities often provide help and guidance to users trying to learn various functionality aspects of the element in question.

user engagement rate—The percentage of audience members who actively engage with a piece of content, including liking, sharing, or commenting on the content.

user interface—The core functionality of an app or program, including the features and items available to a user.

verified accounts—A feature that originated with Twitter but has spread to other social media platforms. On Twitter, verified accounts are signified by a blue check mark next to the name, indicating that Twitter has verified the owner of the account.

video editing—The manipulation of one or more video files into a different format. Video editing generally uses nonlinear editing software to assemble clips into a creative format.

visual effects—A process by which motion graphics and 3D visual effects are applied to video using specialized software.

vocabulary—The collection of words, visual ideas, and other communicative building blocks that serve as the core of your social media approach.

voice—The style and tone of writing or posting that a social media account uses.

well-being—Your emotional, mental, and physical health.

written content—A social media content building block that consists of written text that appears in an interactive frame within a social media app.

References

Chapter 1

Abad-Santos, A. (2018, September 24). Nike's Colin Kaepernick ad sparked a boycott—and earned $6 billion for Nike. *Vox*. Retrieved from www.vox.com/2018/9/24/17895704/nike-colin-kaepernick-boycott-6-billion

Bavishi, J., & Filadelfo, E. (2018, July 17). Insights into the 2018 #WorldCup conversation on Twitter. *Twitter.com*. Retrieved from https://blog.twitter.com/official/en_us/topics/events/2018/2018-World-Cup-Insights.html

Beck, D., & Bosshart, L. (2003). Sports and media. *Communication Research Trends*, 22(4). Retrieved from http://cscc.scu.edu/trends/v22/v22_4.pdf

Clavio, G. (2015). Emerging social media and applications in sport. In P.M. Pedersen (Ed.), *Routledge handbook of sport communication* (pp. 259-268). New York, NY: Routledge.

Cord. (2019, January 19). Most popular Overwatch team by social media following. *Game Guide HQ*. Retrieved from https://gameguidehq.com/biggest-overwatch-team-by-social-media-following

Crupi, A. (2017, July 25). By the numbers: Sports and other live events crowd out scripted series in TV's year so far. *Ad Age*. Retrieved from https://adage.com/article/media/tv-ratings-sports-live-top-50-ncis-big-bang-theory/309906

Crupi, A. (2018, January 2). Despite another ratings slump, the NFL remains TV's top dog. *Ad Age*. Retrieved from https://adage.com/article/media/ratings-slum/311777

Demby, G. (2018, January 4). ESPN's Jemele Hill on race, football, and that tweet about Trump. *NPR*. Retrieved from www.npr.org/sections/codeswitch/2018/01/04/564405968/ask-code-switch-food-culture

Douglas, N. (2006, September 11). What News Corp doesn't want you to know about Myspace: Condensed edition. *Gawker.com*. Retrieved from https://gawker.com/199668/what-news-corp-doesnt-want-you-to-know-about-myspace-condensed-edition

Duhigg, C. (2012, February 16). How companies learn your secrets. *The New York Times Magazine*. Retrieved from www.nytimes.com/2012/02/19/magazine/shopping-habits.html?pagewanted=6&_r=1&hp

eMarketer. (2018, January 9). Social media will hit major milestones in 2018. *eMarketer*. Retrieved from www.emarketer.com/content/social-media-will-hit-major-milestones-in-both-ad-revenues-and-usage-in-2018

Fenton, A. (2018, January 10). Sport and social media's rocky relationship is safe . . . for now. *The Conversation*. Retrieved from https://theconversation.com/sport-and-social-medias-rocky-relationship-is-safe-for-now-89624

Frederick, E.L., & Clavio, G. (2015). Blurred Lines: A qualitative analysis of Twitter use among elite high school athletes. *International Journal of Sport Communication*, 8, 330-344.

Garrahan, M. (2009, December 4). The rise and fall of MySpace. *Financial Times*. Retrieved from www.ft.com/content/fd9ffd9c-dee5-11de-adff-00144feab49a

Goslin, A. (2018, December 11). The 2018 League of Legends World Finals had nearly 100 million viewers. *Rift Herald*. Retrieved from www.riftherald.com/2018/12/11/18136237/riot-2018-league-of-legends-world-finals-viewers-prize-pool

Hale, J. (2018, January 11). Right to free tweets: How Kentucky and other schools deal with athletes on social media. *Louisville Courier Journal*. Retrieved from www.courier-journal.com/story/sports/college/kentucky/2018/01/11/kentucky-football-college-athletes-social-media-twitter-use/848093001

Hall, M. (n.d.). Facebook. *Encyclopedia Britannica*. Retrieved from www.britannica.com/topic/Facebook

Hamilton, T. (2018, October 30). How close is London to getting an NFL franchise? *ESPN.com*. Retrieved from www.espn.com/nfl/story/_/id/25124631/how-close-london-getting-nfl-franchise

Hempel, J. (2018, September 27). Instagram's founders have always had impeccable timing. *Wired.com*. Retrieved from www.wired.com/story/instagrams-kevin-systrom-mike-krieger-exit-facebook/

Hendricks, D. (2013, May 8). Complete history of social media: Then and now. *Small Business Trends*. Retrieved from https://smallbiztrends.com/2013/05/the-complete-history-of-social-media-infographic.html

Herrman, J. (2018, December 12). What happens when Facebook goes the way of Myspace? *The New York Times Magazine*. Retrieved from https://www.nytimes.com/2018/12/12/magazine/what-happens-when-facebook-goes-the-way-of-myspace.html

Hill, K. (2012, February 16). How Target figured out a teen girl was pregnant before her father did. *Forbes*. Retrieved from www.forbes.com/sites/kashmirhill/2012/02/16/how-target-figured-out-a-teen-girl-was-pregnant-before-her-father-did/#530258bf6668

Jackson, N., & Madrigal, A.C. (2011, January 12). The rise and fall of MySpace. *The Atlantic*. Retrieved from https://www.theatlantic.com/technology/archive/2011/01/the-rise-and-fall-of-myspace/69444

Jarvey, N. (2016, July 14). How Instagram's filters got their names. *The Hollywood Reporter*. Retrieved from www.hollywoodreporter.com/news/instagram-filters-history-names-explained-910720

Kaplan, K., & Piller, C. (1999, January 29). Yahoo to buy GeoCities for $3.9 billion in stock. *Los Angeles Times*. Retrieved from http://articles.latimes.com/1999/jan/29/business/fi-2730

Leccesi, J. (2018, May 1). Why do social media "fails" by young athletes keep happening? *USA Today*. Retrieved from https://usatodayhss.com/2018/why-do-social-media-fails-by-young-athletes-keep-happening

Madrigal, A.C. (2019, January 16). Facebook users still don't know how Facebook works. *The Atlantic*. https://www.theatlantic.com/technology/archive/2019/01/facebook-users-still-dont-know-how-facebook-works/580546

Madurai, V. (2018, February 17). Web evolution from 1.0 to 3.0. *Medium.com*. Retrieved from https://medium.com/@vivekmadurai/web-evolution-from-1-0-to-3-0-e84f2c06739

Marketing Charts. (2019, June 24). US online and traditional media advertising outlook, 2019-2023. https://www.marketingcharts.com/advertising-trends-108995

Marketing Dive Team. (2019, February 4). By the numbers: Super Bowl 2019. *Marketing Dive*. Retrieved from www.marketingdive.com/news/super-bowl-2019-by-the-numbers/547612

Molla, R. (2017, June 26). How Apple's iPhone changed the world: 10 years in 10 charts. *Recode*. Retrieved from www.recode.net/2017/6/26/15821652/iphone-apple-10-year-anniversary-launch-mobile-stats-smart-phone-steve-jobs

Moreau, E. (2018, November 26). Is Myspace dead? *Lifewire*. Retrieved from www.lifewire.com/is-myspace-dead-3486012

Moritz, B. (2018, June 5). What's changed about sports journalism: Social media and expectations. *Sports Media Guy*. Retrieved from www.sportsmediaguy.com/blog/2018/6/5/whats-changed-about-sports-journalism-social-media-and-expectations

Murphy, M. (2018, September 24). Professional athletes have become the new "social media influencers." *Instant Sponsor*. Retrieved from https://medium.com/instant-sponsor/professional-athletes-have-become-the-new-social-media-influencers-8cf6915bb791

Pingdom. (2010, October 22). The incredible growth of the Internet since 2000. *Pingdom*. Retrieved from https://royal.pingdom.com/2010/10/22/incredible-growth-of-the-internet-since-2000

Shazi, N. (2018, February 21). 10 most watched sport events in the history of television. *Huffington Post*. Retrieved from www.huffingtonpost.co.za/2018/02/21/10-most-watched-sport-events-in-the-history-of-television_a_23367211

Sloan, G. (2019, October 2019). Facebook reports increases in ad revenue and users in the third quarter. *AdAge*. Retrieved from https://adage.com/article/digital/facebook-reports-increases-ad-revenue-and-users-third-quarter/2211401

Smith, A., & Anderson, M. (2018, March 1). Social media use in 2018. *Pew Research Center*. Retrieved from www.pewinternet.org/2018/03/01/social-media-use-in-2018

Solon, O. (2018, June 6). Meet the people who still use Myspace: "It's given me so much joy." *The Guardian*. Retrieved from www.theguardian.com/technology/2018/jun/06/myspace-who-still-uses-social-network

Umstead, R.T. (2017, March 21). "March Madness" dominates social media. *Multichannel*. Retrieved from www.multichannel.com/news/march-madness-dominates-social-media-411640

Vaynerchuk, G. (2016). The snap generation: A guide to Snapchat's history. *GaryVaynerchuk.com*. Retrieved from www.garyvaynerchuk.com/the-snap-generation-a-guide-to-snapchats-history

Wasserman, T. (2015, February 14). The revolution wasn't televised: The early days of YouTube. *Mashable*. Retrieved from https://mashable.com/2015/02/14/youtube-history/#RVnMIzpiWPqR

Wright, E., Khanfar, N.M., Harrington, C., & Kizer, L.E. (2010). The lasting effects of social media trends on advertising. *Journal of Business & Economics Research*, 8, 73-80.

Yoder, M. (2018, May 18). NBC claims a record number of total viewers for a Premier League season in 2017-18. *Awful Announcing*. Retrieved from https://awfulannouncing.com/soccer/nbc-claims-a-record-number-of-total-viewers-for-a-premier-league-season-in-2017-2018.html

Chapter 2

Angulo, I. (2018, February 13). Snapchat's new interface is already pushing some users to Instagram. *CNBC*. Retrieved from www.cnbc.com/2018/02/13/snapchats-new-interface-is-already-pushing-some-users-to-instagram.html

Facebook Journalism Project. (n.d.). *Facebook Journalism Project*. Retrieved from https://facebookjournalismproject.com

Halliday, J. (2011, May 27). Twitter buys UK's TweetDeck for 25m. *The Guardian*. Retrieved from www.theguardian.com/business/2011/may/27/twitter-buys-tweetdeck

Hootsuite Academy. (n.d.). *Hootsuite Academy*. Retrieved from https://education.hootsuite.com

HubSpot Academy. (n.d.). *Social Media*. Retrieved from https://academy.hubspot.com/courses/social-media

LinkedIn Learning. (n.d.). *LinkedIn Learning*. Retrieved from www.linkedin.com/learning/me

Odisho, J. (n.d.). *Adobe Premiere Pro tutorials* [Video Playlist]. Retrieved from www.youtube.com/playlist?list=PLBrRXoTJAkZBl3XDQEPjVj4okFAHQrVex

/r/FinalCutPro. (n.d.). *Final Cut Pro*. Retrieved from www.reddit.com/r/finalcutpro

Chapter 3

Arens, E. (2019, July 31). Best times to post on social media for 2019. *SproutSocial*. Retrieved from https://sproutsocial.com/insights/best-times-to-post-on-social-media/#how

Cole, S. (2018, June 12). Researchers studied 160 million memes and found most of them come from two websites. *Motherboard*. Retrieved from https://motherboard.vice.com/en_us/article/zm884j/where-do-memes-come-from-researchers-studied-reddit-4chan

Delaney, T. (2007). Pop culture: An overview. *Philosophy Now*. Retrieved from https://philosophynow.org/issues/64/Pop_Culture_An_Overview

Downer, A. (2018). Crying Michael Jordan. *Know Your Meme*. Retrieved from https://knowyourmeme.com/memes/crying-michael-jordan

Emerging Technology from the arXiv. (2018, June 11). This is where Internet memes come from. *MIT Technology Review*. Retrieved from www.technologyreview.com/s/611332/this-is-where-internet-memes-come-from/

Gil, P. (2019, February 5). What is a meme? *Lifewire*. Retrieved from www.lifewire.com/what-is-a-meme-2483702

Ingrassia, N. (2016, May 4). Hawks troll themselves using Crying Jordan meme after Cavs' barrage. *Fox Sports*. Retrieved from https://www.foxsports.com/nba/story/atlanta-hawks-crying-jordan-meme-cleveland-cavaliers-barrage-050416

McGuire, K. (2016, May 5). Atlanta Hawks "Crying Jordan" themselves as Cavs set NBA 3-point record. *Awful Announcing*. Retrieved from https://awfulannouncing.com/nba/atlanta-hawks-crying-jordan-themselves-as-cavs-set-nba-3-point-record.html

Nelson, J. (2019, February 20). Ariana Grande and Piers Morgan bond over drinks after Twitter spat: "We really like each other." *People*. Retrieved from https://people.com/music/ariana-grande-piers-morgan-meet-after-twitter-spat/

Rosati, E. (2018, September 19). The EU's long journey toward "banning memes." *Slate*. Retrieved from https://slate.com/technology/2018/09/european-union-copyright-law-banning-memes.html

Simmons, B. (2019, March 15). The Sports Repodders on James Dolan, Dan Jenkins, and more. *The Ringer*. Retrieved from www.theringer.com/the-bill-simmons-podcast/2019/3/15/18266984/the-sports-repodders-on-james-dolan-dan-jenkins-and-more

Solon, O. (2013, June 20). Richard Dawkins on the Internet's hijacking of the word "meme." *Wired.co.uk*. Retrieved from www.wired.co.uk/article/richard-dawkins-memes

Suler, J. (2004). The online disinhibition effect. *CyberPsychology & Behavior, 7*(3), 321-326.

Teng, E. (2018, September 9). Living the Stream. *ESPN The Magazine*. Retrieved from www.espn.com/espn/feature/story/_/id/24710688/fortnite-legend-ninja-living-stream

TextFixer. (n.d.). Random Word Generator. Retrieved from www.textfixer.com/tools/random-words.php

WordCounter.net. (n.d.). Random Word Generator. Retrieved from https://wordcounter.net/random-word-generator

Chapter 4

Anderson, M., & Jiang, J. (2018, May 31). Teens, social media & technology 2018. *Pew Research Center*. Retrieved from https://www.pewinternet.org/2018/05/31/teens-social-media-technology-2018/

Ashpari, Z. (2012, April 6). Why is Instagram so popular? *PCWorld*. Retrieved from www.pcworld.com/article/253254/why_is_instagram_so_popular_.html

Barron, A. (2019, May 13). It's official: People can't get enough of Snapchat's new gender-swap filter. *BuzzFeed*. Retrieved from www.buzzfeed.com/aliciabarron/snapchat-is-getting-a-lot-of-re-downloads-thanks-to-its-new

Bolt, N. (2011, November 27). Why Instagram is so popular: Quality, audience, & constraints. *TechCrunch*. Retrieved from https://techcrunch.com/2011/11/27/why-instagram-is-so-popular/

Bonnington, C. (2018, April 1). Pinterest isn't a social network. *Slate*. Retrieved from https://slate.com/technology/2018/04/pinterest-isnt-a-social-network-thats-what-makes-it-great.html

Cashmore, P. (2009, June 11). Twitter launches verified accounts. *Mashable*. Retrieved from https://mashable.com/2009/06/11/twitter-verified-accounts-2/

Comscore. (n.d.). More than half of MySpace visitors are now age 35 or older, as the site's demographic composition continues to shift. *ComScore*. Retrieved from https://www.comscore.com/Insights/Press-Releases/2006/10/More-than-Half-MySpace-Visitors-Age-35

Cooper, P. (2019, February 27). 23 Pinterest statistics that matter to marketers in 2019. *Hootsuite*. Retrieved from https://blog.hootsuite.com/pinterest-statistics-for-business/

Gesenhues, A. (2018, November 12). WhatsApp ads are coming: Will advertisers start buying? *Marketing Land*. Retrieved from https://marketingland.com/whatsapp-ads-are-coming-will-advertisers-start-buying-251600

Graham, M. (2019, July 21). As Instagram tests its "like" ban, influencers will have to shift tactics to make money. *CNBC*. Retrieved from www.cnbc.com/2019/07/19/what-instagram-hiding-likes-means-for-influencer-marketing.html?utm_source=fark&utm_medium=website&utm_content=link&ICID=ref_fark

Gramlich, J. (2019, May 16). 10 facts about Americans and Facebook. *Pew Research Center*. Retrieved from www.pewresearch.org/fact-tank/2019/05/16/facts-about-americans-and-facebook/

Hansell, S. (2016, September 12). Site previously for students will be opened to others. *New York Times*. Retrieved from www.nytimes.com/2006/09/12/technology/12online.html

Harrison, S. (2019, July 23). Teen love for Snapchat is keeping Snap afloat. *Wired.com*. Retrieved from www.wired.com/story/teen-love-snapchat-keeping-snap-afloat/

Holmes, R. (2019, August 28). Is TikTok a time bomb? *Fast Company*. Retrieved from www.fastcompany.com/90395898/is-tiktok-a-time-bomb

Iqbal, M. (2019, February 19). WhatsApp revenue and usage statistics 2019. *Business of Apps*. Retrieved from www.businessofapps.com/data/whatsapp-statistics/

Isaac, M. (2015, July 3). Reddit moderators shut down parts of site over employee's dismissal. *The New York Times*. Retrieved from www.nytimes.com/2015/07/04/technology/reddit-moderators-shut-down-parts-of-site-over-executives-dismissal.html?ref=technology

Lee, A. (2011, August 30). Myspace collapse: How the social network fell apart. *HuffPost*. Retrieved from www.huffpost.com/entry/how-myspace-fell-apart_n_887853

Manjoo, F. (2016, December 21). For millions of immigrants, a common language: WhatsApp. *The New York Times*. Retrieved from www.nytimes.com/2016/12/21/technology/for-millions-of-immigrants-a-common-language-whatsapp.html?module=inline

Perrin, A., & Anderson, M. (2018, April 10). Share of U.S. adults using social media, including Facebook, is mostly unchanged since 2018. *Pew Research*. Retrieved from www.pewresearch.org/fact-tank/2019/04/10/share-of-u-s-adults-using-social-media-including-facebook-is-mostly-unchanged-since-2018/

Perrin, A., & Duggan, M. (2015, June 26). Americans Internet Access: 2000-2015. *Pew Internet*. Retrieved from https://www.pewinternet.org/2015/06/26/americans-internet-access-2000-2015/

Pew Internet. (2018, February 5). *Mobile Fact Sheet*. Retrieved from https://www.pewinternet.org/fact-sheet/mobile/

Pew Research Center. (2019, April 10). *Facebook, YouTube continue to be the most widely used online platforms among U.S. adults*. Retrieved from www.pewresearch.org/fact-tank/2019/04/10/share-of-u-s-adults-using-social-media-including-facebook-is-mostly-unchanged-since-2018/ft_19-04-10_socialmedia2019_facebookyoutube_2/

Phillips, S. (2007, July 25). A brief history of Facebook. *The Guardian*. Retrieved from www.theguardian.com/technology/2007/jul/25/media.newmedia

Schulze, E. (2019, April 25). Facebook's user growth in Europe is bouncing back, defying stricter privacy laws. *CNBC*. Retrieved from www.cnbc.com/2019/04/25/facebook-q1-2019-user-growth-in-europe-is-bouncing-back-despite-gdpr.html

Statcounter. (2019, September 1). *Social Media Stats Europe*. Retrieved from https://gs.statcounter.com/social-media-stats/all/europe

Stewart, E. (2019, May 23). Facebook has taken down billions of fake accounts, but the problem is still getting worse. *Vox.com*. Retrieved from www.vox.com/recode/2019/5/23/18637596/facebook-fake-accounts-transparency-mark-zuckerberg-report

Van Kessel, P., Toor, S., & Smith, A. (2019, July 25). A week in the life of popular YouTube channels. *Pew Internet*. Retrieved from www.pewinternet.org/2019/07/25/a-week-in-the-life-of-popular-youtube-channels/

Wang, S. (2019, April 13). Snapchat is projected to lose users in the U.S. for the first time. *The Denver Post*. Retrieved from www.denverpost.com/2019/04/13/snapchat-losing-users/

Webster, T. (2019, June 18). Unfriending Facebook: New research on why people like Facebook less. *The Startup*. Retrieved from https://medium.com/swlh/unfriending-facebook-new-research-on-why-people-like-facebook-less-74894b927a0

Yasak, M. (2019, July 11). How Texas Tech and Jarrett Culver won together with an athlete-driven social strategy. Opendorse. Retrieved from https://opendorse.com/blog/tech-culver-case-study/

Chapter 5

Ajzen, I. (1991). The theory of planned behavior. *Organizational Behavior and Human Decision Process, 50,* 179-211.

Amnesty International. (n.d.). *Toxic Twitter—A toxic place for women.* Retrieved from www.amnesty.org/en/latest/research/2018/03/online-violence-against-women-chapter-1/

Associated Press. (2019, September 27). Des Moines *Register* reporter out after past offensive tweets. Retrieved from www.apnews.com/8795a1eb19864171921c889c32d62644

Benedikt, A., Kirk, C., & Kois, D. (2014, December 17). The year of outrage. *Slate.* Retrieved from www.slate.com/articles/life/culturebox/2014/12/the_year_of_outrage_2014_everything_you_were_angry_about_on_social_media.html

Clarke, T. (2019, February 28). Social media trolls: A practical guide for dealing with impossible people. *Hootsuite.* Retrieved from https://blog.hootsuite.com/how-to-deal-with-trolls-on-social-media/

Clavio, G. (2008). Demographics and usage profiles of collegiate sport message board users. *International Journal of Sport Communication, 1*(4), 434-443.

Clavio, G., & Vooris, R. (2018). ESPN and the hostile media effect. *Communication and Sport, 6*(6), 728-744, DOI: 10.1177/2167479517739835.

Crist, A. (2019, April 27). NFL player prompts online outrage for tweeting "Avengers: Endgame" spoilers. *The Hollywood Reporter.* Retrieved from www.hollywoodreporter.com/heat-vision/lesean-mccoy-tweets-avengers-endgame-spoilers-draws-online-outrage-1205417

Deitsch, R. (2017, May 7). Behind the Peabody-winning #MoreThanMean video and its almost-scrapped launch. *Sports Illustrated.* Retrieved from www.si.com/tech-media/2017/05/07/peabody-awards-more-than-mean-sarah-spain-julie-dicaro

Favale, D. (2017, July 7). Banana boats and emoji wars: The day DeAndre Jordan turned Twitter upside down. *Bleacher Report.* Retrieved from https://bleacherreport.com/articles/2719108-banana-boats-and-emoji-wars-the-day-deandre-jordan-turned-twitter-upside-down

Feiner, L. (2019, June 9). Trolls use a little-known Twitter feature to swarm others with abuse, and their targets say Twitter hasn't done much to stop it. *CNBC.* Retrieved from www.cnbc.com/2019/06/07/how-trolls-use-twitter-lists-to-target-and-harass-other-users.html

Friedsdorfer, C. (2018, December 30). Reflections on a year of outrage. *The Atlantic.* Retrieved from www.theatlantic.com/ideas/archive/2018/12/year-of-outrage/579100/

Front Office Sports. (2018, September 19). *Rob Perez's journey from ticketing entrepreneur to NBA personality* [Podcast]. Retrieved from https://frntofficesport.com/rob-perez-nba-personality/

Graham, J. (2015, June 26). ESPN's Michelle Beadle takes on Twitter trolls. *USA Today.* Retrieved from www.usatoday.com/story/tech/2015/06/26/espns-michelle-beadle-takes--twitter-trolls/29186535/

Johnson, T. (2014, September 10). Michelle Beadle on Ray Rice, Twitter trolls, and Stephen A. Smith. *The Washington Post.* Retrieved from www.washingtonpost.com/news/early-lead/wp/2014/09/10/michelle-beadle-on-ray-rice-twitter-trolls-and-stephen-a-smith/

Laird, S. (2017, June 6). MLB legend Mike Schmidt apologizes after inciting Twitter outrage. *Mashable.* Retrieved from https://mashable.com/2017/06/06/mike-schmidt-comments/

Lorenz, T. (2018, October 15). Instagram has a massive harassment problem. *The Atlantic.* Retrieved from www.theatlantic.com/technology/archive/2018/10/instagram-has-massive-harassment-problem/572890/

Lucia, J. (2014, December 29). Michelle Beadle goes nuclear on Twitter troll. *Awful Announcing.* Retrieved from https://awfulannouncing.com/2014/michelle-beadle-goes-nuclear-twitter-troll.html

Maese, R. (2018, May 31). NBA Twitter: A sports bar that doesn't close, where the stars pull up a seat next to you. *Washington Post.* Retrieved from www.washingtonpost.com/news/sports/wp/2018/05/31/nba-twitter-a-sports-bar-that-doesnt-close-where-the-stars-pull-up-a-seat-next-to-you/

Mettler, J. (2016, April 28). The disgustingly obscene "everyday" harassment of sports media women: A lesson for men. *The Washington Post.* Retrieved from www.washingtonpost.com/news/morning-mix/wp/2016/04/28/morethanmean-a-graphic-lesson-for-men-in-the-everyday-harassment-of-women-in-sports-media/

Miller, J.A. (2018, October 1). James Andrew Miller: Jemele Hill waves goodbye to ESPN and hello to "Places where discomfort is OK." *The Hollywood Reporter.* Retrieved from www.hollywoodreporter.com/news/jemele-hill-interview-leaving-espn-joining-atlantic-1148171

Moreau, E. (2019, July 20). Internet trolling: How do you spot a real troll? *Lifewire.* Retrieved from www.lifewire.com/what-is-internet-trolling-3485891

Risdon, J. (2019, October 14). Twitter explodes at the horrible officiating that hands the Packers a win. *USA Today.* Retrieved from https://lionswire.usatoday.com/2019/10/14/twitter-explodes-at-the-horrible-officiating-that-hands-the-packers-a-win/

Smith, D. (2019, July 14). Craigslist's Craig Newmark: "Outrage is profitable. Most online outrage is faked for profit." *The Guardian.* Retrieved from www.theguardian.com/technology/2019/jul/14/craigslist-craig-newmark-outrage-is-profitable-most-online-outrage-is-faked-for-profit?utm_source=fark&utm_medium=website&utm_content=link&ICID=ref_fark

Spector, J. (2018, August 21). How WNBA players fought back against the Twitter trolls. *The Guardian.* Retrieved from www.theguardian.com/sport/2018/aug/21/why-wnba-players-became-the-most-ferocious-athletes-on-social-media

Strauss, B. (2019, July 26). As ESPN tries to stick to sports, President Jimmy Pitaro must define what that means. *The Washington Post.* Retrieved from www.washingtonpost.com/sports/2019/07/26/jimmy-pitaro-espn-president-politics/

Suler, J. (2004). The online disinhibition effect. *CyberPsychology & Behavior, 7*(3), 321-326.

Sussman, G. (2016, May 31). Michelle Beadle has the perfect responses to Twitter trolls. *SportsGrid.* Retrieved from www.sportsgrid.com/real-sports/nba/michelle-beadle-has-the-perfect-responses-to-twitter-trolls/

Chapter 6

Adler, K.C. (2019, July 1). All ESPN streaming content now exclusively on the ESPN app. *ESPN Front Row.* Retrieved from www.espnfrontrow.com/2019/07/all-espn-streaming-content-now-exclusively-on-the-espn-app/

Apple. (2010, January 27). Apple launches iPad. *Apple.com.* Retrieved from www.apple.com/newsroom/2010/01/27Apple-Launches-iPad/

Farokhmanesh, M. (2018, June 21). Young people still love Twitter—as screenshots on Instagram. *The Verge.* Retrieved from www.theverge.com/2018/6/21/17442028/instagram-twitter-meme-accounts-screenshots-text

Fry, J. (2012, July 6). ESPN faces challenges in Twitter era. *ESPN.* Retrieved from www.espn.com/blog/poynterreview/post/_/id/373/espn-faces-challenges-in-twitter-era

Gallegos, J.A. (2019, October 19). An easy guide to creating social media videos that drive results. *Social Media Today.* Retrieved from www.socialmediatoday.com/news/an-easy-guide-to-creating-social-media-videos-that-drive-results/565381/?fbclid=IwAR1G3z2uDcYo-FEeDRSMixcCo2vzx-GaaZFLz4sDWAEZh-CLZt_rENxdcSL4

Garrison, C. (2020, January 3). Here's how to get the Instagram Disney filter to find your character. *Elite Daily.* Retrieved from www.elitedaily.com/p/heres-how-to-get-the-instagram-disney-filter-to-find-your-character-19741575

Giphy. (n.d.). *Explore NBA memes GIFs.* Retrieved from https://giphy.com/explore/nba-memes

Mastorakis, G. (2018, July 10). How augmented reality will influence future social media trends. *Mentionlytics.* Retrieved from www.mentionlytics.com/blog/how-augmented-reality-will-influence-future-social-media-trends/

McClinton, D. (2019, April 17). Global attention span is narrowing and trends don't last as long, study reveals. *The Guardian.* Retrieved from www.theguardian.com/society/2019/apr/16/got-a-minute-global-attention-span-is-narrowing-study-reveals

Saad, L. (2018, February 16). Gallup Vault: Misjudging cellphone adoption. *Gallup.* Retrieved from https://news.gallup.com/vault/227810/gallup-vault-misjudging-cellphone-adoption.aspx

Sperling, L. (2019, October 7). Jeffrey Katzenberg's mobile start-up, Quibi, makes a deal with ESPN. *The New York Times.* Retrieved from www.nytimes.com/2019/10/07/business/media/quibi-espn-katzenberg.html?smid=tw-nytimesbusiness&smtyp=cur

Torrance, L. (2019, January 15). YinzCam develops mobile app for English Premier League club. *Pittsburgh Business Times.* Retrieved from www.bizjournals.com/pittsburgh/news/2019/01/15/yinzcam-develops-mobile-app-for-english-premier.html

Chapter 7

Andrews, M. (2018, March 17). Man behind U.M.B.C. Twitter account also takes a victory lap. *New York Times.* Retrieved from www.nytimes.com/2018/03/17/sports/ncaabasketball/umbc-twitter.html

Atkinson, T. (2016, August 8). The importance of the Atlanta Hawks' social media presence. *Soaring Down South.* Retrieved from https://soaringdownsouth.com/2016/08/18/importance-atlanta-hawks-social-media-presence/

Brooke, T. (2015, February 4). Atlanta Hawks thriving off court thanks to rebranding, embracing social media. *Bleacher Report.* Retrieved from https://bleacherreport.com/articles/2352775-atlanta-hawks-thriving-off-court-thanks-to-rebranding-embracing-social-media

Burns, P. (2013, July 26). What I learned from a year of watching SportsCenter. *Deadspin.* Retrieved from https://deadspin.com/what-i-learned-from-a-year-of-watching-sportscenter-5979510

Denham, B.E. (2004). *Sports Illustrated*, the mainstream press and the enactment of drug policy in Major League Baseball. *Journalism, 5,* 51-68.

Denham, B.E. (2014). Intermediate attribute agenda setting in the *New York Times*: The case of animal abuse in U.S. horse racing. *Journalism & Mass Communication Quarterly, 91*(1), 17-37.

Feldman, J. (2019, February 7). New York Jets QB Sam Darnold talks Adam Gase memes, podcasting and social media. *Sports Illustrated.* Retrieved from www.si.com/media/2019/02/07/sam-darnold-new-york-jets-qb-adam-gase-podcast-social-media

Frederick, E.L., & Clavio, G. (2015). Blurred lines: An examination of high school football recruits' self-presentation on Twitter. *International Journal of Sport Communication, 8*(3), 330-344.

Frederick, E.L., Lim, C., Clavio, G., Pedersen, P.M., & Burch, L.M. (2014). Choosing between the one-way or two-way street: An exploration of relationship promotion by professional athletes on Twitter. *Communication & Sport, 2,* 80-99.

Goffman, E. (1974). *Frame analysis: An essay on the organization of experience.* New York: Harper & Row.

Jennings, R. (2019, October 9). Two British footballers' wives are feuding. It's the perfect Brexit palate cleanser. *Vox.* Retrieved from www.vox.com/the-goods/2019/10/9/20906753/rebekah-vardy-coleen-rooney-instagram-feud

Lang, G.E., & Lang, K. (1983). *The battle for public opinion: The president, the press, and the polls during Watergate.* New York: Columbia University Press.

Lebel, K., & Danylchuk, K. (2012). How tweet it is: A gendered analysis of professional tennis players' self-presentation on Twitter. *International Journal of Sport Communication, 5,* 461-480.

Lorenz, T. (2019, July 3). Emma Chamberlain is the most important YouTuber today. *The Atlantic.* Retrieved from www.theatlantic.com/technology/archive/2019/07/emma-chamberlain-and-rise-relatable-influencer/593230/

McCombs, M. & Shaw, D. (1972). The agenda-setting function of mass media. *Public Opinion Quarterly, 36,* 176-187.

Mirer, M., & Mederson, M. (2017). Leading with the head: How NBC's Football Night in America framed football's concussion crisis: A Case Study. *Journal of Sports Media, 12*(1), 21-44.

NFL on ESPN. (2019, September 8). Antonio Brown sought advice from social media consultants on how he could accelerate his release from the Raiders, accoring to @mortreport. [Twitter post]. Retrieved from https://twitter.com/ESPNNFL/status/1170707387482857476?s=20

Prada, M. (2014, June 3). Meet the man behind the best Twitter account in sports. *SB Nation.* Retrieved from www.sbnation.com/nba/2014/6/3/5776210/atlanta-hawks-twitter-interview-nba

Rooney, C. (2019, October 9). This has been a burden in my life for a few years now and finally I have got to the bottom of it . . . [Twitter Post]. Retrieved from https://twitter.com/ColeenRoo/status/1181864136155828224?s=20

Rosenthal, G. (2019, March 13). Steelers trade Antonio Brown to Raiders: Who won, who lost? *NFL.com.* Retrieved from www.nfl.com/news/story/0ap3000001021716/article/steelers-trade-antonio-brown-to-raiders-who-won-who-lost

Sanderson, J. (2008). The blog is serving its purpose: Self-presentation strategies on 38pitches.com. *Journal of Computer Mediated Communication, 13,* 912-936.

Sanderson, J. (2013a). Social media and sport communication. In P.M. Pedersen. (Ed.), *Routledge Handbook of Sport Communication.* London, England: Routledge.

Sanderson, J. (2013b). Stepping into the (social media) game: Building athlete identity via Twitter. In R. Luppicini (Ed.), *Handbook of research on technoself: Identity in a technological society* (pp. 419-438). New York: Idea Group Global. doi:10.4018/978-1-4666-2211-1.ch023

Springer, S. (2019, January 7). 7 ways to improve coverage of women's sports. *Nieman Reports.* Retrieved from https://niemanreports.org/articles/covering-womens-sports/

Tasch, J. (2019, September 8). Antonio Brown took absurd measures to force Raiders release. *New York Post.* Retrieved from https://nypost.com/2019/09/08/antonio-brown-took-absurd-measures-to-force-raiders-release/

Waterson, J. (2019, October 9). Coleen Rooney accuses Rebekah Vardy of leaking stories to Sun. *The Guardian.* Retrieved from www.theguardian.com/media/2019/oct/09/coleen-rooney-accuses-rebekah-vardy-leaking-stories-sun

Weintraub, R. (2012, August 6). ESPN's Tim Tebow lovefest. *Columbia Journalism Review.* Retrieved from https://archives.cjr.org/full_court_press/espn_nbc_olympics_coverage_tim.php

Chapter 8

Cuban, M. (2011, April 4). What's the role of media for sports teams? *Blog Maverick.* Retrieved from http://blogmaverick.com/2011/04/04/whats-the-role-of-media-for-sports-teams/

Curtis, B. (2015, March 20). Distant Thunder: What did Oklahoma City's media do to piss off Russell Westbrook and Kevin Durant? *Grantland.* Retrieved from https://grantland.com/the-triangle/nba-russell-westbrook-kevin-durant-oklahoma-city-thunder-sports-media/

Curtis, B. (2019, May 29). "The bane of my existence": U.K. sportswriting's access crisis. *The Ringer.* Retrieved from www.theringer.com/sports/2019/5/29/18643311/uk-sportswriting-embargo-access-champions-league-independent

Deitsch, R. (2015, April 19). Sports media members on changes to industry; Britt McHenry aftermath. *Sports Illustrated.* Retrieved from www.si.com/more-sports/2015/04/19/sports-media-panel-adam-schefter-joe-buck-britt-mchenry-espn

ESPN. (2011, August). Social networking. *ESPN Front Row*. Retrieved from www.espnfrontrow.com/wp-content/uploads/2011/08/social-networking-v2-2011.pdf

Harris, T. (2019, June 30). Tobias Harris: "I'm a Philadelphia 76er." *ESPN*. Retrieved from www.espn.com/nba/story/_/id/27090540/tobias-harris-philadelphia-76er

James, L. (2014, July 11). LeBron: I'm coming back to Cleveland. *Sports Illustrated*. Retrieved from www.si.com/nba/lebron-james-cleveland-cavaliers

Layden, T. (2017, December 20). Root, root, root for my team: Sports reporting continues to move further away from objectivity. *Sports Illustrated*. Retrieved from www.si.com/tech-media/2017/12/20/sports-media-reporting-objective-journalism-fans

Middleton, K. (2019, June 29). Khris Middleton: Why I'm staying in Milwaukee. *ESPN*. Retrieved from www.espn.com/nba/story/_/id/27083386/khris-middleton-why-staying-milwaukee

Moritz, B. (2011, April 5). Mark Cuban on the role of sports reporters. *Sports Media Guy*. Retrieved from www.sportsmediaguy.com/blog/2011/04/06/mark-cuban-on-the-role-of-sports-reporters

Reigstad, L. (2016, November 7). Mark Cuban just revoked Mavs media credentials for two ESPN reporters. *Texas Monthly*. Retrieved from www.texasmonthly.com/the-daily-post/mark-cuban-just-revoked-mavs-media-credentials-two-espn-reporters/

Valade, J. (2014, July 11). How SI's Lee Jenkins got the biggest LeBron James scoop of all. *Cleveland Plain Dealer*. Retrieved from www.cleveland.com/cavs/2014/07/how_sis_lee_jenkins_got_the_bi.html

Chapter 9

BBC. (2019, October 14). *The Hong Kong protests explained in 100 and 500 words*. Retrieved from www.bbc.com/news/world-asia-china-49317695

Bird, H. (2018, August 8). "It's not tolerable": How offensive tweets are spurring an evolution in sports. *Boston.com*. Retrieved from www.boston.com/sports/sports-news/2018/08/08/josh-hader-sean-newcomb-tweets

Brunt, C. (2018, July 28). Old tweets by athletes highlight teams' fears of social media. *Honolulu Star Advertiser*. Retrieved from www.staradvertiser.com/2018/07/29/sports/sports-breaking/old-tweets-by-athletes-highlight-teams-fears-of-social-media/

Caporoso, J. (2016, February 16). How athletes can optimize social media on and off the field. *Adweek*. Retrieved from www.adweek.com/digital/joe-caporoso-guest-post-athletes-optimize-social-media/

Deb, S. (2019, October 17). N.B.A. Commissioner: China asked us to fire Daryl Morey. *The New York Times*. Retrieved from www.nytimes.com/2019/10/17/sports/basketball/nba-china-adam-silver.html

de la Cretaz, B. (2018, September 19). The person running your favorite football team's Twitter is probably a woman. *The Verge*. Retrieved from www.theverge.com/2018/9/19/17852628/sports-social-media-women-twitter-nfl-nba-mlb

Eisenberg, J. (2018, December 18). Inside one of sports' most abhorrent trends: The unearthing of old tweets. *Yahoo! Sports*. Retrieved from https://sports.yahoo.com/inside-one-sports-abhorrent-trends-unearthing-old-tweets-194202602.html

Farmer, S. (2019, October 26). These NFL blunders have been amplified by social media. *The Los Angeles Times*. Retrieved from www.latimes.com/sports/story/2019-10-26/what-to-look-for-in-week-8-of-the-nfl-season

FC Bayern Munich. (2019, December 29). *What happens at a football medical?* [Video File]. Retrieved from www.youtube.com/watch?v=waXOtLVJT7M

Freberg, K. (2018). *Social media for strategic communication*. Los Angeles: Sage. ISBN: 978-1-5443-5475-0

Frederick, E.L. & Clavio, G. (2015). Blurred Lines: A qualitative analysis of Twitter use among elite high school athletes. *International Journal of Sport Communication, 8*, 330-344.

Gonzalez, J. (2019, October 6). Daryl Morey's Hong Kong tweet has put his relationship with the Rockets in limbo. *The Ringer*. Retrieved from www.theringer.com/nba/2019/10/6/20901828/daryl-morey-hong-kong-china-houston-rockets-tweet-controversy

Hale, J. (2018, January 11). Don't feed the trolls: Highlights from colleges' social media policies for athletes. *Louisville Courier Journal*. Retrieved from www.courier-journal.com/story/sports/college/kentucky/2018/01/11/kentucky-football-college-athletes-social-media-twitter-use/848093001/

Heim, M. (2019, August 28). Top 18 most popular college football players on social media include Alabama stars. *AL.com*. Retrieved from www.al.com/sports/g66l-2019/08/c5db3a36df3467/top-18-most-popular-college-football-players-on-social-media-include-alabama-stars-.html

Hickman, A. (2019, October 22). Man City calls on influencers to build hype for Champions League home games. *PR Week*. Retrieved from www.prweek.com/article/1663345/man-city-calls-influencers-build-hype-champions-league-home-games

Kahler, K. (2019, April 24). How NFL draft prospects are learning to protect themselves from social media snafus. *Sports Illustrated*. Retrieved from www.si.com/nfl/2019/04/24/nfl-draft-social-media-kyler-murray-nick-bosa-josh-allen-old-tweets-cleanup

Lane, B. (2019, October 16). Cristiano Ronaldo reportedly makes more money being an influencer on Instagram than he does playing soccer for Juventus. *Business Insider*. Retrieved from www.businessinsider.com/cristiano-ronaldo-makes-more-money-from-instagram-than-juventus-2019-10/

Lucken, S. (2019, January 29). Move aside influencers—Athletes are becoming the faces of new brand strategies. *Adweek*. Retrieved from www.adweek.com/tv-video/move-aside-influencers-athletes-are-becoming-the-faces-of-new-brand-strategies/

Mozur, P., & Qin, A. (2019, October 10). China's NBA fans feel the tug of loyalty toward Beijing. *The New York Times*. Retrieved from www.nytimes.com/2019/10/10/business/china-nba-hong-kong-basketball-fans.html

Nielsen. (2019, July 8). Predicting performance of athletes as influencers: On-court performance doesn't always dictate marketability. Retrieved from www.nielsen.com/us/en/insights/article/2019/predicting-performance-of-athletes-as-influencers-on-court-performance-doesnt-always-dictate-marketability/

Olojede, Z. (2017, December 31). The worst sports social media fails of 2017. *Complex*. Retrieved from www.complex.com/sports/worst-sports-social-media-fails-2017/

Patterson, M. (2015, August 24). Social media in sports: 5 strategies from the pros. *SproutSocial*. Retrieved from https://sproutsocial.com/insights/social-media-in-sports/

Pitcher, L. (2019, May 29). How female athletes are becoming social media's newest "influencers." *Vice*. Retrieved from https://i-d.vice.com/en_us/article/a3xnkj/how-female-athletes-are-becoming-social-medias-newest-influencers

talkSPORT. (2017, July 26). *10 hilarious football social media mistakes*. Retrieved from www.youtube.com/watch?v=DR1c_aT69G8

Tan, J. (2019, August 10). F1: Lewis Hamilton can earn "insane" amount of money per Instagram post. *International Business Times*. Retrieved from www.ibtimes.com/f1-lewis-hamilton-can-earn-insane-amount-money-instagram-post-2812110

Temming, S. (2018, December 24). Year in review: Top sports social media fails of 2018. *Yahoo! News*. Retrieved from https://news.yahoo.com/year-review-top-sports-social-media-fails-2018-182357379.html

University of Southern California. (2012). *Social media policy & guidelines for student-athletes*. Retrieved from https://saas.usc.edu/files/2012/08/USC-Student-Athlete-Social-Media-Policy-Sign-Off.pdf

Vadaj, R. (2020, January 1). Myles Garrett speaks out for the first time on Twitter since his indefinite suspension was upheld in November. *Cleveland 19*. Retrieved from www.cleveland19.com/2020/01/02/myles-garrett-speaks-out-first-time-twitter-since-his-indefinite-suspension-was-upheld-november/

Yeung, J., & Levenson, E. (2019, October 15). LeBron James says NBA exec was "misinformed" in his tweet supporting Hong Kong protests. *CNN*. Retrieved from www.cnn.com/2019/10/14/us/lebron-james-nba-china-intl-hnk-scli/index.html

Chapter 10

Auxier, B.E., & Vitak, J. (2019). Factors motivating customization and echo chamber creation within digital news environments. *Social Media + Society, 5*(2), April-June. DOI: https://doi.org/10.1177/2056305119847506

Bromwich, J.E. (2019, July 9). The evolution of Emma Chamberlain. *The New York Times*. Retrieved from www.nytimes.com/2019/07/09/style/emma-chamberlain-youtube.html?smid=tw-nytimes&smtyp=cur

Brown, E. (2019, February 19). 7 ways for social marketers to avoid social media burnout. *Hootsuite*. Retrieved from https://blog.hootsuite.com/ways-to-avoid-social-media-burnout/

de la Cretaz, B. (2018, September 19). The person running your favorite football team's Twitter is probably a woman. *The Verge*. Retrieved from www.theverge.com/2018/9/19/17852628/sports-social-media-women-twitter-nfl-nba-mlb

Draper, K., & Bromwich, J.E. (2018, December 18). Ninja would like to get some sleep. *The New York Times*. Retrieved from www.nytimes.com/2018/12/18/sports/ninja-fortnite.html?module=inline

Front Office Sports. (2018, September 19). *Rob Perez's journey from ticketing entrepreneur to NBA personality* [Podcast]. Retrieved from https://frntofficesport.com/rob-perez-nba-personality/

Haberstroh, T. (2018, October 1). Is social media addiction in the NBA out of control? *Bleacher Report*. Retrieved from https://bleacherreport.com/articles/2798257-is-social-media-addiction-in-the-nba-out-of-control

Labarre, S. (2018, March 14). Creatives are overworked. *Fast Company*. Retrieved from www.fastcompany.com/90164035/creatives-are-overworked

Owen, L.H. (2019, May 28). Want to feel less anxious about the state of the world? Try diversifying your online news sources. *Nieman Lab*. Retrieved from www.niemanlab.org/2019/05/want-to-feel-less-anxious-about-the-state-of-the-world-try-diversifying-your-online-news-sources/

Proctor, K. (2019, September 15). Stop engaging with online trolls altogether, public figures say. *The Guardian*. Retrieved from www.theguardian.com/society/2019/sep/16/stop-engaging-with-online-trolls-altogether-public-figures-say

Index

Note: The italicized *f* and *t* following page numbers refer to figures and tables, respectively.

Galen Clavio, PhD, is widely regarded as one of the brightest minds in social media in sports research, with a background in both sport management and sports communication. He serves as an associate professor of sports media, head of the sports media program, and director of the National Sports Journalism Center at Indiana University (IU). His teaching draws upon his professional experience as a broadcaster, reporter, and media relations director to teach courses in sportscasting and play-by-play, applied uses of social media in sports communication, sports and society, and the intersection of academic theory and social media.

Galen Clavio

Clavio's research focuses on the effects of digital media on the interactions between sport entities and sports consumers. He has authored nearly 50 peer-reviewed publications, the vast majority of which focus on social media utilization of fans, teams, and individuals within the sports environment. He is the senior editor for scholarly outreach for *Communication & Sport* and has served as a guest editor of three separate social media–focused special issues in respected journals (*International Journal of Sport Communication*, 2010; *Online Information Review*, 2016; and *Journal of Legal Aspects of Sport*, 2017).

A native of Indiana, Clavio graduated from IU as an undergraduate in 2001 and worked for several years in the sports media field before earning his PhD from IU in 2008.

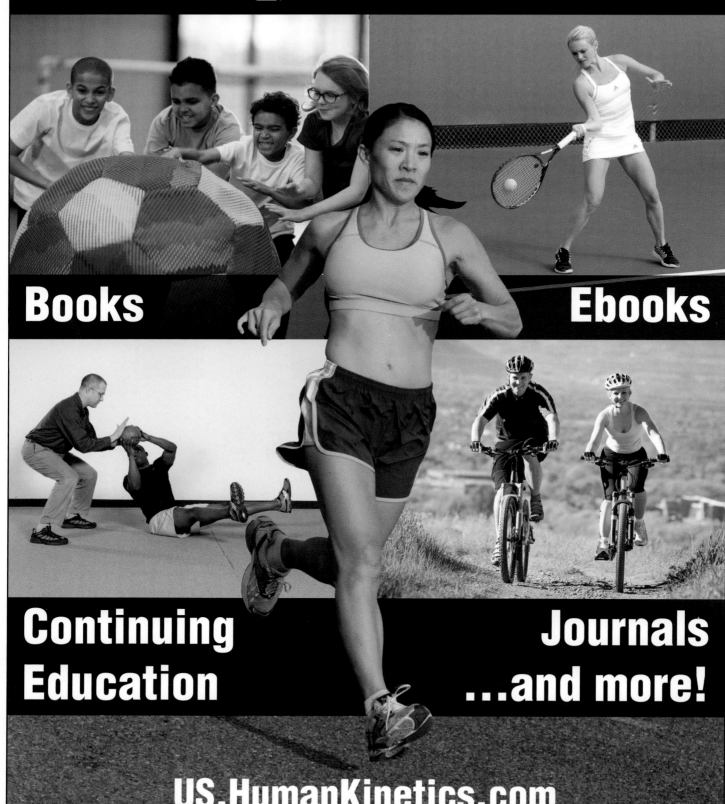